Relief from Judgment in North Carolina Civil Cases

Ann M. Anderson

2015

UNC
SCHOOL OF
GOVERNMENT

The School of Government at the University of North Carolina at Chapel Hill works to improve the lives of North Carolinians by engaging in practical scholarship that helps public officials and citizens understand and improve state and local government. Established in 1931 as the Institute of Government, the School provides educational, advisory, and research services for state and local governments. The School of Government is also home to a nationally ranked graduate program in public administration and specialized centers focused on information technology and environmental finance.

As the largest university-based local government training, advisory, and research organization in the United States, the School of Government offers up to 200 courses, webinars, and specialized conferences for more than 12,000 public officials each year. In addition, faculty members annually publish approximately 50 books, manuals, reports, articles, bulletins, and other print and online content related to state and local government. Each day that the General Assembly is in session, the School produces the *Daily Bulletin Online*, which reports on the day's activities for members of the legislature and others who need to follow the course of legislation.

The Master of Public Administration Program is offered in two formats. The full-time, two-year residential program serves up to 60 students annually. In 2013 the School launched MPA@UNC, an online format designed for working professionals and others seeking flexibility while advancing their careers in public service. The School's MPA program consistently ranks among the best public administration graduate programs in the country, particularly in city management. With courses ranging from public policy analysis to ethics and management, the program educates leaders for local, state, and federal governments and nonprofit organizations.

Operating support for the School of Government's programs and activities comes from many sources, including state appropriations, local government membership dues, private contributions, publication sales, course fees, and service contracts. Visit www.sog.unc.edu or call 919.966.5381 for more information on the School's courses, publications, programs, and services.

Printed in the United States of America

21 20 19 18 17   2 3 4 5 6

ISBN 978-1-56011-855-8

Contents

About This Book

There are many reasons a party to a civil action may seek relief from a final judgment or order of North Carolina's trial courts. Litigants often, of course, take their arguments to the state's appellate division. But for many issues, the North Carolina Rules of Civil Procedure provide methods for first seeking relief directly from the trial courts themselves. These rules, presented in Chapter 1A of the North Carolina General Statutes, and North Carolina case law interpreting them, are the focus of this book. The discussion proceeds in two parts.

Part I covers motions for immediate post-trial relief. These motions include

1. *Judgment notwithstanding the verdict (JNOV)*. A motion for JNOV is a continuation of a party's directed verdict motion made at the close of evidence pursuant to Rule 50, and it challenges the sufficiency of the evidence to support the jury's verdict. With this motion, a party asks the trial judge to upend the decision of the jury and the judgment on which it is based and instead grant judgment for the movant. The law permits this remedy only where the evidence on which the judgment was based was insufficient as a matter of law—an exacting standard reviewable *de novo* on appeal. Rule 50 governs motions for JNOV.
2. *New trial*. This less sweeping but nonetheless quite significant remedy is available in a much wider range of situations—nine enumerated grounds—all but one of which are matters of the court's discretion. Governed by Rule 59, new trial motions often are coupled with JNOV motions.

3. *Amendment of judgment.* For judgments after non-jury trials, Rule 52(b) allows motions to amend the findings in the court's written judgment. Rule 59 also permits motions to alter or amend a judgment after a non-jury trial for any of the pertinent grounds listed for new trial.

The time frame for each of these motions is a mere ten days after entry of the judgment.

Part II covers motions brought under Rule 60(b), which allows relief from a "final judgment, order, or proceeding" based on any of six specific grounds that are based largely in equity and, in general, are discretionary. The range of final orders from which relief may be sought is much broader than the range discussed in Part I, and the motion may be made within a reasonable time after judgment, limited to one year for the first three grounds. This motion is not a substitute for a proper appeal of the order or a timely motion under Rule 50, Rule 52(b), or Rule 59.

As to each of these types of motions for post-judgment relief, there are important procedural requirements to which the parties and the trial courts must give careful attention. Failure to comply with certain aspects of the rules may affect the trial court's jurisdiction over a motion and appeal of the court's decision.

The focus of this book is North Carolina case law, primarily cases that interpret the Rules of Civil Procedure governing these motions rather than cases discussing the common law upon which the rules are based or statutes that preceded them. On many occasions, however, pre-rules case law is helpful to provide context or to explain the basis for a particular Rule of Civil Procedure, and this book attempts to note these older cases whenever useful. Appendix B provides a table of authorities for reference to the sources noted throughout the text.

Ann M. Anderson
Fall 2015

Part I Post-Trial Relief: JNOV, New Trial, and Amendment of Judgment

Chapter 1

JNOV—Rule 50(b)

Introduction

There is a single method for seeking relief from judgment at the trial court level on grounds that the evidence was legally insufficient to support the jury's verdict. The losing party may, within ten days of entry of the judgment, move for entry of judgment in its favor despite the verdict the jury returned.[1] This is called making a motion for judgment *non obstante veredicto*—"notwithstanding the verdict"—or JNOV.[2] Governed by Rule of Civil Procedure 50(b), a motion for JNOV is a renewal of the party's Rule 50(a) motion for a directed verdict made at the close of evidence.[3] Because JNOV is, in essence, "a directed verdict granted after the jury verdict,"[4] a JNOV motion cannot be granted unless the party also moved for a directed verdict after the close of all the evidence.[5] Rule 50(b)(1) states,

> Whenever a motion for a directed verdict made at the close of all the evidence is denied or for any reason is not granted, the submission of the action to the jury shall be deemed to be subject to a later determination of the legal questions raised by the motion. Not later than 10 days after entry of judgment, a party who has moved for a directed verdict may move to have the verdict and any judgment entered thereon

---

1. Section 1A-1, Rule 50(b)(1), of the North Carolina General Statutes (hereinafter G.S.).

2. *See* Comment (original) to Rule 50.

3. Bryant v. Nationwide Mut. Fire Ins. Co., 313 N.C. 362, 368–69, 329 S.E.2d 333, 338 (1985) (citing Dickinson v. Pake, 284 N.C. 576, 201 S.E.2d 897 (1974)); Moon v. Bostian Heights Volunteer Fire Dep't, 97 N.C. App. 110, 111, 387 S.E.2d 225, 226 (1990); Nytco Leasing, Inc. v. Se. Motels, Inc., 40 N.C. App. 120, 132, 252 S.E.2d 826, 834 (1979)).

4. Brissett v. First Mount Vernon Indus. Loan Ass'n, 756 S.E.2d 798, 808 (N.C. Ct. App. 2014) (quoting Tomika Invs., Inc. v. Macedonia True Vine Pentecostal Holiness Church of God, Inc., 136 N.C. App. 493, 498, 524 S.E.2d 591, 595 (2000)).

5. Rule 50(b)(1); *Bryant*, 313 N.C. at 369, 329 S.E.2d at 338 (noting that it is "elementary" that the movant must first have moved for directed verdict at the close of the evidence); Coates v. Niblock Dev. Corp., 161 N.C. App. 515, 516, 588 S.E.2d 492, 493–94 (2003).

> set aside and to have judgment entered in accordance with his motion for a directed verdict[.][6]

JNOV is required if and *only* if a "directed verdict could properly have been granted."[7] The standard for granting JNOV is precisely the same as that for a directed verdict.[8] A directed verdict—and therefore JNOV—are appropriate only if the evidence before the jury was insufficient *as a matter of law* to support the jury's verdict.[9] The JNOV motion must be denied if there is "more than a scintilla" of evidence to support each element of the non-moving party's claim.[10] In determining whether a scintilla of evidence exists, the trial court must consider the evidence in the light most favorable to the non-moving party and must view as true all evidence that supports the non-movant's claim.[11] The non-movant

---

6. Rule 50(b)(1).

7. *Id.*; *see* Raintree Homeowners Ass'n, Inc. v. Bleimann, 342 N.C. 159, 164, 463 S.E.2d 72, 75 (1995); *Bryant,* 313 N.C. at 369, 329 S.E.2d at 338 (citing Manganello v. Permastone, Inc., 291 N.C. 666, 231 S.E.2d 678 (1977)).

8. Abels v. Renfro Corp., 335 N.C. 209, 214, 436 S.E.2d 822, 825 (1993); Smith v. Price, 315 N.C. 523, 527, 340 S.E.2d 408, 411 (1986); *Coates,* 161 N.C. App. at 517, 588 S.E.2d at 494; *Moon,* 97 N.C. App. at 111, 387 S.E.2d at 226; Kiousis v. Kiousis, 130 N.C. App. 569, 572, 503 S.E.2d 437, 440 (1998).

9. West v. Slick, 313 N.C. 33, 40–41, 326 S.E.2d 601, 605–06 (1985); Bodine v. Harris Village Prop. Owners Ass'n, Inc., 207 N.C. App. 52, 58, 699 S.E.2d 129, 134 (2010); Maxwell v. Michael P. Doyle, Inc., 164 N.C. App. 319, 322, 595 S.E.2d 759, 761 (2004).

10. Fisk v. Murphy, 212 N.C. App. 667, 670, 713 S.E.2d 100, 102 (2011) (citing Austin v. Bald II, L.L.C., 189 N.C. App. 338, 342, 658 S.E.2d 1, 4 (2008); Rhue v. Rhue, 189 N.C. App. 299, 303, 658 S.E.2d 52, 57 (2008); Hodgson Constr., Inc. v. Howard, 187 N.C. App. 408, 412, 654 S.E.2d 7, 11 (2007) (quoting Cox v. Steffes, 161 N.C. App. 237, 243, 587 S.E.2d 908, 912–13 (2003)); Bahl v. Talford, 138 N.C. App. 119, 122, 530 S.E.2d 347, 350 (2000); Edwards v. West, 128 N.C. App. 570, 573, 495 S.E.2d 920, 923 (1998); Lyon v. May, 119 N.C. App. 704, 707, 459 S.E.2d 833, 836 (1995); Ace Chem. Corp. v. DSI Transports, Inc., 115 N.C. App. 237, 242, 446 S.E.2d 100, 103 (1994).

Note, however, that the North Carolina Supreme Court recently detailed a different standard for assessing JNOV motions related to a punitive damages verdict. For a discussion of this distinction, *see infra* section titled "The Punitive Damages Variation."

11. *Bryant,* 313 N.C. at 368–69, 329 S.E.2d at 338; *West,* 313 N.C. at 40–41, 326 S.E.2d at 606; Boggess v. Spencer, 173 N.C. App. 614, 618, 620 S.E.2d 10, 13 (2005).

must be given the benefit of every reasonable inference that may legitimately be drawn from the evidence.[12] Contradictions, conflicts, and inconsistencies must be resolved in that party's favor.[13] The judge does not, therefore, weigh disputed evidence[14] or assess credibility of witnesses when credibility is at issue.[15] Whether JNOV is appropriate is a question of law and is renewed *de novo* on appeal.[16]

"Close Call": Why Is JNOV Necessary?

If the standard for granting JNOV is the same as for directed verdict, why is JNOV necessary? In other words, why is the jury allowed to address an issue that the court could have disposed of as a matter of law on directed verdict? The primary answer is largely practical: to avoid unnecessary retrials after appeal. Deciding whether there is "more than a scintilla" of evidence to support a verdict sometimes requires a difficult analysis resulting in a very close call. A judge inclined to direct a verdict may be wary of doing so in a close case because of the potential for reversal, which would then require a new trial before a new jury.[17] The procedural mechanism of JNOV allows the judge to make a final assessment of the evidence after the jury has done its work. If the jury finds in favor of the party who moved for directed

12. *Smith*, 315 N.C. at 527, 340 S.E.2d at 411; *Fisk*, 212 N.C. App. at 679–70, 713 S.E.2d at 102; *Tomika Investments*, 136 N.C. App. at 498, 524 S.E.2d at 595.

13. *Smith*, 315 N.C. at 527, 340 S.E.2d at 411; *Coates*, 161 N.C. App. 515, 516–17, 588 S.E.2d at 494.

14. *Tomika Investments*, 136 N.C. App. at 499, 524 S.E.2d at 595; Deal v. Pilot Life Ins. Co., 20 N.C. App. 30, 33, 200 S.E.2d 420, 423 (1973).

15. *Smith*, 315 N.C. at 527, 340 S.E.2d at 411; Burris v. Shumate, 77 N.C. App. 209, 212, 334 S.E.2d 514, 516 (1985) ("[T]he testimony of the plaintiff's witnesses must be accepted at face value.") (citations omitted).

16. *In re* Will of Buck, 350 N.C. 621, 624, 516 S.E.2d 858, 860 (1999); Weaver v. Sheppa, 186 N.C. App. 412, 418, 651 S.E.2d 395, 398 (2007); *Maxwell*, 164 N.C. App. at 323, 595 S.E.2d at 761 (citing Denson v. Richmond Cty., 159 N.C. App. 408, 411, 583 S.E.2d 318, 320 (2003)).

17. *See* Kuykendall v. Turner, 61 N.C. App. 638, 642, 301 S.E.2d 715, 718 (1983).

verdict, the matter is no longer at issue.[18] If the jury does not find in favor of the moving party, the judge may then grant JNOV either on his or her own motion or on the party's motion.[19] If the JNOV order is reversed on appeal, the jury's verdict may be reinstated (assuming no other appeal issues alter the outcome) and no new trial is required.[20] Indeed, to prevent "the expense and delay involved in a retrial,"[21] the appellate courts have described such restraint as "the better practice" where "the question of granting a directed verdict is a close one[.]"[22]

Evidence to Be Considered

When deciding a motion for JNOV, the trial court assesses *all* the relevant evidence in the light most favorable to the non-moving party.[23] The court, therefore, considers any evidence elicited from the moving

---

18. Harman v. Belk, 165 N.C. App. 819, 827, 600 S.E.2d 43, 49 (2004); Atl. Tobacco Co. v. Honeycutt, 101 N.C. App. 160, 163, 398 S.E.2d 641, 642 (1990).

19. The court must, of course, be careful not to be influenced by what the jury decided but, instead, must consider only what the evidence actually permitted, which is the sole question before the court on JNOV. Odell v. Lipscomb, 12 N.C. App. 318, 321, 183 S.E.2d 299, 301 (1971).

20. *Kuykendall*, 61 N.C. App. at 642, 301 S.E.2d at 718. If, however, the trial judge has conditionally granted a new trial when granting JNOV, a new trial will proceed after remand unless the appellate court directs otherwise. *See infra* section titled "Conditional Rulings on Combined New Trial Motions."

21. *Kuykendall*, 61 N.C. App. at 642, 301 S.E.2d at 720.

22. Turner v. Duke Univ., 325 N.C. 152, 158, 381 S.E.2d 706, 710 (1989); Manganello v. Permastone, Inc., 291 N.C. 666, 669–70, 231 S.E.2d 678, 680 (1977). In *Partin v. Carolina Power & Light Co.*, the Court of Appeals took particular note of the closeness issue, stating that "between those cases holding contributory negligence as a matter of law and those cases holding the evidence was for the jury, the line is thin and at some places obscure or nebulous"; in such a case it is "advisable" to reserve ruling on directed verdict. 40 N.C. App. 630, 639–40, 253 S.E.2d 605, 612–13 (1979).

23. Cox v. Steffes, 161 N.C. App. 237, 242, 587 S.E.2d 908, 912 (2003); Stallings v. Food Lion, Inc., 141 N.C. App. 135, 136–37, 539 S.E.2d 331, 332 (2000).

party that is favorable to the non-movant.[24] Evidence by the moving party that clarifies its opponent's case may be considered, but evidence that contradicts or refutes the opponent's case is not considered.[25]

In addition, all admitted evidence, whether competent or not, is considered in evaluating a JNOV motion.[26] For example, in an action to recover allegedly excessive attorney fees, the trial court granted JNOV in favor of the defendant law firm.[27] On appeal, the Court of Appeals reviewed "in some detail" the evidence in the record, including the testimony of plaintiff's two expert witnesses.[28] The defendant argued that this evidence should not be considered because the experts had been unqualified to testify and had applied a theory of law not applicable in North Carolina.[29] The Court of Appeals disagreed, stating that "once admitted, both competent and incompetent evidence must be considered on a motion for directed verdict and the subsequent motion for judgment notwithstanding the verdict."[30] "The reason for this rule

24. Dickinson v. Pake, 284 N.C. 576, 583, 201 S.E.2d 897, 902 (1974); Envtl. Landscape Design Specialist v. Shields, 75 N.C. App. 304, 305, 330 S.E.2d 627, 628 (1985); Am. Home Products Corp. v. Howell's Motor Freight, Inc., 46 N.C. App. 276, 279, 264 S.E.2d 774, 777 (1980); Nytco Leasing, Inc. v. Se. Motels, Inc., 40 N.C. App. 120, 132, 252 S.E.2d 826, 834 (1979).

25. Forsyth Cty. v. Shelton, 74 N.C. App. 674, 676, 329 S.E.2d 730, 732 (1985); *American Home Products Corp.*, 46 N.C. App. at 279, 264 S.E.2d at 777; Tate v. Bryant, 16 N.C. App. 132, 134, 191 S.E.2d 433, 434 (1972).

26. Dixon v. Edwards, 265 N.C. 470, 476, 144 S.E.2d 408, 412–13 (1965) ("All relevant evidence admitted by the trial court, whether competent or not, must be accorded its full probative force[.]"); J.T. Russell & Sons, Inc. v. Silver Birch Pond, L.L.C., 217 N.C. App. 290, 295, 721 S.E.2d 699, 703 (2011) (citing Hart v. Warren, 46 N.C. App. 672, 678, 266 S.E.2d 53, 58 (1980)); McCollum v. Grove Mfg. Co., 58 N.C. App. 283, 286, 293 S.E.2d 632, 635 (1982); Bishop v. Roanoke Chowan Hosp., Inc., 31 N.C. App. 383, 385, 229 S.E.2d 313, 314 (1976).

27. Williams v. Randolph, 94 N.C. App. 413, 418, 380 S.E.2d 553, 556 (1989).

28. *Id.* at 418, 380 S.E.2d 557.

29. *Id.* at 421–22, 380 S.E.2d at 559.

30. *Id.* at 422, 380 S.E.2d at 559 (citing Haney v. Alexander, 71 N.C. App. 731, 733–34, 323 S.E.2d 430, 432 (1984)).

is that the admission of such [incompetent] evidence may have caused the plaintiff to omit competent evidence of the same import."[31]

JNOV in Negligence Cases

It is unusual for JNOV to be properly awarded against the plaintiff in a negligence case because, typically, the elements of negligence—most notably reasonableness and causation—are issues of fact for a jury.[32] As with any other type of claim, however, if plaintiff fails as a matter of law to establish one or more elements of negligence, the defendant

---

31. *Haney*, 71 N.C. App. at 733–43, 323 S.E.2d at 432 (citing Huff v. Thornton, 23 N.C. App. 388, 390, 209 S.E.2d 401, 403 (1974), *aff'd*, 287 N.C. 1, 213 S.E.2d 198 (1975)).

32. Turner v. Duke Univ., 325 N.C. 152, 162, 381 S.E.2d 706, 712 (1989) (reversing JNOV for medical providers and noting that "proximate cause is ordinarily a jury question"); Taylor v. Walker, 320 N.C. 729, 734, 360 S.E.2d 796, 799 (1987) ("[A]pplication of the prudent man test, or any other applicable standard of care, is generally for the jury."); Weaver v. Sheppa, 186 N.C. App. 412, 416–18, 651 S.E.2d 395, 398–99 (2007) (noting factual nature of causation and reversing JNOV in medical negligence action); Jones v. Durham Anesthesia Assocs., P.A., 185 N.C. App. 504, 510, 648 S.E.2d 531, 536 (2007) (JNOV inappropriate where admission regarding breach of standard of care was equivocal and evidential rather than judicial); Cameron v. Canady, 157 N.C. App. 132, 134, 577 S.E.2d 700, 701–02 (2003) (error to grant JNOV for plaintiff as to contributory negligence due to sufficient issues of fact); Burchette v. Lynch, 139 N.C. App. 756, 762, 535 S.E.2d 77, 81 (2000) (contributory negligence was question of fact where plaintiff applied brakes when seeing oncoming car); Blackmon v. Bumgardner, 135 N.C. App. 125, 134–35, 519 S.E.2d 335, 341 (1999) (denial of JNOV proper "because the parties did not stipulate to the issues of proximate cause and damages"); Cook v. Wake County Hosp. Sys., Inc., 125 N.C. App. 618, 621–23, 482 S.E.2d 546, 549–50 (1997) (evidence allowed jury to conclude plaintiff had slipped on floor defendant should reasonably have known was wet); Thomas v. Dixson, 88 N.C. App. 337, 339–41, 363 S.E.2d 209, 211–12 (1988) (question of failure to maintain premises in reasonably safe condition was for the jury); Radford v. Norris, 74 N.C. App. 87, 88–89, 327 S.E.2d 620, 621–22 (1985) ("[S]ince negligence usually involves issues of due care and reasonableness of actions under the circumstances, it is especially appropriate for determination by the jury.").

is entitled to judgment.[33] In *Hall v. Torero's II, Inc.*,[34] for example, the estate of a man killed by a drunk driver sued the restaurant that had served the driver alcohol. A jury returned a verdict for plaintiff exceeding $1.2 million. The trial judge granted the restaurant JNOV on the basis that the restaurant had no duty under North Carolina law to take affirmative steps to prevent the man from driving given the circumstances of the case.[35] The plaintiff could not, therefore, establish the first element of negligence. In a lengthy opinion, the Court of Appeals affirmed,[36] noting that JNOV is appropriate against a plaintiff in a negligence case only in "exceptional cases" but that one such case is where the plaintiff is unable as a matter of law to offer evidence to establish an element of the claim.[37] And in the recent case of *Wilmoth v. Hemrich*,[38] the trial court erred in failing to grant judgment for defendants on plaintiff's negligence claim for injuries he received when defendant's straying cow charged at him. Because plaintiff failed to offer evidence that the cow was "at large" due to some negligence of defendants, such as an inadequate fence or infrequent surveillance, or that prior to plaintiff's injury defendants knew or should have known that the cows had escaped, plaintiff failed as a matter of law to demonstrate breach of a duty of care.[39]

---

33. Hawkins v. SSC Hendersonville Operating Co., LLC, 202 N.C. App. 707, 714–15, 690 S.E.2d 35, 40–41 (2010) (Rule 50 motion should have been granted where expert's testimony failed as a matter of law to address required standard of care); McMurray v. Surety Fed. Savs. & Loan Ass'n, 82 N.C. App. 729, 348 S.E.2d 162 (1986) (directed verdict for defendant appropriate where plaintiff could not establish a duty); Cowan v. Laughridge Constr. Co., 57 N.C. App. 321, 323–24, 291 S.E.2d 287, 289 (1982); Oliver v. Royall, 36 N.C. App. 239, 242, 243 S.E.2d 436, 439 (1978). Likewise, if the evidence raises only a "mere conjecture" of contributory negligence, the issue should not be submitted to a jury. Whisnant v. Herrera, 166 N.C. App. 719, 722, 603 S.E.2d 847, 850 (2004) (determining that circumstances of a car accident did more than raise mere conjecture).

34. 176 N.C. App. 309, 626 S.E.2d 861 (2006).

35. *Id.* at 312, 626 S.E.2d at 864.

36. *Id.* at 330, 626 S.E.2d at 874.

37. *Id.* at 313, 626 S.E.2d at 865.

38. 768 S.E.2d 570 (N.C. Ct. App. 2014).

39. *Id.* at 572.

JNOV in Favor of Party with Burden of Proof

Any party is permitted to move for JNOV if the verdict does not go its way. But if the moving party bore the burden of proof on the issue, the court should examine the evidence with particular rigor.[40] Such judgments are rarely granted because, even if the party with the burden of proof "succeeds in the difficult task of establishing a clear and uncontradicted prima facie case, there will ordinarily remain in issue the credibility of [that party's] evidence."[41] The trial court must not grant JNOV to such a party unless credibility is manifest as a matter of law.[42] Although "there are neither constitutional nor procedural impediments to granting JNOV for the party with the burden of proof,"[43] the evidence "must so clearly establish the fact in issue that no reasonable inferences to the contrary can be drawn."[44]

---

40. Williams v. Randolph, 94 N.C. App. 413, 418, 380 S.E.2d 553, 556 (1989).

41. N.C. Nat'l Bank v. Burnette, 297 N.C. 524, 536, 256 S.E.2d 388, 395 (1979); Allis-Chalmers Corp. v. Davis, 37 N.C. App. 114, 118, 245 S.E.2d 566, 570 (1978). This rule applies not just to a prima facie case, but also to an affirmative defense. Because defendants have the burden of proof of their affirmative defenses, the granting of JNOV as to an affirmative defense likewise will "be more closely scrutinized." Bryant v. Nationwide Mut. Fire Ins. Co., 313 N.C. 362, 369, 329 S.E.2d 333, 338 (1985); Hodgson Constr., Inc. v. Howard, 187 N.C. App. 408, 412, 654 S.E.2d 7, 11 (2007).

42. Smith v. Price, 315 N.C. 523, 527–28, 340 S.E.2d 408, 411 (1986); *Burnette*, 297 N.C. at 536, 256 S.E.2d at 395.

43. *Burnette*, 297 N.C. at 537, 256 S.E.2d at 396 ("The constitutional right to trial by jury, N.C. Const., Art. I, § 25, is not absolute; rather, it is premised upon a preliminary determination by the trial judge that there indeed exist genuine issues of fact and credibility which require submission to the jury.").

44. Murdock v. Ratliff, 310 N.C. 652, 659, 314 S.E.2d 518, 522 (1984); *see also* Wilburn v. Honeycutt, 135 N.C. App. 373, 519 S.E.2d 744 (1999) (court erred in granting JNOV for defendant in accident case on issue of plaintiff's contributory negligence).

For this reason, JNOV should not be granted on a disputed issue merely because the movant is the only party to give evidence on the matter. Even uncontradicted evidence on a disputed issue does not permit judgment as a matter of law if the credibility of that evidence is in question. Cutts v. Casey,

Whether the credibility of a party's evidence is "manifest"—or essentially incontrovertible—depends on a case's unique facts: "[I]t would be futile to attempt to state a general rule[.]"[45] In *North Carolina National Bank v. Burnette,* however, the North Carolina Supreme Court articu-

---

278 N.C. 390, 417, 180 S.E.2d 297, 311 (1971) ("[T]he judge cannot direct a verdict upon any controverted issue in favor of the party having the burden of proof even though the evidence is uncontradicted."); Smith v. Carolina Coach Co., 120 N.C. App. 106, 110, 461 S.E.2d 362, 364 (1995). In *Lowe's of Greensboro, Inc. v. Curry,* plaintiff argued that, because it was the only party offering evidence as to the amount of a debt, plaintiff was entitled to judgment on that issue. 29 N.C. App. 229, 223 S.E.2d 909 (1976). The trial court disagreed, stating,

> Plaintiff's evidence that there was no limit on the amount of defendant's guarantee was uncontradicted by defendant. Nevertheless it was not Admitted by defendant. Plaintiff's evidence that the corporation was indebted to it and its evidence as to the amount of the debt was not contradicted by defendant. Nevertheless, neither by pleading nor evidence did defendant Admit the company debt or the amount thereof. . . . The verdict may not be directed merely because the material facts are uncontradicted. The uncontradicted evidence must be submitted to the jury with instructions as to how to answer the issues if they believe the evidence.

Id. at 231, 223 S.E.2d at 911. Along similar lines, in *Austin v. R.W. Raines Enterprises, Inc.,* the Court of Appeals reversed a directed verdict for an accounting firm that had sued to recover fees for its services. 45 N.C. App. 709, 264 S.E.2d 121 (1980). The court stated that the

> only evidence of the value of plaintiff's services in this case was the testimony of one partner in the firm that he "felt" $16.00 an hour to be a "reasonable" fee. No independent or objective evidence of the reasonable worth of such services was offered. Plaintiff's proof clearly depends completely upon the credibility of its witness. Although the defendant offered no evidence respecting the reasonable value of the services rendered it, it did deny that their worth as determined by the plaintiff was reasonable. Such is sufficient to raise an issue of fact as to the reasonable value of the services, and that question is for the jury.

Id. at 710–11, 264 S.E.2d at 122.

45. *Burnette,* 297 N.C. at 537, 256 S.E.2d at 396.

lated the following three "recurrent situations" where credibility tends to be established definitively:

1. Where non-movant establishes proponent's case by admitting the truth of the basic facts upon which the claim of proponent rests,
2. Where the controlling evidence is documentary and non-movant does not deny the authenticity or correctness of the documents,
3. Where there are only latent doubts as to the credibility of oral testimony and the opposing party has "failed to point to specific areas of impeachment and contradictions."[46]

The court in *Burnette* held that plaintiff's evidence that it mailed a notice of sale to the defendants' proper address in compliance with the Uniform Commercial Code was credible as a matter of law. Thus the jury was not "at liberty to disbelieve" it, and plaintiff was entitled to JNOV in its action to collect a deficiency.[47] In *Goodwin v. Investors Life Insurance Co. of North America*,[48] the court determined that an insurer was entitled to judgment as a matter of law on its affirmative defense. Plaintiff sued the insurer to recover the proceeds of a life insurance policy on her husband. After the husband's death in a car accident, the insurer discovered multiple moving violations and auto accidents the husband had failed to report on his policy application.[49] The insurer rescinded the policy. At trial, the jury found in favor of the plaintiff, and the trial court refused to grant JNOV for the insurer. The Supreme Court reversed, finding that the plaintiff denied neither the evidence of her husband's misrepresentations nor the authenticity of the insurer's written underwriting guidelines regarding false applications. Thus the "credibility of defendant['s] documentary evidence was manifest,"[50] and because the company established that the false information would have

46. *Id.* at 537–38, 256 S.E.2d at 396 (citations omitted).
47. *Id.* at 538, 256 S.E.2d at 396.
48. 332 N.C. 326, 419 S.E.2d 766 (1992).
49. *Id.* at 328, 419 S.E.2d at 767.
50. *Id.* at 330, 419 S.E.2d at 768.

affected its underwriting decision, it established its affirmative defense as a matter of law and "fully overcame plaintiff's prima facie case."[51]

In the more recent case of *Primerica Life Insurance Co. v. James Massengill & Sons Construction Co.*,[52] plaintiff Primerica issued a life insurance policy to defendant JMS insuring the lives of two of its owners and listing the company as beneficiary. Later, during a policy renewal process, JMS changed the beneficiaries, designating the wives of the respective insured. In a complicated series of missteps, Primerica processed the beneficiary change erroneously. One of the insureds later died, and Primerica sent the claimant form to JMS rather than to the decedent's widow. JMS claimed, received, and promptly spent nearly all of the $1 million benefit. Soon thereafter, the widow sued Primerica claiming the $1 million. Primerica, apparently conceding it had paid JMS in error, paid $1 million to the widow and sued JMS to recover the first $1 million. The jury found in favor of JMS. The trial court then granted JNOV to Primerica.[53] The Court of Appeals affirmed, holding that the undisputed terms of the policy established that only JMS could change a beneficiary designation and that no mistake by Primerica in processing the changes JMS had made could alter those terms.[54] It also found that "JMS's own admissions established that JMS had not authorized the [erroneous] changes made to the beneficiary and ownership designations[.]"[55] The trial court, therefore, correctly determined that Primerica had established all elements of its claim as a matter of law.[56]

In addition, JNOV for defendant on its affirmative defense of plaintiff's contributory negligence is appropriate only in the unusual event

---

51. *Id.* at 332–33, 419 S.E.2d 766, 769–70; *see also* Paccar Fin. Corp. v. Harnett Transfer, Inc., 51 N.C. App. 1, 10, 275 S.E.2d 243, 248–49 (1981) (affirming grant of JNOV to plaintiff regarding immediate entitlement to possession of collateral); Price v. Conley, 21 N.C. App. 326, 329–30, 204 S.E.2d 178, 180–81 (1974) (evidence of plaintiff's waiver of breach of lease established defendant's affirmative defense as a matter of law).

52. 211 N.C. App. 252, 712 S.E.2d 670 (2011).

53. *Id.* at 253–56, 712 S.E.2d at 673–75.

54. *Id.* at 262–63, 712 S.E.2d at 678–79.

55. *Id.* at 263, 712 S.E.2d at 679.

56. *Id.* at 264, 712 S.E.2d at 679.

that the evidence, considered in the light most favorable to plaintiff "so clearly establishes the defense . . . that no other conclusion can reasonably be drawn."[57] Examples include cases involving voluntary consumption of alcohol before driving,[58] the case of a driver who was unreasonable as a matter of law in pulling out into traffic,[59] and the "clear cut" case of a man who was hit by a car after running into the road in the middle of the night.[60]

The Punitive Damages Variation

As discussed above, when considering a JNOV motion, the trial judge views the evidence in the light most favorable to the non-movant to determine whether there was "more than a scintilla" of evidence to support the jury's verdict.[61] Before 2009, the same standard applied to all aspects of the jury's verdict, including an award of punitive

---

57. Stallings v. Food Lion, Inc., 141 N.C. App. 135, 138, 539 S.E.2d 331, 333 (2000); Smith v. Wal-Mart Stores, Inc., 128 N.C. App. 282, 286, 495 S.E.2d 149, 151 (1998) (quoting Peeler v. S. Ry. Co., 32 N.C. App. 759, 760, 233 S.E.2d 685, 686 (1977); *see also* Barber v. Presbyterian Hosp., 147 N.C. App. 86, 93, 555 S.E.2d 303, 308 (2001) (judgment for defendant improper where step plaintiff used was obstructed by doorway); Cowan v. Laughridge Constr. Co., 57 N.C. App. 321, 326, 291 S.E.2d 287, 290 (1982) (whether working on a ramp without guardrails constituted contributory negligence was question for jury); Everhart v. LeBrun, 52 N.C. App. 139, 142, 277 S.E.2d 816, 818–19 (1981) (whether plaintiff should have pursued a safer route was question for the jury); Seaman v. McQueen, 51 N.C. App. 500, 504, 277 S.E.2d 118, 120 (1981) (mere failure of plaintiff to look left in traffic accident did not permit judgment as a matter of law as to contributory negligence).

58. *See, e.g.*, Sorrells v. M.Y.B. Hospitality Ventures of Asheville, 332 N.C. 645, 648–49, 423 S.E.2d 72, 74 (1992) (contributory negligence established as a matter of law where plaintiff drove after becoming highly intoxicated); Mohr v. Matthews, 768 S.E.2d 10, 13–14 (N.C. Ct. App. 2014) (same).

59. Williams v. Davis, 157 N.C. App. 696, 702, 580 S.E.2d 85, 89 (2003).

60. Widener v. Fox, 11 N.C. App. 525, 529, 181 S.E.2d 731, 733 (1971).

61. Taylor v. Walker, 320 N.C. 729, 733, 360 S.E.2d 796, 799 (1987).

damages.[62] In 2009, the North Carolina Supreme Court held that a different review standard applies to motions for JNOV as to punitive damages. In *Scarborough v. Dillard's, Inc.*,[63] the majority held that the standard for reviewing a jury award of punitive damages is "whether the nonmovant has produced clear and convincing evidence from which a jury could reasonably find one or more of the aggravating factors" required by statute for a punitive damages verdict (fraud, malice, or willful or wanton conduct).[64] In *Scarborough*, a shoe salesman sued his employer for malicious prosecution and was awarded $30,000 in compensatory damages and $77,000 in punitive damages. The employer moved for JNOV as to the punitive damages award, arguing that the plaintiff had not produced "clear and convincing" evidence of punitive damages as required by G.S. 1D-15(b). The trial court agreed and granted JNOV for the employer. The Court of Appeals reversed, holding that the standard for a judge to apply on a JNOV motion is whether there is "more than a scintilla" of evidence to support the verdict.[65]

---

62. Shugar v. Guill, 304 N.C. 332, 339, 283 S.E.2d 507, 511 (1981); Williams v. Boylan-Pierce, 69 N.C. App. 315, 319–21, 317 S.E.2d 17, 20 (1984); *see also* Cockerham-Ellerbee v. Jonesville, 190 N.C. App. 150, 157, 660 S.E.2d 178, 182 (2008) ("the weight and credibility of . . . evidence of willful or wanton conduct . . . [are] for a jury, not for this Court").

63. 363 N.C. 715, 693 S.E.2d 640 (2009), *cert denied*, 131 S. Ct. 2456, 179 L. Ed. 2d 1211 (2011).

64. *Id.* at 721–22, 693 S.E.2d at 644. G.S. 1D-15(a) provides that punitive damages may be awarded "only if the claimant proves that the defendant is liable for compensatory damages and that one of the following aggravating factors was present and was related to the injury for which compensatory damages were awarded:

(1) Fraud.
(2) Malice.
(3) Willful or wanton conduct."

The aggravating factor must be proven by clear and convincing evidence. G.S. 1D-15(b).

65. Scarborough v. Dillard's, Inc., 188 N.C. App. 430, 431, 655 S.E.2d 875, 876 (2008).

The Supreme Court reversed, noting that the statutory standard for proving liability for punitive damages is that the defendant engaged in an aggravating factor of fraud, malice, or willful or wanton conduct pursuant to G.S. 1D-15(a) and that the plaintiff must prove the aggravating factor by "clear and convincing evidence" pursuant to G.S. 1D-15(b). The court went on to hold that

> in reviewing a trial court's ruling on a motion for judgment notwithstanding the verdict on punitive damages, our appellate courts must determine whether the non-movant produced clear and convincing evidence from which a jury could reasonably find one or more of the statutory aggravating factors required by N.C.G.S. § 1D-15(a) and that that aggravating factor was related to the injury for which compensatory damages were awarded. Reviewing the trial court's ruling under the "more than a scintilla" of evidence standard does not give proper deference to the statutory mandate that the aggravating factor be proved by clear and convincing evidence. Evidence that is only more than a scintilla cannot as a matter of law satisfy the nonmoving party's threshold statutory burden of clear and convincing evidence.[66]

---

66. *Scarborough*, 363 N.C. at 722, 693 S.E.2d at 644. In a vigorous dissent, two justices argued that, by applying a "clear and convincing" standard to JNOV, the majority had confused the concepts of burden of production and burden of proof.

> Determining whether a plaintiff has met the burden of persuasion by producing "clear and convincing" evidence is in the exclusive province of the fact finder. . . . Contrary to the majority's assertions, the trial court does not alter its review of the plaintiff's *burden of production* upon a motion for judgment notwithstanding the verdict merely because the *burden of persuasion* is higher or lower in each case.

Id. at 732–33, 693 S.E.2d at 650.

Given this "clear and convincing" review standard, the court also emphasized the statutory requirement of G.S. 1D-50.[67] The statute states,

> When reviewing the evidence regarding a finding by the trier of fact concerning liability for punitive damages . . . the trial court shall state in a written opinion its reasons for upholding or disturbing the finding or award. In doing so, the court shall address with specificity the evidence, or lack thereof, as it bears on the liability for or the amount of punitive damages, in light of the requirements of this Chapter.[68]

The court stated that these trial court opinions "are not binding on the appellate court, [but] provide valuable assistance to the appellate court in determining whether as a matter of law the evidence, in the light most favorable to the nonmoving party, is sufficient to be considered by the jury as clear and convincing evidence on the issue of punitive damages."[69] In light of *Scarborough*, the Court of Appeals has been "constrained to" hold that opinions under G.S. 1D-50 are mandatory and has remanded orders on JNOV motions regarding punitive damages where the trial court has not produced the opinion.[70]

Table 1 presents a hypothetical example of how a JNOV motion is to be reviewed, in a case in which the jury finds defendant liable for breach of fiduciary duty and fraud and imposes compensatory and punitive damages. In sum, when a JNOV motion involves punitive damages, the trial judge is in the position of evaluating not just the presence or absence of evidence, but also its weight and persuasiveness, a role the judge is accustomed to when finding facts in a bench trial but not when evaluating dispositive motions. As a result, a party's argument for JNOV as to punitive damages may more closely resemble

67. *Id.* at 721, 693 S.E.2d at 643.

68. G.S. 1D-50.

69. *Scarborough*, 363 at 722, 693 S.E.2d at 644–45.

70. Springs v. City of Charlotte, 209 N.C. App. 271, 281, 704 S.E.2d 319, 326 (2011); Hudgins v. Wagoner, 204 N.C. App. 480, 495, 694 S.E.2d 436, 447–48 (2010).

Table 1. Hypothetical Review of a JNOV Motion

Claim/Award	Trial Court's JNOV Review Standard	Appellate JNOV Review Standard
Breach of fiduciary duty and fraud† **(and corresponding compensatory damages)**	Traditional standard: Whether there was more than a scintilla of evidence to support the verdict.	Traditional standard: Whether there was more than a scintilla of evidence to support the verdict.
Punitive damages	Whether the non-movant produced "clear and convincing evidence" by which a jury could find one or more statutory aggravating factors. *(Analysis reflected in trial court's written opinion pursuant to* G.S. 1D-50.)	Whether the non-movant produced "clear and convincing evidence" by which a jury could find one or more statutory aggravating factors. *(Written opinion pursuant to* G.S. 1D-50 *is "valuable assistance" to appellate court. If trial court produces no opinion, matter remanded to trial court.*)

† Because fraud is one of the aggravating factors under G.S. 1D-15, it appears that the court will have to assess the evidence relating to fraud a second time under the standard articulated in *Scarborough* when assessing the JNOV motion relating to punitive damages.

a jury argument than a JNOV argument, particularly as to the nine factors a jury may consider under the punitive damages statutes.[71] The end result of *Scarborough* is that judges have considerably more room on a JNOV motion to set aside punitive damages than liability and compensatory damages.

A question unanswered by *Scarborough* is whether its holding extends to a trial court's directed verdict analysis. As discussed above, JNOV is, in short, a renewal of a directed verdict motion, and the traditional directed verdict and JNOV standards are identical. It seems that a trial court's decision to grant a directed verdict on punitive damages would therefore be reviewed under the same standard established for JNOV in *Scarborough*, but that no written opinion would be required pursuant to G.S. 1D-50.

71. *See* G.S. 1D-35.

Procedure and Jurisdiction

The Motion

Motions for Directed Verdict Mandatory

As discussed above, a JNOV motion is technically a renewal of the moving party's earlier motion for directed verdict. A party has no right to JNOV if that party did not first move for directed verdict at the close of all the evidence:[72] "A motion for directed verdict at the close of all evidence is an absolute prerequisite to the post verdict motion for judgment notwithstanding the verdict."[73]

Timing of Motion

A motion for JNOV must be made not later than ten days after entry of judgment.[74] The trial court has no authority under Rule of Civil Procedure 6(b) to extend the time for making a JNOV motion.[75] Nor may the parties agree to extend the deadline by stipulation or otherwise.[76] The ten-day deadline for making a motion begins with entry of judgment.[77] "Entry" is defined by Rule of Civil Procedure 58,

---

72. Rule 50(b)(1); Bryant v. Nationwide Mut. Fire Ins. Co., 313 N.C. 362, 369, 329 S.E.2d 333, 338 (1985); Graves v. Walston, 302 N.C. 332, 338, 275 S.E.2d 485, 489 (1981) ("The plain meaning of the quoted rule is that a motion for judgment notwithstanding the verdict must be preceded by a motion for directed verdict at the close of all the evidence."); Coates v. Niblock Dev. Corp., 161 N.C. App. 515, 516, 588 S.E.2d 492, 493–94 (2003); Tatum v. Tatum, 79 N.C. App. 605, 609–10, 339 S.E.2d 817, 819–20, *aff'd as modified*, 318 N.C. 407, 348 S.E.2d 813 (1986).

73. Boone Lumber, Inc. v. Sigmon, 103 N.C. App. 798, 800, 407 S.E.2d 291, 293 (1991).

74. Rule 50(b)(1). If there was no verdict, the motion must be made within ten days after the jury was discharged. *Id.*

75. Rule 6(b) gives the trial court broad discretion to extend deadlines established in the Rules of Civil Procedure, but it explicitly excludes most significant post-trial motions for relief: "[N]either the court nor the parties may extend the time for taking any action under Rules 50(b), 52, 59(b), (d), (e), 60(b), except to the extent and under the conditions stated in them." Rule 50 includes no extension provisions of its own.

76. Rule 6(b).

77. Rule 50(b)(1).

which states that "a judgment is entered when it is reduced to writing, signed by the judge, and filed with the clerk of court." [78] Neither the rendering of the verdict nor the reading of the verdict is entry of judgment,[79] nor is a trial court's announcement of a judgment in open court.[80] If the court's judgment is served by one of the parties by mail, the movant's time to make a JNOV motion is extended by three days.[81] If a party is not timely served the judgment as required by Rule 58, the time limit for making a JNOV motion is tolled for the duration of any period of noncompliance with Rule 58's service requirement but not "longer than 90 days from the date the judgment is entered." [82] Service and filing of a written JNOV motion are governed by Rule of Civil Procedure 5.[83]

---

78. G.S. 1A-1, Rule 58.

79. Griffith v. N.C. Dep't of Corr., 210 N.C. App. 544, 549, 709 S.E.2d 412, 416–17 (2011); Olson v. McMillian, 144 N.C. App. 615, 619, 548 S.E.2d 571, 574 (2001); Sheehan v. Harper Builders, Inc. v. Hazelwood Constr. Co., Inc., 83 N.C. App. 630, 631, 351 S.E.2d 114, 115 (1986).

80. *Griffith*, 210 N.C. App. at 549, 709 S.E.2d at 417 (citing Worsham v. Richbourg's Sales & Rentals, 124 N.C. App. 782, 784, 478 S.E.2d 649, 650 (1996)); Muse v. Charter Hosp. of Winston-Salem, 117 N.C. App. 468, 480–81, 452 S.E.2d 589, 598, *aff'd per curiam*, 342 N.C. 403, 464 S.E.2d 44 (1995).

81. The rule reads as follows:

> The party designated by the judge or, if the judge does not otherwise designate, the party who prepares the judgment, shall serve a copy of the judgment upon all other parties within three days after the judgment is entered. Service and proof of service shall be in accordance with Rule 5. If service is by mail, three days shall be added to the time periods prescribed by Rule 50(b), Rule 52(b), and Rule 59.

G.S. 1A-1, Rule 58.

82. Rule 58.

83. *See* G.S. 1A-1, Rule 5(a), (b), (d), (e)(1). Rule 5(b) permits motions to be served upon a party's attorney of record by delivery to the attorney (handing to the attorney, leaving it at the attorney's office, or faxing it to the attorney's office) or by mailing to the attorney's office. Absent an attorney of record (or upon court order), service is to be made upon the party by hand delivery to the party, mailing to the party's last known address, or, if no address is known, filing it with the clerk of court.

Effect on Appeal Deadlines

The general deadline for filing and service of a written notice of appeal of a civil judgment is thirty days after entry of judgment.[84] If, however, a party has made a timely motion for JNOV under Rule 50(b), the "thirty day period for taking appeal is tolled as to all parties until entry of an order disposing of the motion[.]"[85] The appeal period begins to run again from the date the trial court enters an order on the Rule 50(b) motion (or from the date of untimely service of the order as directed by Rule 3(c)).[86]

Stating the "Specific Grounds"

Rule 50(a) also requires that a motion for directed verdict "state the specific grounds therefor." This direction is mandatory,[87] and failure to comply can be "sufficient grounds standing alone for the trial court to overrule the motion."[88] But what exactly does it mean to "state the specific grounds" under Rule 50? There is only one standard for a Rule 50 motion: that the evidence is legally insufficient to go to a jury. If the basis for a Rule 50 motion is, by its nature, so limited, what does the "specific grounds" mandate require?

---

84. N.C. R. App. P. 3(c). The deadline is thirty days "after entry of judgment if the party has been served with a copy of the judgment within the three day period prescribed by Rule 58 of the Rules of Civil Procedure; or (2) within thirty days after service upon the party of a copy of the judgment if service was not made within that three day period[.]" N.C. R. App. P. 3(c)(1), (2). But see *Wilkins Family Medicine, P.A., v. WakeMed*, ___ S.E.2d ___ (N.C. Ct. App. Jan. 5, 2016), and *Magazian v. Creagh*, 759 S.E.2d 130, 131 (N.C. Ct. App. 2014), for the effect of *actual notice* of a final order on the three-day service period.

85. N.C. R. App. P. 3(c)(3); G.S. 1-279.1; *see* Middleton v. Middleton, 98 N.C. App. 217, 220, 390 S.E.2d 453, 455 (1990). Note, however, that despite the plain language of appellate Rule 3(c)(3) tolling the deadline as to "all parties," the Court of Appeals recently permitted tolling only as to the party who had made the Rule 50 motion. Estate of Hurst *ex rel.* Cherry v. Moorehead I, LLC, 228 N.C. App. 571, 586, 748 S.E.2d 568, 579 n.2 (2013).

86. N.C. R. App. P. 3(c)(3).

87. Anderson v. Butler, 284 N.C. 723, 729, 202 S.E.2d 585, 588 (1974).

88. Byerly v. Byerly, 38 N.C. App. 551, 552–53, 248 S.E.2d 433, 435 (1978) (citing Dixon v. Shelton, 9 N.C. App. 392, 176 S.E.2d 390 (1970)).

In many—if not most—civil trials, there are multiple claims, each of which likely has multiple elements, and there may also be multiple defenses, some of which involve complicated applications. When it is time for a party to ask a court for judgment as a matter of law under Rule 50, the court needs to know what part of the case it is being asked to assess. As the Court of Appeals recently noted, "In complex civil cases . . . where the parties have argued multiple defenses and theories of liability, it is critical that the movant direct the trial court with specificity to the grounds for its motion for a directed verdict."[89] The movant must, therefore, state which particular claim, defense, element, or other evidentiary component of the case is at issue in the motion. Not only does this requirement give the trial court important direction; it also gives the other party a chance to correct an evidentiary failing, if possible. The courts have stated that the "specific grounds" requirement "allow[s] the adverse party to meet any defects with further proof and avoid the entry of a judgment notwithstanding the verdict at the close of the trial, on a ground that could have been met with proof had it been suggested earlier."[90]

In *Jones v. Allred*,[91] for example, defendants argued that the trial court's directed verdict as to negligence should be upheld due to evidence of plaintiff's contributory negligence. Disagreeing, the Court of Appeals noted that defendants had cited only the absence of their own negligence—and not the presence of contributory negligence—when arguing for a directed verdict before the trial court. Thus the issue of contributory negligence was not preserved.[92] In a complex fraudulent transfer case, plaintiffs asserted that the trial court erred

---

89. Plasma Ctrs. of Am., LLC v. Talecris Plasma Res., Inc., 222 N.C. App. 83, 88, 731 S.E.2d 837, 841 (2012)).

90. *Byerly*, 38 N.C. App. at 553, 248 S.E.2d at 435; *see also* Love v. Pressley, 34 N.C. App. 503, 511, 239 S.E.2d 574, 580 (1977) (stating the rationale); Hedden v. Hall, 23 N.C. App. 453, 457, 209 S.E.2d 358, 361 (1974) (noting that requirement of specificity is a matter of fairness to the party with the burden of proof). Failure to include a specific basis also, of course, makes appellate review more cumbersome. Browne v. Macaulay, 65 N.C. App. 708, 710, 309 S.E.2d 704, 705 (1983).

91. 52 N.C. App 38, 278 S.E.2d 521 (1981).

92. *Id.* at 46, 278 S.E.2d at 526.

in not granting a JNOV on grounds of lack of valuable consideration.[93] In arguing this point, however, plaintiffs relied on two principles of fraudulent conveyance that they had not argued on directed verdict. Thus the appellate court refused to consider the additional points, holding that "plaintiffs are procedurally precluded from making the evidentiary showing necessary to set aside the jury verdict[.][94]

No new grounds in JNOV motion.

The moving party should be as inclusive as possible when crafting a directed verdict motion because the subsequent JNOV motion is not an opportunity to include areas not covered the first time. Because a "motion for judgment notwithstanding the verdict is technically only a renewal of the motion for a directed verdict made at the close of all the evidence, . . . [a] movant cannot assert grounds not included in the motion for directed verdict."[95] In a products liability case, plaintiffs argued in their JNOV motion that defendant's spoliation of evidence precluded him from pursuing a certain defense as a matter of law.[96] The Court of Appeals rejected this JNOV argument because the spoliation allegations had not been part of plaintiffs' directed verdict motion.[97] And, in a negligence case, plaintiff initially moved for a directed verdict "on the issue of negligence" but did not argue that he was entitled to judgment on the issue of proximate cause. He was therefore precluded from later arguing proximate cause on his JNOV motion.[98] In *Munie v. Tangle Oaks Corp.*,[99] defendants argued both the statute of limita-

---

93. Tiber Holding Corp. v. Diloreto, 160 N.C. App. 583, 585, 586 S.E.2d 538, 539 (2003).

94. *Id.* at 585–86, 586 S.E.2d at 539–40.

95. Lee v. Capitol Tire Co., Inc., 40 N.C. App. 150, 156, 252 S.E.2d 252, 256–57 (1979) (quoting *Love*, 34 N.C. App. at 511, 239 S.E.2d at 580); *Hedden*, 23 N.C. App. at 457, 209 S.E.2d at 361.

96. Jones v. GMRI, Inc., 144 N.C. App. 558, 564, 551 S.E.2d 867, 871–72 (2001).

97. *Id.* at 564, 551 S.E.2d at 872.

98. Lassiter v. English, 126 N.C. App. 489, 493, 485 S.E.2d 840, 843 (1997), *overruled on other grounds by In re* Will of Buck, 350 N.C. 621, 516 S.E.2d 858 (1999).

99. 109 N.C. App. 336, 427 S.E.2d 149 (1993).

tions and insufficiency of the evidence as grounds for JNOV. Because only the statute of limitations argument was raised on directed verdict, defendants were limited to arguing statute of limitations on JNOV.[100] And in a recent opinion, the Court of Appeals rejected JNOV arguments made on grounds that there was no evidence (1) of mutual assent or (2) plaintiff's willingness to perform its obligations. Because the directed verdict argument was based only on statute of frauds and lack of waiver, the moving party could not properly raise additional issues in its JNOV motion.[101]

No new grounds on appeal.

Likewise, a basis for a Rule 50 motion not raised before the trial court will not be reviewed on appeal.[102] A defendant in a trespass and conversion case whose directed verdict motion raised only lawful occupation and property removal could not appeal the denial of directed verdict on the basis of insufficient evidence of damages.[103] And where defendant appealed the denial of directed verdict on four separate grounds, the Court of Appeals declined to review two of those grounds because they had not been asserted before the trial court.[104]

The Court of Appeals has also specifically held that a basis raised in a directed verdict motion, but then not included among the issues

---

100. *Id.* at 342, 427 S.E.2d at 152.

101. Plasma Ctrs. of Am., LLC v. Talecris Plasma Res., Inc., 222 N.C. App. 83, 87–88, 731 S.E.2d 837, 841 (2012).

102. Maxwell v. Michael P. Doyle, Inc., 164 N.C. App. 319, 323, 595 S.E.2d 759, 762 (2004); Tiber Holding Corp. v. Diloreto, 160 N.C. App. 583, 586, 586 S.E.2d 538, 540 (2003); Williams v. Davis, 157 N.C. App. 696, 701, 580 S.E.2d 85, 88 (2003) (citing Leatherwood v. Ehlinger, 151 N.C. App. 15, 18, 564 S.E.2d 883, 886 (2002)); Smith v. Carolina Coach Co., 120 N.C. App. 106, 461 S.E.2d 362 (1995); Freese v. Smith, 110 N.C. App. 28, 34, 428 S.E.2d 841, 845–46 (1993); Mobley v. Hill, 80 N.C. App. 79, 84, 341 S.E.3d 46, 49 (1986); Broyhill v. Coppage, 79 N.C. App. 221, 225, 339 S.E.2d 32, 36 (1986); Lee v. Keck, 68 N.C. App. 320, 328, 315 S.E.2d 323, 329 (1984); Oxendine v. Moss, 64 N.C. App. 205, 206, 306 S.E.2d 831, 832 (1983); Worrell v. Hennis Credit Union, 12 N.C. App. 275, 278, 182 S.E.2d 874, 876 (1971).

103. Love v. Pressley, 34 N.C. App. 503, 510–11, 239 S.E.2d 574, 579–80 (1977).

104. Ellis v. Vespoint, 102 N.C. App. 739, 743, 403 S.E.2d 542, 545 (1991).

renewed on JNOV, will not be reviewed on appeal. In *Rhue v. Rhue*,[105] a constructive trust case involving land parcels, defendant made a directed verdict motion as to "Issue No. 1," which addressed parcels C and D. In his JNOV motion, he asked for judgment "in accordance with his 'previous motion for [a] directed verdict as to Issue No. 1.'" On appeal, he argued that judgment should have been granted under Rule 50(b) as to parcels C and D as well as A, B, and E. The Court of Appeals held that defendant had waived his arguments regarding A, B, and E because they were not included among the grounds renewed on JNOV.[106]

Further, if a Rule 50 motion is reviewed by the trial court on one ground, the appellate courts may not uphold the decision on a different basis. In a construction dispute, the trial court granted a directed verdict to defendant, and the trial transcript showed that defendant had based its motion solely on the expiration of the statute of limitations.[107] The Court of Appeals, however, affirmed directed verdict not on that basis, but on grounds that plaintiff had failed to establish a prima facie case for fraud.[108] The Supreme Court reversed, holding that allowing an appellate court to affirm a Rule 50 order on a basis not raised at trial would "completely frustrate the notice purpose" of Rule 50(a)'s specificity requirement.[109]

A party moving for judgment under Rule 50 should ensure that the record reflects the grounds upon which the party based the motion before the trial court. Ideally the grounds will appear in a written motion.[110] Written motions are often impractical for directed verdict, which is addressed in the midst of trial. Written motions may generally be expected, however, at the JNOV stage. If a Rule 50 motion is made

---

105. 189 N.C. App. 299, 658 S.E.2d 52 (2008).

106. *Id.* at 304, 658 S.E.2d at 57.

107. Feibus & Co., Inc. v. Godley Constr. Co., Inc., 301 N.C. 294, 299–300, 271 S.E.2d 385, 389–390 (1980).

108. *Id.* at 297–98, 271 S.E.2d at 388.

109. *Id.* at 301, 271 S.E.2d 390.

110. Hensley v. Ramsey, 283 N.C. 714, 726, 199 S.E.2d 1, 8 (1973) (noting that written motions are "the better practice").

orally, an appellate court will review an oral statement of the grounds if a transcript of that statement is included in the record on appeal.[111]

Flexible application.

While the courts have long held that the specificity provision is mandatory, it may be excused in cases where the trial court and the parties are well aware of the grounds.[112] This occurs, naturally, in cases where the legal questions are less complex or there are few distinct matters in dispute. The appellate courts opted not to "inflexibly enforce" the requirement in a straightforward contract dispute where it "was clear the determinative issue was whether the plaintiff's paving job complied with the terms of the paving contract";[113] in a medical negligence case where the "obvious" basis was lack of actionable negligence;[114] in a will caveat where the issues of testamentary capacity and undue influence

---

111. *Id.*; *Feibus*, 301 N.C. at 298, 271 S.E.2d at 387; *see also* Davis v. Peacock, 10 N.C. App. 256, 257, 178 S.E.2d 133, 135 (1970) ("Litigants would be well advised to include in the record the specific grounds stated in the motion for a directed verdict. A failure to do so could result in a dismissal of the appeal."). *But see* Warren v. Canal Indus., Inc., 61 N.C. App. 211, 213, 300 S.E.2d 557, 559 (1983) (reviewing grounds not otherwise included in the record because they were "apparent from the judge's response to defendants' motion and from the briefs"). Whether in writing or oral, the statement should actually recite a ground and not merely cite a relevant case. Grant v. Greene, 11 N.C. App. 537, 540, 181 S.E.2d 770, 772 (1971).

112. Anderson v. Butler, 284 N.C. 723, 729, 202 S.E.2d 585, 588–89 (1974); J.T. Russell & Sons, Inc. v. Silver Birch Pond, L.L.C., 217 N.C. App. 290, 295, 721 S.E.2d 699, 703 (2011); Humphrey v. Hill, 55 N.C. App. 359, 363, 285 S.E.2d 293, 296 (1982). Note also that, if grounds were adequately stated in a motion for directed verdict after plaintiff's evidence, but no specific basis was stated on a renewed motion after the close of all the evidence, the specificity requirement is excusable if it is apparent that the grounds were the same. *In re* Will of Yelverton, 178 N.C. App. 267, 280, 631 S.E.2d 180, 187 (2006); Hodges v. Hodges, 37 N.C. App. 459, 464, 246 S.E.2d 812, 815 (1978).

113. *J.T. Russell*, 217 N.C. App. at 295, 721 S.E.2d at 702–03.

114. Lindsey v. The Clinic for Women, 40 N.C. App. 456, 461, 253 S.E.2d 304, 307 (1979).

were clearly identified throughout trial;[115] and in an adverse possession case where the obvious ground was insufficiency of the evidence.[116]

Objection required.

If a Rule 50 motion is granted by the trial court, another party may not appeal on the basis that the motion did not state specific grounds unless that party raised the deficiency at trial.[117] In *Humphrey v. Hill*, for example, the court noted that, even if defendant's Rule 50 motion was indeed too general, the plaintiff had "waived his objection" when he did not argue that contention before the trial judge.[118] Raising an objection at trial gives the movant, if possible, a chance to correct the omission[119] so that the court and non-moving party can be fully aware of the purpose of the motion.

Motions by the Court

Rule 50 also allows a court essentially to grant or deny JNOV without a motion by a party. The rule states that a judge on his or her own motion may "grant, deny, or redeny a motion for directed verdict made at the close of all the evidence that was denied or for any reason was not granted."[120] A court has no authority to make a JNOV ruling on its own motion unless the relevant party moved for directed verdict at the close of the evidence.[121] The court may make its ruling with or without

115. *In re* Will of Jones, 114 N.C. App. 782, 784–85, 443 S.E.2d 363, 364 (1994).

116. Herbert v. Babson, 74 N.C. App. 519, 521, 328 S.E.2d 796, 798 (1985).

117. Johnson v. Dunlap, 53 N.C. App. 312, 315, 280 S.E.2d 759, 762 (1981); Byerly v. Byerly, 38 N.C. App. 551, 553, 248 S.E.2d 433, 435 (1978); Builders Supplies Co. v. Gainey, 10 N.C. App. 364, 368, 178 S.E.2d 794, 797 (1971); Pergerson v. Williams, 9 N.C. App. 512, 516–17, 176 S.E.2d 885, 888 (1970). In *Browne v. Macaulay*, the court was compelled to review the Rule 50 order because appellant failed to object, but the court went on to note that failure to state a specific basis nevertheless "unduly complicates the process of appellate review." 65 N.C. App. 708, 710, 309 S.E.2d 704, 705 (1983).

118. 55 N.C. App. 359, 363, 285 S.E.2d 293, 296 (1982).

119. *Byerly*, 38 N.C. App. at 553, 248 S.E.2d at 435.

120. Rule 50(b)(1).

121. *Id.*

further notice and hearing.[122] The court's order—not just its motion—must be entered no later than ten days after entry of judgment.[123]

Combined Motions for JNOV and New Trial

A party moving for JNOV may combine the JNOV motion with a motion for new trial under Rule 59.[124] The party is not *required* to make a combined motion, however, and a motion for directed verdict or JNOV is not a prerequisite to a new trial motion.[125] The two types of relief are independent of each other, are based on different grounds, and are subject to different review standards. The procedure for the court's disposition of a combined motion is discussed below.[126]

The Court's Order

Hearing

When the trial judge grants, denies, or redenies relief under Rule 50(b)(1) on his or her own motion, the judge is not required to first hold a hearing.[127] There also is no explicit requirement that the judge conduct a formal hearing on a motion by a party, but a hearing may happen by operation of court practice if duly noticed pursuant to Rule of Civil Procedure 6(d), or if it appears on a motions calendar pursuant to court calendaring rules or policy.[128] If the court conducts

---

122. *Id.*

123. *Id.* If there is no verdict, the ruling must be made within ten days after the jury was discharged. *Id.*

124. Rule 50(b)(1) ("A motion for a new trial may be joined with this motion, or a new trial may be prayed for in the alternative."). Motions for a new trial are discussed in Chapter 2.

125. Garrison v. Garrison, 87 N.C. App. 591, 595, 361 S.E.2d 921, 924 (1987) ("Rule 50(b) merely establishes a procedure whereby a movant may, *if he chooses*, join the new trial motion with one for judgment notwithstanding the verdict.").

126. *See infra* section titled "Conditional Rulings on Combined New Trial Motions."

127. Rule 50(b)(1).

128. Rule of Civil Procedure 5(a) requires service of every written notice applicable to the action. *See* G.S. 1A-1, Rule 5(a). Rule 6(d) sets out the general timing requirements for notices of hearing. *See* G.S. 1A-1, Rule

a hearing on a party's Rule 50 motion, there must be adequate notice to the adverse party or parties and opportunity to respond. In a case decided in the similar context of a new trial motion, the trial court granted plaintiff's motion after conducting a hearing without defendants or their counsel present, and the record revealed no actual notice or attempted notice to defendants of the hearing date.[129] The Court of Appeals reversed and remanded for a new hearing, holding that the lack of notice deprived defendants of an opportunity to object in violation of their right to due process.[130]

Timing of Order and Stay of Execution

An order on the court's own motion under Rule 50(b)(1) must be made within ten days of entry of judgment.[131] When the motion for JNOV is by a party, however, there is no specified timeframe in the Rules of Civil Procedure within which the court must enter an order.[132] When the party's motion is timely, it tolls the period for appeal of the underlying judgment until the trial court enters an order on the JNOV motion, and the trial court may rule on the motion after the underlying appeal period (typically thirty days) has expired.[133] The court may also enter an order on a JNOV motion after expiration of the session of court in which the motion was heard.[134] As with all orders, the court should

---

6(d). Many local court rules include preferred procedures and forms for requesting a hearing on a motion. *See, e.g.,* Local Rules for Civil Superior Court, Tenth Judicial District, North Carolina, Local Form 1, available at www.nccourts.org/Courts/CRS/Policies/LocalRules.

129. Otto v. Certo, 210 N.C. App. 468, 472–73, 708 S.E.2d 183, 186 (2011).

130. *Id.* at 473, 708 S.E.2d at 186.

131. Rule 50(b)(1). *See supra* section titled "Motions by the Court."

132. Local court rules may dictate certain time requirements where not provided by statute.

133. N.C. R. App. P. 3(c)(3).

134. Rule of Civil Procedure 6(c) provides as follows:

> The period of time provided for the doing of any act or the taking of any proceeding is not affected or limited by the continued existence or expiration of a session of court. The continued existence or expiration of a session of court in no way affects the power of a court to do any act or take any

dispose of post-trial motions in a timely manner, with due consideration for fairness, judicial efficiency, the parties' need for finality, and the benefits of ruling on matters when they are fresh in the judge's mind.

The filing of a Rule 50(b) motion does not automatically stay enforcement of the underlying judgment past the automatic (thirty-day) stay allowed in Rule 62(a).[135] The trial court, therefore, has discretion under Rule 62(b) to stay execution of proceedings to enforce the judgment while a motion for JNOV is pending.[136]

> proceeding, but no issue of fact shall be submitted to a jury out of session.

G.S. 1A-1, Rule 6(c); *see also* Hous., Inc. v. Weaver, 305 N.C. 428, 440, 290 S.E.2d 642, 649 (1982) (holding that a court may grant a JNOV motion "after the adjournment of the term during which the judgment was entered."). For a discussion of a court's ability to enter an order after a term or session of court has ended, see Michael Crowell, *Out-of-Term, Out-of-Session, Out-of-County*, ADMIN. OF JUST. BULL. 2008/05 (UNC School of Government, Nov. 2008).

135. *See* G.S. 1A-1, Rule 62(a).

136. *See* Rule 62(b), which states,

> In its discretion and on such conditions for the security of the adverse party as are proper, the court may stay the execution of or any proceedings to enforce a judgment pending the disposition of a motion for a new trial or to alter or amend a judgment made pursuant to . . . a motion for judgment made pursuant to Rule 50[.] If the time provided in the controlling statute or rule of appellate procedure for giving notice of appeal from the judgment had not expired before a stay under this subsection was entered, that time shall begin to run immediately upon the expiration of any stay under this section, and no execution shall issue nor shall proceedings be taken for enforcement of the judgment until the expiration of that time.

The authority to issue a stay also applies to Rule 59 motions, motions under Rule 52(b), and Rule 60 motions.

No Findings of Fact

Rule 52 of the Rules of Civil Procedure requires a judge, when ruling on a motion, to make written findings of fact *if a party requests them.*[137] Based on this language, occasionally a party may request such findings when making its JNOV motion, or, similarly, a party submitting a draft JNOV order may include findings of fact for the judge to consider. Regardless of the language of Rule 52, however, findings of fact are *not* appropriate in a JNOV order. Orders on certain dispositive motions, including Rule 50, cannot properly include findings of fact. To make a finding of fact, a court is required to weigh competing evidence and decide ("find") what is true. The decision on a motion for JNOV is simply whether sufficient evidence existed upon which the jury could have based its verdict for the non-moving party; the court does not engage in any fact finding based on that evidence.[138] As the Court of Appeals has explained,

---

137. G.S. 1A-1, Rule 52(a)(2).

138. This exception applies also to orders on the other dispositive motions, including summary judgment, where the question is simply whether a party has met its threshold burden of production. At summary judgment, the court's task is to determine only whether genuine issues of material fact exist, not to decide those facts in favor of one party or another. *See* Hodges v. Moore, 205 N.C. App. 722, 723, 697 S.E.2d 406, 406 (2010); Broughton v. McClatchy Newspapers, Inc., 161 N.C. App. 20, 33–34, 588 S.E.2d 20, 30 (2003). The court may recite the *undisputed* facts in order to give the parties and appellate courts a better understanding of its decision but should do so with caution in order to avoid the appearance that it has resolved disputed evidence. As the court of appeals observed in *War Eagle, Inc. v. Belair,*

> By making findings of fact on summary judgment, the trial court demonstrates to the appellate courts a fundamental lack of understanding of the nature of summary judgment proceedings. We understand that a number of trial judges feel compelled to make findings of fact reciting those "uncontested facts" that form the basis of their decision. When this is done, any findings should clearly be denominated as "uncontested facts" and not as a resolution of contested facts. In the instant case, there was no statement that any of the findings were of "uncontested facts."

> When a judge decides that a directed verdict [or JNOV] is appropriate, actually he is deciding that the question has become one exclusively of law and that the jury has no function to serve. . . . [D]efendants [are mistaken] that deference is due the trial court's findings of fact in the case *sub judice.* Rather, the trial court's findings of fact and conclusions of law have no legal significance in an order granting JNOV. . . . Therefore, "we consider the matter anew and . . . freely substitute our judgment for that of the trial court regardless of whether the trial court made findings of fact and conclusions of law."[139]

Note that while findings of fact are inappropriate in a JNOV order, when assessing a JNOV motion regarding *punitive damages*, the court is required to issue a written opinion pursuant to G.S. 1D-50 stating its reasons for upholding or disturbing the award.[140]

Conditional Rulings on Combined New Trial Motions

As noted above, a party moving for JNOV may combine that motion with a motion for new trial under Rule 59. The rule states as follows:

> A motion for a new trial may be joined with this motion, or a new trial may be prayed for in the alternative. If a verdict was returned the judge may allow the judgment to stand or may set aside the judgment and either order a new trial or direct the entry of judgment as if the requested verdict had been directed. If no verdict was returned the judge may direct the entry of judgment as if the requested verdict had been directed or may order a new trial.[141]

---

204 N.C. App. 548, 552, 694 S.E.2d 497, 500 (2010).

139. Hodgson Constr., Inc. v. Howard, 187 N.C. App. 408, 411–412, 654 S.E.2d 7, 10–11 (2007) (citations omitted); *see also* N.C. Indus. Capital, LLC v. Clayton, 185 N.C. App. 356, 370–71, 649 S.E.2d 14, 24–25 (2007) (findings of fact not required in order on JNOV even where party requested them under Rule 52(a)).

140. *See supra* section titled "The Punitive Damages Variation."

141. Rule 50(b)(1).

When the judge receives a combined motion and denies the JNOV motion, the court then may grant or deny the new trial motion. When the judge receives a combined motion and grants the JNOV motion, the judge must also make a conditional ruling on the new trial motion.[142] This procedure avoids serial appeals, allowing the appellate court to review the new trial determination in the event it reverses the grant of JNOV. The trial court must determine whether the new trial motion should be granted if JNOV is vacated or reversed on appeal and must specify the grounds for conditionally granting or denying the new trial motion.[143] Thus upon granting JNOV,

- If the trial court conditionally grants new trial,[144] and the order granting JNOV is then reversed on appeal, the new trial proceeds unless the appellate court directs otherwise.[145]
- If the trial court conditionally denies new trial,[146] the party may assert error in the denial of the new trial motion. If the order

142. Rule 50(c)(1); *In re* Will of Buck, 350 N.C. 621, 623, 516 S.E.2d 858, 860 (1999); Bryant v. Nationwide Mut. Fire Ins. Co., 313 N.C. 362, 379, 329 S.E.2d 333, 343 (1985); Graves v. Walston, 302 N.C. 332, 339, 275 S.E.2d 485, 489 (1981); Lyon v. May, 119 N.C. App. 704, 708, 459 S.E.2d 833, 836 (1995).

143. Rule 50(c)(1). The grounds and standards for granting a new trial are discussed in Chapter 2. If the appellate court affirms the trial court's grant of JNOV, review of the new trial order is not necessary.

144. The conditional grant of a new trial "does not affect the finality of the judgment." Rule 50(c)(1).

145. Rule 50(c)(1); *see, e.g.,* Williams v. Randolph, 94 N.C. App. 413, 423–24, 380 S.E.2d 553, 560 (1989) (reversing JNOV but affirming conditional grant of new trial on grounds that verdict was against greater weight of evidence).

146. It is unlikely that a trial court would grant JNOV and then conditionally deny new trial. At the very least, if the court concludes that the evidence was insufficient as a matter of law to support the verdict under Rule 50, it seems likely that the court would also grant new trial under Rule 59(a)(7) on grounds that the verdict was against the greater weight of the evidence. But the grant of a new trial under this basis is discretionary, so it is possible that a trial court could opt not to order such relief. See section in Chapter 2 titled "Insufficiency of the Evidence to Justify Verdict; Verdict Contrary to Law—Rule 59(a)(7)."

granting JNOV is then reversed on appeal, the matter proceeds in accordance with the appellate court's disposition.[147]

The court's order granting JNOV and conditional new trial on a combined motion should contain language clearly showing the conditional nature of the grant of new trial. Where an order granted JNOV, but then also granted new trial and ordered the negligence and damages issues to be re-calendared, the order was "legally inconsistent," and the motions were remanded for rehearing.[148] In a fraud case, the court granted JNOV—thus judicially determining that defendant did not commit fraud—and also granted new trial, returning the fraud issue to a new jury. The appellate court acknowledged that the trial judge's "apparent intent" was to make the new trial order conditional, but because the order instead granted the motion "alternatively, and additionally," it did not conform to Rule 50(c)(1).[149]

The party whose verdict has been set aside upon the trial court's grant of JNOV may serve a motion for new trial under Rule 59 not later than ten days after entry of the JNOV.[150] The standards and procedures applicable to new trial motions are discussed in Chapter 2.

Jurisdiction over JNOV Motions after Appeal

If the underlying matter has been appealed, the trial court lacks authority to rule on a JNOV motion:[151] "The general rule is that an appeal takes the case out of the jurisdiction of the trial court. Thereafter,

---

147. Rule 50(c)(1).

148. Streeter v. Cotton, 133 N.C. App. 80, 83, 514 S.E.2d 539, 542 (1999).

149. S. Furn. Hardware, Inc. v. Branch Banking & Trust Co., 136 N.C. App. 695, 703–04, 526 S.E.2d 197, 201–02 (2000).

150. Rule 50(c)(2).

151. Estrada v. Jaques, 70 N.C. App. 627, 637–38, 321 S.E.2d 240, 247 (1984); Wiggins v. Bunch, 280 N.C. 106, 108, 184 S.E.2d 879, 880 (1971); Am. Aluminum Products, Inc. v. Pollard, 97 N.C. App. 541, 545, 389 S.E.2d 589, 592 (1990); Jim Walter Homes, Inc. v. Peartree, 24 N.C. App. 579, 580, 211 S.E.2d 457, 458 (1975); *see also* G.S. 1-294 ("When an appeal is perfected . . . it stays all further proceedings in the court below upon the judgment appealed from, or upon the matter embraced therein[.]"); *cf.* Seafare Corp. v. Trenor Corp., 88 N.C. App. 404, 411, 363 S.E.2d 643, 649 (1988)

pending the appeal, the trial judge is *functus officio*."[152] This general rule has "two exceptions and one qualification": The trial judge retains jurisdiction to make rulings in the case (1) during the session in which the judgment appealed from was entered and (2) for the purpose of settling the case on appeal; and the judge, after notice and a proper showing, may determine that the appeal has been abandoned and thereby regain jurisdiction over the case.[153]

Appeal of JNOV Order

The sufficiency of the evidence to support a verdict is a question of law; JNOV orders, therefore, are reviewed *de novo* on appeal.[154] The appellate court reviews the evidence under the same standard as the trial court—whether the evidence in the light most favorable to the non-movant was sufficient to support a verdict in that party's favor.[155]

The appeals court generally will only review a JNOV motion on the same grounds for which the motion was made before the trial court.[156]

(holding, in the context of new trial motion, that court divested of jurisdiction even when motion made at same time as appeal).

152. *Estrada*, 70 N.C. App. at 637, 321 S.E.2d at 247.

153. *Estrada*, 70 N.C. App. at 637–38, 321 S.E.2d at 247 (quoting Bowen v. Hodge Motor Co., 292 N.C. 633, 635–36, 234 S.E.2d 748, 749 (1977)); *Pollard*, 97 N.C. App. at 545, 389 S.E.2d at 592.

154. *In re* Will of Buck, 350 N.C. 621, 624, 516 S.E.2d 858, 860 (1999); Primerica Life Ins. Co. v. James Massengill & Sons Constr. Co., 211 N.C. App. 252, 258, 712 S.E.2d 670, 676 (2011); Weaver v. Sheppa, 186 N.C. App. 412, 418, 651 S.E.2d 395, 398 (2007); Maxwell v. Michael P. Doyle, Inc., 164 N.C. App. 319, 322, 595 S.E.2d 759, 761 (2004) (citing Denson v. Richmond Cty., 159 N.C. App. 408, 411, 583 S.E.2d 318, 320 (2003)).

155. Rayfield v. Clark, 283 N.C. 362, 366, 196 S.E.2d 197, 199 (1973); Bahl v. Talford, 138 N.C. App. 119, 122, 530 S.E.2d 347, 350 (2000).

156. Rhue v. Rhue, 189 N.C. App. 299, 304, 658 S.E.2d 52, 57 (2008). For further discussion of this specificity requirement, *see supra* section titled "Stating the 'Specific Grounds.'"

If a Rule 50 motion is reviewed by the trial court on one basis, the appellate court may not uphold the decision on a different basis.[157]

When a JNOV motion is denied, the party who prevailed on the motion may, as appellee, assert entitlement to a new trial on the appropriate grounds provided in Rule 59(a). If the appellate court decides the JNOV motion should have been granted, the court may then review the opposing party's new trial arguments and either (1) determine whether a new trial is appropriate or (2) direct the trial court to make that determination.[158]

Note also that, when directed verdict at the close of the evidence is denied, a timely JNOV motion by either the party or the judge is a prerequisite to the appellate court's ability to direct judgment for that party. Rule 50(b)(2) states,

> An appellate court, on finding that a trial judge should have granted a motion for directed verdict made at the close of all the evidence, may not direct entry of judgment in accordance with the motion unless the party who made the motion for a directed verdict also moved for judgment in accordance with Rule 50(b)(1) or the trial judge on his own motion granted, denied or redenied the motion for a directed verdict in accordance with Rule 50(b)(1).[159]

In the absence of the JNOV motion, the appellate court is limited to granting a new trial for the party in whose favor directed verdict should have been granted.[160]

---

157. Feibus & Co., Inc. v. Godley Constr. Co., Inc., 301 N.C. 294, 299–301, 271 S.E.2d 385, 389–90 (1980).

158. Rule 50(d).

159. Rule 50(b)(2); *see* Britt v. Allen, 291 N.C. 630, 636–37, 231 S.E.2d 607, 612 (1977); Hodges v. Hodges, 37 N.C. App. 459, 470, 246 S.E.2d 812, 818 (1978).

160. *Britt*, 291 N.C. at 637–38, 231 S.E.2d at 613–14; Campbell v. Connor, 77 N.C. App. at 631, 335 S.E.2d at 791 (1985), *aff'd*, 316 N.C. 548, 342 S.E.2d 391 (1986); *Hodges*, 37 N.C. App. at 470, 246 S.E.2d at 818.

Chapter 2

New Trial—Rule 59

Introduction

As discussed in Chapter 1, after a trial the losing party is entitled to judgment notwithstanding the verdict (JNOV) *only* where the evidence fails as a matter of law to support the prevailing party's case. The less sweeping remedy of a new trial, however, is available in a far broader range of circumstances. Under Rule of Civil Procedure 59, a party may seek a new trial whether or not it also has moved for JNOV.[1] Rule 59 sets out nine specific bases for a new trial—including a general "catch-all"—covering a wide range of potential arguments. The list is intended simply to formalize and not in any way to diminish the very broad, traditional, discretionary authority of trial judges to award new

1. *See infra* section titled "Combined Motions for JNOV and New Trial."

trials.[2] Under Rule 59, a new trial may be granted "for any of the following causes or grounds":

1. Any irregularity by which any party was prevented from having a fair trial;
2. Misconduct of the jury or prevailing party;
3. Accident or surprise which ordinary prudence could not have guarded against;
4. Newly discovered evidence material for the party making the motion which he could not, with reasonable diligence, have discovered and produced at the trial;
5. Manifest disregard by the jury of the instructions of the court;
6. Excessive or inadequate damages appearing to have been given under the influence of passion or prejudice;
7. Insufficiency of the evidence to justify the verdict or that the verdict is contrary to law;
8. Error in law occurring at the trial and objected to by the party making the motion; or
9. Any other reason heretofore recognized as grounds for new trial.[3]

Eight of these grounds—1 through 7 and 9—are considered discretionary, and appellate review of a decision under any of them is "strictly limited to a determination of whether the record affirmatively demonstrates a manifest abuse of discretion by the trial judge."[4] An order

2. Burgess v. Vestal, 99 N.C. App. 545, 548–49, 393 S.E.2d 324, 326 (1990) (citing Britt v. Allen, 291 N.C. 630, 635, 231 S.E.2d 607, 611–12 (1977)); *see also* Comment to Section 1A-1, Rule 59 of the North Carolina General Statutes (hereinafter G.S.): "In listing the grounds for new trial, the rule goes beyond the prior statutory law . . . to include all those grounds for new trial which have been approved by North Carolina case law."

3. G.S. 1A-1, Rule 59 (hereinafter Rule 59).

4. Worthington v. Bynum, 305 N.C. 478, 482, 290 S.E.2d 599, 602 (1982); *see also* Greene v. Royster, 187 N.C. App. 71, 78, 652 S.E.2d 277, 282 (2007) (restating the discretionary standard).

either granting or denying a motion under these grounds should not be disturbed unless the appellate court is "reasonably convinced by the cold record that the trial judge's ruling probably amounted to a substantial miscarriage of justice."[5] Although courts should exercise their discretion with care and reluctance,[6] our appellate courts generally have "great faith and confidence" in trial judges' ability to make new trial decisions "fairly and without partiality."[7] As the North Carolina Supreme Court has said,

> [O]ur Court has had many opportunities, if it were so inclined, to formulate a "precise" test for determining when an abuse of discretion has occurred in the trial judge's grant or denial of a motion for a new trial. . . . [O]ur Court has not, however, found it logically necessary or wise to attempt to define what an abuse of discretion might be in the abstract concerning any ground upon which a new trial may be granted. For well over one hundred years, it has been a sufficiently workable standard of review to say merely that a manifest abuse of discretion must be made to appear from the record as a whole with the party alleging the existence of an abuse bearing the heavy burden of proof.[8]

---

5. Bryant v. Nationwide Mut. Fire Ins. Co., 313 N.C. 362, 382, 329 S.E.2d 333, 345 (1985) (quoting *Worthington,* 305 N.C. at 487, 290 S.E.2d at 605); Pelzer v. United Parcel Serv., Inc., 126 N.C. App. 305, 311, 484 S.E.2d 849, 853 (1997) (citing Anderson v. Hollifield, 345 N.C. 480, 483, 480 S.E.2d 661, 663 (1997)); Edge v. Metro. Life Ins. Co., 78 N.C. App. 624, 626, 337 S.E.2d 672, 673–74 (1985).

6. *In re* Will of Buck, 350 N.C. 621, 626, 516 S.E.2d 858, 861 (1999); Boykin v. Wilson Medical Ctr., 201 N.C. App. 559, 561, 686 S.E.2d 913, 915 (2009).

7. Chambliss v. Health Scis. Found., Inc., 176 N.C. App. 388, 395, 626 S.E.2d 791, 796 (2006); *Burgess,* 99 N.C. App. 545, 550, 393 S.E.2d 324, 327 (1990).

8. *Buck,* 350 N.C. at 629, 516 S.E.2d at 863 (quoting *Worthington,* 305 N.C. at 484, 290 S.E.2d at 604). Our courts often have emphasized the "heavy burden" a movant faces when attempting to demonstrate abuse of the trial court's discretion. *See* Fisk v. Murphy, 212 N.C. App. 667, 670, 713

Rule 59 is not limited to the eight discretionary grounds: Rule 59(a)(8) also gives the court an opportunity to address prejudicial legal errors to which an objection was made at trial. When an order granting or denying a new trial is based on an asserted error of law, review is de novo.[9] Rule 59(a)(8) and the *de novo* review standard are discussed in further detail later in this chapter.

Rule 59 is intended as a remedy for matters that come to the party's attention during or very shortly after trial, so, as discussed below, the time limit for serving a motion under this rule is ten days from entry of judgment.[10] For certain grounds that arise later, or for relief from a broader range of final orders, parties may invoke Rule 60(b), which is discussed in Part II.

A judge may grant a new trial in either a jury or non-jury trial.[11] In a non-jury trial, the judge is the finder of fact, so typically it is more practical for the judge to reopen relevant portions of the evidence, if necessary, reconsider the record, and amend his or her written findings and conclusions. Rule 59(a) provides for reopening evidence and altering and amending such judgments. That procedure is discussed in Chapter 3.

S.E.2d 100, 102 (2011); Yorke v. Novant Health, Inc., 192 N.C. App. 340, 357, 666 S.E.2d 127, 139 (2008); Taylor v. Ellerbee, 146 N.C. App. 56, 58, 552 S.E.2d 667, 669 (2001).

9. Harrell v. Sagebrush of N.C., LLC, 191 N.C. App. 381, 386, 663 S.E.2d 444, 447 (2008) (reversing new trial where trial court erred in concluding it was error of law to exclude deposition testimony); Kinsey v. Spann, 139 N.C. App. 370, 373, 533 S.E.2d 487, 490 (2000); Heart of the Valley Motel, Inc. v. Edwards, 111 N.C. App. 896, 898–99, 433 S.E.2d 466, 467–68 (1993).

10. *See infra* section titled "Time Requirements."

11. Some of the nine grounds listed in Rule 59(a) will not, however, apply in non-jury trials, most notably misconduct of the jury, (a)(2), and jury disregard of instructions, (a)(5).

Applicability of Rule 59

By its language, Rule 59 clearly is intended to provide relief after a "trial." Accordingly, several of the listed grounds explicitly relate to juries and verdicts or are otherwise grounded in the context of a trial. And, of course, the stated remedy is itself a *new* "trial." Given the language of the rule, to what extent may a party nevertheless use it to seek relief from judgments not resulting from a jury or non-jury trial? In the recent case of *Bodie Island Beach Club Ass'n, Inc. v. Wray,*[12] the defendant appealed the trial court's denial of its motions under Rule 59(a) to set aside default and summary judgment. The Court of Appeals determined that the motions were not properly brought under Rule 59 "[b]ecause both Rule 59(a)(8) and (9) are properly made after a trial, and the case *sub judice* concluded at the summary judgment stage."[13] And in the earlier case of *Garrison ex rel. Chavis v. Barnes,* the Court of Appeals also held that "Rule 59 is an inappropriate vehicle to challenge the denial of a Rule 60 motion."[14] However, in a series of other cases in which the parties did not expressly challenge Rule 59's applicability, the court has tacitly allowed the use of the rule to seek relief from summary judgment,[15]

---

12. 215 N.C. App. 283, 716 S.E.2d 67 (2011).

13. *Id.* at 287, 716 S.E.2d at 72.

14. 117 N.C. App. 206, 211, 450 S.E.2d 554, 557 (1994); *cf.* Curry v. First Fed. Savs. & Loan Ass'n of Charlotte, 125 N.C. App. 108, 112, 479 S.E.2d 286, 289 (1997) (noting that Rule 59(e) motion was inappropriate to challenge denials of class certification and intervention motions because those orders were not "judgments").

15. Elliott v. Enka-Candler Fire & Rescue Dep't, Inc., 213 N.C. App. 160, 169, 713 S.E.2d 132, 138–39 (2011) (analyzing substance of Rule 59 motion, apparently based on improper notice, to set aside summary judgment); Broughton v. McClatchy Newspapers, Inc., 161 N.C. App. 20, 34, 588 S.E.2d 20, 30 (2003) (affirming denial of Rule 59 relief from summary judgment as a matter of the court's discretion without discussing procedural propriety); Muse v. Charter Hosp. of Winston-Salem, 117 N.C. App. 468, 480–81, 452 S.E.2d 589, 598 (1995) (affirming relief under Rule 59 from order granting summary judgment as to punitive damages). In two other cases, the court concluded that relief from summary judgment under Rule 59 was not proper because the motions had not properly invoked one of the Rule 59 grounds but, instead, had been used merely to re-argue summary judgment. Neither case addressed whether Rule 59 was a proper means of seeking

dismissal of claims as a discovery sanction,[16] and default judgment.[17] In the most recent case to address the issue directly, the court reversed a trial court's denial of a Rule 59 motion seeking to amend a summary judgment order.[18] The dissenting judge argued that Rule 59 was "simply not applicable" to the case because the judgment was neither a verdict nor the result of a trial and had been used improperly to make legal arguments not made at the summary judgment hearing.[19] The Supreme Court affirmed the majority's opinion *per curiam* but with an equally divided panel, thus leaving the Court of Appeals opinion undisturbed and standing without precedential value.[20]

Whatever the future of the law on this question, in light of *Bodie Island* parties should be very cautious in seeking relief under Rule 59 from any appealable judgment that was not the result of trial. As discussed in further detail later in this chapter, a proper Rule 59 motion tolls the period for appeal of the underlying judgment. If a court determines that Rule 59 was not the appropriate vehicle for the party's argument, the motion will not have tolled the appeal period. If the appeal deadline (typically thirty days) runs during the time the moving party's

---

relief from summary judgment generally. Sellers v. Ochs, 180 N.C. App. 332, 335, 638 S.E.2d 1, 3 (2006); Smith v. Johnson, 125 N.C. App. 603, 606, 481 S.E.2d 415, 417 (1997).

16. Batlle v. Sabates, 198 N.C. App. 407, 416–17, 681 S.E.2d 788, 795–96 (2009) (holding that plaintiff's Rule 59 motion stated a sufficient basis for relief). The court in *Batlle* noted, however, that "no party to this proceeding has contended that a litigant is not entitled to seek relief from an order imposing sanctions . . . under . . . Rule 59, and we do not, for that reason, express an opinion on that issue here." *Id.* at 413 n.1, 681 S.E.2d at 793.

17. Jackson v. Culbreth, 199 N.C. App. 531, 538–39, 681 S.E.2d 813, 818 (2009). In *Jackson*, the court held that the trial judge erred in denying a Rule 59 motion to amend a default judgment. The default judgment contained findings of fact, however, as would be required after a non-jury trial, so the court seemed to treat the trial judge's disposition as though it had resulted from a non-jury trial. *See id.* at 537–38, 681 S.E.2d at 817–18.

18. Rutherford Plantation, LLC v. Challenge Golf Grp. of the Carolinas, LLC, 225 N.C. App. 79, 83, 737 S.E.2d 409, 412–13 (2013).

19. *Id.* at 86, 737 S.E.2d at 414–15.

20. Rutherford Plantation, LLC v. Challenge Golf Grp. of the Carolinas, LLC, 367 N.C. 197, 197, 753 S.E.2d 152, 153 (2014).

purported Rule 59 motion is pending, the party may lose its right to appeal.[21] This was indeed the conclusion in *Bodie Island*, where the Court of Appeals noted that the improper Rule 59 motions "did not toll the appeal, permitting us to dismiss the appeal[.]"[22]

Grounds for New Trial

Irregularities Preventing Fair Trial—Rule 59(a)(1)

The first basis for relief under Rule 59 is broad, allowing the court to grant a new trial for "any irregularity by which any party was prevented from having a fair trial."[23] An irregularity is an occurrence that is contrary to the usual and accepted practice of the court.[24] Under this basis, the court has wide latitude to determine that a new trial is warranted.[25] A trial judge did not err, for example, in reopening a bench trial under this rule after determining that he had acted too hastily and wanted to have all the facts before him.[26] While the court's authority is expansive, the irregularity must have created some prejudice to the movant's case: "New trials are not awarded because of technical error.

---

21. *See infra* section titled "Effect on Appeal Deadlines."

22. 215 N.C. App. 283, 287–88, 716 S.E.2d 67, 72 (2011). The court nevertheless went on to grant *certiorari* over the issue (*id.* at 288, 716 S.E.2d at 73) and then again concluded that the trial court did not err in denying the Rule 59 motions because they were "post-trial motions and because the instant case concluded at the summary judgment stage"; *id.* at 294–95, 716 S.E.2d at 77.

23. Rule 59(a)(1). Given the breadth of this definition, motions based on arguments that could fall within the definition of an "irregularity" may at times be brought under the "catch-all" category in Rule 59(a)(9), discussed later in this chapter. *See, e.g.*, Boykin v. Wilson Med. Ctr., 201 N.C. App. 559, 562–63, 686 S.E.2d 913, 915–16 (2009) (granting new trial based on "marathon schedule" imposed by court because of impending holiday weekend).

24. Taylor v. Triangle Porsche-Audi, Inc., 27 N.C. App. 711, 717, 220 S.E.2d 806, 811 (1975).

25. Philco Fin. Corp. v. Mitchell, 26 N.C. App. 264, 267, 215 S.E.2d 823, 825 (1975).

26. *Id.*

The error must be prejudicial."[27] A party may also waive a potential argument if the moving party made no objection to the irregularity when appropriate.[28] The following sections focus on several categories of missteps, mistakes, and lapses that our courts have acknowledged as potential irregularities warranting new trial.

Improper Statements by the Court

Misconduct by the trial court is irregular by its nature; it may, when prejudicial, form the basis for a new trial. In particular, a judge is prohibited from making certain comments to the jury regarding the facts that weigh more in one party's favor than the other: "Every litigant in the courts of this State is entitled by the law to have his cause considered with the cold neutrality of the impartial judge and the equally unbiased mind of a properly instructed jury."[29] Rule of Civil Procedure 51(a) provides that "In charging the jury in any action governed by these rules, a judge shall not give an opinion as to whether or not a fact is fully or sufficiently proved[.]"[30] For example, in an action to

---

27. Turner v. Turner, 261 N.C. 472, 474–75, 135 S.E.2d 12, 14 (1965); Dixon v. Weaver, 41 N.C. App. 524, 528 S.E.2d 322, 325 (1979). "[T]he party asserting the error must demonstrate that he has been prejudiced thereby." Robinson v. Seaboard Sys. R.R., Inc., 87 N.C. App. 512, 528, 361 S.E.2d 909, 919 (1987). *See, e.g.*, Sisk v. Sisk, 221 N.C. App. 631, 635, 729 S.E.2d 68, 70–71 (2012) (court's review of materials submitted by opposing counsel after hearing was not prejudicial); Gardner v. Harriss, 122 N.C. App. 697, 700, 471 S.E.2d 447, 450 (1996) (court's error in allowing exhibit into jury room not basis for new trial unless prejudicial).

28. *See, e.g.*, State *ex rel.* Everett v. Hardy, 65 N.C. App. 350, 354, 309 S.E.2d 280, 283 (1983) (refusing to consider an argument regarding witness misconduct where no objection was raised before the trial court).

29. Russell v. Town of Morehead City, 90 N.C. App. 675, 679, 370 S.E.2d 56, 59 (1988) (*quoting* Withers v. Lane, 144 N.C. 184, 192, 56 S.E. 855, 857–58 (1907)).

30. G.S. 1A-1, Rule 51(a) (titled "Judge to explain law but give no opinion on facts."). Reflecting this requirement, North Carolina Pattern Instruction (Civil) 150.20 (No Opinion) states,

> The law requires the presiding judge to be impartial and express no opinions as to the facts. You are not to draw any inference from any ruling that I have made. You must not let any inflection in my voice, expression on my face (or any

establish paternity, a new trial was required where the judge implied that more weight should be given to the testimony of plaintiff's mother than to that of defendant's witnesses.[31] A new trial also was required in a wrongful death case where the judge's charge referred to plaintiff's witness as "of perhaps weak mentality" though nothing in evidence related to the witness's mental condition.[32]

Rule 51(a) states also that, in charging the jury, "If the judge undertakes to state the contentions of the parties, he shall give equal stress to the contentions of each party."[33] In *Key v. Merritt-Holland*

> question I have asked a witness) or anything else that I have done during this trial influence your findings. It is your duty to find the facts of this case from the evidence as presented.

31. Searcy v. Justice, 20 N.C. App. 559, 562, 202 S.E.2d 314, 316 (1974). The trial judge told the jury,

> Now she testified that she dated the defendant from August 1963 until October 1970, that she neither dated nor had intercourse with any other man during that time, as the Court remembers her testimony. The defendant, on the other hand says that she told him of five men that she had had intercourse with during this interim we're talking about. Now as the Court recalls, no person who has gone upon the stand has testified that any person had intercourse with the plaintiff ten lunar months before the birth of this child on August the 26, 1964. The plaintiff contending that she had intercourse with the defendant, all along and had intercourse with no one else and that the defendant, therefore, was father of the child.

32. Burkey v. Kornegay, 261 N.C. 513, 513, 135 S.E.2d 204, 205 (1964); *see also* State Highway Comm'n v. Ferry, 19 N.C. App. 332, 336, 198 S.E.2d 773, 775–76 (1973) (new trial where trial judge suggested jury give more weight to defendant's professional appraisers than to plaintiff's lay witnesses); *In re* Holland's Will, 16 N.C. App. 398, 399–400, 192 S.E.2d 98, 99–100 (1972) (judge prejudicially invaded province of jury in will caveat by suggesting jury give more weight to one of propounder's witnesses than they "would to another witness").

33. G.S. 1A-1, Rule 51(a). Such summaries of the evidence are in the judge's discretion: "[A] judge . . . shall not be required to state, summarize or recapitulate the evidence[.]" *Id.* North Carolina Pattern Instruction (Civil) 101.00 (Admonition to Trial Judge) advises trial judges as follows:

> No future pattern charge or replacement will direct the trial judge to state, summarize or recapitulate the evidence. . . . It

Welding Supplies, Inc., a new trial was required because the trial court's summary devoted considerably more attention to defendant's evidence than to plaintiff's and made overly generous assessments of defense testimony.[34]

The prohibition against improper comments applies to the entire trial, not just the charge conference.[35] As our appellate courts have stated: "The trial judge occupies an exalted station. Juries entertain great respect for his opinion, and are easily influenced by any suggestion coming from him. As a result, he must abstain from conduct or language which tends to discredit or prejudice (any party) or his cause with the jury."[36] In a trespass and civil assault case in which defendants were a town mayor and other town officials, a judge made numerous remarks in front of the jury disparaging public officials, as follows:

- When asked if some of the defendants could be excused for a portion of the evidence to attend town business and a ship's dedication, he replied, "It would suit me just fine if they never come back" and "All politicians go to all meetings. I imagine they will have a pigpicking on the grounds."

> is the opinion of the Civil Subcommittee that, in view of . . . Rule 51(a), the mandate should be limited to a summary of the elements of the applicable law. Of course, there may be occasions when the evidence should be stated or the application of the law to the evidence should be explained. These instances are left to the reasoned judgment of the trial judge.

34. 273 N.C. 609, 613–14, 160 S.E.2d 687, 690–91 (1968); *see also* York v. N. Hosp. Dist. of Surry Cty., 88 N.C. App. 183, 195–96, 362 S.E.2d 859, 868 (1987) (noting that a judge opting to apply the law to the evidence must "instruct completely and without omission").

35. Russell v. Town of Morehead City, 90 N.C. App. 675, 680, 370 S.E.2d 56, 59 (1988) ("[T]he rule in this State is that the trial judge is prohibited from making comments at any time during the trial which amount to expressions of opinion as to what has or what has not been shown by the evidence."); Saintsing v. Taylor, 57 N.C. App. 467, 472, 291 S.E.2d 880, 883–84 (1982); Worrell v. Hennis Credit Union, 12 N.C. App. 275, 278, 182 S.E.2d 874, 876–77 (1971).

36. *Searcy*, 20 N.C. App. at 561, 202 S.E.2d at 316 (quoting State v. Carter, 233 N.C. 581, 583, 65 S.E.2d 9, 10 (1951)).

- When a witness testified to seeing public works defendants on disputed property, the judge "interjected": "Typical, public service workers sitting around doing nothing."
- Before the charge conference, he gave the jury an extended speech about constitutional protections of citizens against government. He also encouraged the jurors to read an article about the constitution and to "think about the fact that you live in a country in which the government itself is subject to law."
- Before the charge conference, he indicated in front of the jury that the charge conference likely would not take long and stated: "I have already got my mind made up."[37]

The Court of Appeals ordered a new trial because of the "cumulative prejudicial effect" of the judge's comments on defendant's case.[38] Likewise, in a personal injury action, the cumulative effect of thirty-seven remarks reflecting antagonism toward defendant and defense counsel warranted a new trial.[39] And in *Board of Transportation v. Wilder*,[40] the trial court attempted to curtail cross-examination of plaintiff's witness. After flustered counsel responded in frustration, the court threatened, "About two remarks like that, you are going to have more trouble than you have in your life." Combined with further "sharp remarks," the

---

37. *Russell*, 90 N.C. App. at 680–82; 370 S.E.2d at 59–61.

38. *Id.* at 683, 370 S.E.2d at 61.

39. McNeill v. Durham Cty. ABC Bd., 322 N.C. 425, 430, 368 S.E.2d 619, 622 (1988). In this case involving an Alcoholic Beverage Control Commission agent, the remarks ranged from several comments on defense counsel's examination, such as, "I'm bored with the repetition, frankly, and I think everybody else is" and "I don't know why we're getting so torn to pieces by a little liquor and gambling going on" to various jokes about defendants and their association with alcoholic beverages. At the same time, the judge was openly complimentary of one of plaintiff's damages witnesses, telling him as he left the stand, "Thank you for being here, sir. I enjoyed your explanation." *Id.* at 429, 368 S.E.2d at 622.

40. 28 N.C. App. 105, 220 S.E.2d 183 (1975).

judge's statement "tended to discredit defendants' counsel, and hence their cause, in the eyes of the jury in violation of G.S. 1A-1, Rule 51(a)."[41]

Whether an improper statement constitutes grounds for new trial depends on its impact on the jury. The movant must show that the statement was in fact prejudicial, and "the probable effect upon the jury, and not the motive of the judge, is determinative."[42] The statement

---

41. *Id.* at 107–08, 220 S.E.2d at 184–85; *see also* Worrell v. Hennis Credit Union, 12 N.C. App. 275, 279, 182 S.E.2d 874, 877 (1971) (judge sustained own objections to ten questions by defense counsel to defense witness, struck defense testimony on own motion, and displayed "persistence" and "antagonistic attitude" toward defendant).

42. Colonial Pipeline Co. v. Weaver, 310 N.C. 93, 103, 310 S.E.2d 338, 344 (1984). A trial court's comments may, of course, evince prejudice against one side in a non-jury trial as well. But, in general, "less judicial restraint is required during a bench trial" because

> the ordinary rules as to the competency of evidence applied in a trial before a jury are to some extent relaxed, for the reason that the judge with knowledge of the law is able to eliminate from the testimony he hears that which is immaterial and incompetent, and consider only that which tends properly to prove the facts to be found.

Gemini Drilling & Found., LLC v. National Fire Ins. Co. of Hartford, 192 N.C. App. 376, 385, 665 S.E.2d 505, 511 (2008) (citations omitted). In *Gemini Drilling*, a contract case, defendant argued that the judge's "lack of decorum" and "inexplicably hostile" comments were an irregularity requiring a new trial. The judge, for example, told both attorneys, "Just as an observation, neither one of [you] do a whole lot of trial work, do you?" He also declared, "In the 16 years I have been a Superior Court judge and the five years I was a District Court judge, I have never, to this day, understood why contract cases ever go to trial." Such comments continued through trial, and at closing the judge "opined,"

> Of course, my observation is that in all the cases involving contracts and business, they're all subject to being looked at as a heck of a way to run a railroad. I find it absolutely—lots of things I find absolutely astounding in so-called, quote, "business situations." But that's okay. Go ahead and finish your argument, and then [opposing counsel] can be heard, and then you can be heard again, and then he can be heard.
>
> Each of you can be heard ad nauseam, as long as you want to.

The Court of Appeals agreed that the comments were "not at all kind," but because they did not affect a jury and were directed at both parties, they did

will be evaluated "in light of the circumstance in which it was made" because "a word is not a crystal, transparent and unchanged; it is the skin of a living thought and may vary greatly in color and content according to the circumstances and the time in which it is used."[43] In *Bowden v. Bell*, for example, the judge's use of the phrase "the negligent defendant" in a last clear chance instruction was not prejudicial in the context of the entire jury charge.[44] And in an action for money owed, a judge's instruction to the jury to examine a particular exhibit "very carefully" was not a prejudicial comment on the exhibit's probative force.[45] In short, judges may—and sometimes must—take an active role in controlling the proceedings: "[R]emarks made by the trial court in the jury's presence do not always constitute prejudicial error. Judges are not merely mute observers of the legal drama before them. They

---

not constitute a basis for a new trial. *Id.* at 385–86, 665 S.E.2d at 510–11; *see also* Lacey v. Kirk, 767 S.E.2d 632, 641 (N.C. Ct. App. 2014) (comments to defendant that she was wasting jury's time and being "coy" not prejudicial because made outside of jury's presence), *review denied*, 771 S.E.2d 321 (N.C. 2015).

43. *Colonial Pipeline*, 310 N.C. at 103, 310 S.E.2d at 344.

44. 116 N.C. App. 64, 72–73, 446 S.E.2d 816, 822 (1994).

45. Mack Fin. Corp. v. Harnett Transfer, Inc., 42 N.C. App. 116, 123, 256 S.E.2d 491, 496 (1979); *see also, e.g., Lacey*, 767 S.E.2d at 639–41 (various statements aimed at preventing evasive and repetitive testimony were not prejudicial); O'Mara v. Wake Forest Univ. Health Scis., 184 N.C. App. 428, 441, 646 S.E.2d 400, 408 (2007) (judge's own extensive questioning of expert was for clarification and not prejudicial); Ward v. McDonald, 100 N.C. App. 359, 362, 396 S.E.2d 337, 339 (1990) (no prejudice where judge remarked to the jury that trial needed to be shortened); Lenins v. K-Mart Corp., 98 N.C. App. 590, 594–95, 391 S.E.2d 843, 846 (1990) (court's "informal and even jocular" comments not prejudicial in light of all facts and circumstances); *Colonial Pipeline*, 310 N.C. at 103–04, 310 S.E.2d at 344–45 (no prejudice where judge interrupted cross-examination and stated, "I don't believe that is relevant."); Brenner v. Little Red School House, Ltd., 59 N.C. App. 68, 71, 295 S.E.2d 607, 609–10 (1982) (no error for judge to instruct jury to apply the law as the court states it rather than as counsel present it; defendant suffered no prejudice because the instruction applied to both counsel); Saintsing v. Taylor, 57 N.C. App. 467, 472–73, 291 S.E.2d 880, 883–84 (1982) (no prejudice where judge was "somewhat harsh" regarding counsel's continuous objections).

are the most important participants in the search for truth through trial by jury."[46]

Failure of Court to Reveal Conflict

Trial judges are bound to certain ethical standards to promote fairness in the judicial process and protect the integrity of the judiciary.[47] Among other duties, a judge is required to disqualify himself or herself "in a proceeding in which the judge's impartiality may reasonably be questioned."[48] When a breach of judicial responsibility creates a prejudicial irregularity, a new trial is in order. A matter that arose in the context of arbitration is a useful example. In *William C. Vick Construction Co. v. North Carolina Farm Bureau Federation*,[49] petitioner moved to vacate the award of an appointed arbitrator after discovering that the arbitrator had numerous relationships with respondent's counsel and had willfully failed to disclose them.[50] After the motion was denied, petitioner moved under Rule 59 to alter, amend, or reopen the judgment. The Court of Appeals found that the arbitrator

> did not disclose numerous social, business, and professional relationships with partners in the law firm representing [respondent]. . . . Additionally, we find that these relationships were likely to affect impartiality or reasonably create an appearance of partiality or bias. We also note that the

---

46. *Colonial Pipeline*, 310 N.C. at 103, 310 S.E.2d at 344; *see also Brenner*, 59 N.C. App. at 71, 295 S.E.2d at 609 ("It should be remembered by defendant that a trial judge can control the course of a trial, including admonishing counsel not to pursue a prohibited line of questioning.").

47. North Carolina Code of Judicial Conduct, Preamble.

48. North Carolina Code of Judicial Conduct, Canon 3.C (Disqualification).

49. 123 N.C. App. 97, 472 S.E.2d 346 (1996).

50. *Id.* at 99, 472 S.E.2d at 347. While neutral arbitrators are not bound to the Code of Judicial Conduct, they nevertheless have "an affirmative duty to disclose any prior dealings with a party" (Ruffin Woody & Assocs. v. Person Cty., 92 N.C. App. 129, 139, 374 S.E.2d 165, 171 (1988)), and under the Revised Uniform Arbitration Act, a court must vacate an arbitrator's award in the event of "evident partiality by an arbitrator[.]" G.S. 1-569.23(a)(2)a.

> relationships involved in the case before us are not merely trivial in nature. Indeed, [the arbitrator] had significant business relationships and friendships with respondent's counsel. Because of [the arbitrator's] failure to affirmatively disclose these relationships, the trial court erred in not granting [petitioner]'s Rule 59 motion.[51]

Improper Closing Argument

A closing argument, generally speaking, is a critically important part of a litigant's case or defense. Unlike the opening statement, the closing is the party's chance to *argue* to the jury how and why both the facts and the law support a verdict in its favor.[52] North Carolina law gives the parties wide latitude to make their arguments,[53] but there are limits, and when the boundaries are crossed, new trials may be appropriate.[54] When a statement in a closing argument is improper, and the opposing party makes a timely objection, the court is obligated to sustain the objection and take appropriate action. At a minimum, the court should "correct the transgression by clear instructions" to the jury.[55] Often a clear and complete limiting instruction will suffice.[56] If the statement is grossly improper or egregious, however, a new trial may be necessary.[57]

---

51. *Vick*, 123 N.C. App. at 102, 472 S.E.2d at 349.

52. G.S. 7A-97 ("In jury trials the whole case as well of law as of fact may be argued to the jury."). *See generally* GEN. R. P. SUPER. & DIST. CTS. 10.

53. Seafare Corp. v. Trenor Corp., 88 N.C. App. 404, 414–15, 363 S.E.2d 643, 651–52 (1988); Corwin v. Dickey, 91 N.C. App. 725, 728, 373 S.E.2d 149, 151 (1988).

54. Couch v. Private Diagnostic Clinic, 133 N.C. App. 93, 98, 515 S.E.2d 30, 35 (1999) ("Jury argument . . . is not without limitations.") (quoting State v. Sanderson, 336 N.C. 1, 15, 442 S.E.2d 33, 42 (1994)).

55. Crutcher v. Noel, 284 N.C. 568, 572, 201 S.E.2d 855, 857 (1974); *Couch*, 133 N.C. App. at 97–98, 515 S.E.2d at 35; *see also* Wilcox v. Glover Motors, Inc., 269 N.C. 473, 478, 153 S.E.2d 76, 81 (1967) (trial court should have "instructed the jury to disregard this portion of counsel's argument").

56. *See, e.g.*, Clemons v. Lewis, 23 N.C. App. 488, 489–90, 209 S.E.2d 291, 292 (1974) (trial court's instruction to disregard the statements was appropriate).

57. *See, e.g.*, Johnson v. Amethyst Corp., 120 N.C. App. 529, 536–37, 463 S.E.2d 397, 402 (1995) (new trial required for counsel's "shockingly

If a party fails to object to an improper closing argument, the court nevertheless has an obligation to intervene *ex mero motu* if the statement is "grossly improper."[58] A grossly improper statement often will merit the granting of a new trial, but, depending on surrounding circumstances, a clear limiting instruction may be enough.[59]

A motion for a new trial under Rule 59 may be based on the trial court's failure to sustain an objection to an improper closing or to take appropriate action to limit the effects of the argument on the jury's decision. The motion is an opportunity for the trial court to reevaluate—in light of the jury's decision—its earlier response to an objectionable closing.

Closing arguments must, as a starting point, be supported by the evidence in the record. An attorney may not "'travel outside the record and inject into his argument facts of his own knowledge or other facts not included in the evidence.'"[60] In *Crutcher v. Noel*,[61] plaintiff's counsel

---

inappropriate" comments); *see also* Fincher v. Rhyne, 266 N.C. 64, 70–71, 145 S.E.2d 316, 320–21 (1965) (new trial warranted where counsel discussed liability insurance).

58. Watson v. White, 309 N.C. 498, 507, 308 S.E.2d 268, 274 (1983); *Seafare*, 88 N.C. App. at 414, 363 S.E.2d at 651. The Court of Appeals has stressed, however, that "It is only when the error and the unfair prejudice are extreme that a court *must* intervene." Hudgins v. Wagoner, 204 N.C. App. 480, 498, 694 S.E.2d 436, 449 (2010) (citing Smith v. Hamrick, 159 N.C. App. 696, 699, 583 S.E.2d 676, 679 (2003)).

59. *See, e.g.*, *Couch*, 133 N.C. App. at 99–100, 515 S.E.2d at 35–36 (holding no new trial where grossness of the statement was balanced by overwhelming evidence of negligence); O'Carroll v. Texasgulf, Inc., 132 N.C. App. 307, 315, 511 S.E.2d 313, 319 (1999) (holding that numerous statements about plaintiff's counsel's "agenda" to make money and get the "big guy" were improper but not so egregious as to warrant new trial).

60. Karriker v. Sigmon, 43 N.C. App. 224, 225–26, 258 S.E.2d 473, 474 (1979) (quoting *Crutcher*, 284 N.C. at 572, 201 S.E.2d at 857). In *Callicutt v. Smith*, 267 N.C. 252, 252–53, 148 S.E.2d 9, 10 (1966), for example, a vehicle negligence case, defendant's attorney was properly prohibited from using a large chart in his closing showing defendant's life expectancy and various other computations. Counsel was "in effect . . . attempting to use this chart as an exhibit which had never been introduced into evidence."

61. 284 N.C. 568, 201 S.E.2d 855 (1974).

stated that defendant had planned to call several doctors to testify on defendant's behalf, but the witnesses were not called. He argued that if these doctors were able to give favorable testimony, defendant would have called them. In response, defendant's counsel indicated that those doctors would have testified favorably toward his client and that their testimony would merely have been duplicative. The Supreme Court ordered a new trial for plaintiff, holding that

> the weight of the medical testimony was the paramount issue. . . . [Counsel's] statement . . . that twelve doctors . . . would have testified to the same thing his client testified to, offered facts outside the record which effectively buttressed his client's testimony on this crucial issue . . . [and] weighted the verdict in defendant's favor.[62]

Closing arguments must also include "[o]nly the legitimate inferences that may be drawn from the evidence."[63] Misstatements of the evidence are not permitted.[64] In addition, closing arguments must not include statements of the facts and outcomes of other cases as a basis for arguing that the jury must come to the same conclusion in the case before the court.[65]

---

62. *Id.* at 573, 201 S.E.2d at 858; *see also Karriker,* 43 N.C. App. at 225–26, 258 S.E.2d at 474 (an argument about car damage was improper in a bodily injury case where car's condition not in evidence).

63. Johnson v. Amethyst Corp., 120 N.C. App. 529, 535, 463 S.E.2d 397, 401–02 (1995) (citing Wilson v. Commercial Fin. Co., 239 N.C. 349, 359–60, 79 S.E.2d 906, 916 (1954)).

64. *Amethyst Corp.,* 120 N.C. App. at 535, 463 S.E.2d at 402; *see also* Gen. R. P. Super. & Dist. Cts. 12 ("Counsel shall not knowingly misinterpret the contents of a paper, the testimony of a witness, [or] the language or argument of opposite counsel.").

65. Joines v. Moffitt, 226 N.C. App. 61, 66, 739 S.E.2d 177, 182 (2013) (citing Wilcox v. Glover Motors, Inc., 269 N.C. 473, 479, 153 S.E.2d 76, 81 (1967)). In *Wilcox,* defendant's counsel read fact and conclusion portions of three opinions and stated, "I say to you that the facts in this case are the same as the facts in the case I have just read . . . and that the defendant . . . is no more liable here than the defendants in the other cases." *Id.* at 478, 153 S.E.2d at 80. The Supreme Court held that such an argument was "highly

Evidence of efforts to settle may not be introduced during trial to prove liability.[66] Likewise, closing arguments should not reference such efforts.[67] In most negligence actions, the presence or absence of liability insurance is not relevant to the jury's determination, and the mention of such insurance in a closing statement in either a positive or negative manner creates impermissible prejudice.[68] It also is improper to make reference in closing argument to collateral sources of payment, such as public assistance, to argue that a plaintiff has suffered no damages.[69]

---

prejudicial to plaintiffs" and that "[i]t is not sufficient merely to stop such an argument without an appropriate direction to the jury." *Id.* at 478, 153 S.E.2d at 81. As the court explained,

> In order to make meaningful a statement of a rule of law found in a reported decision, it is sometimes necessary to recount some of the facts which the court had before it when it pronounced the rule in question. For this purpose, counsel, in his argument in a subsequent case, may not only read the rule of law stated in the published opinion in the former case but may also state the facts before the court therein. . . .
>
> It is not permissible argument for counsel to read, or otherwise state, the facts of another case, together with the decision therein, as premises leading to the conclusion that the jury should return a verdict favorable to his client in the case on trial. That is, counsel may not properly argue: The facts in the reported case were thus and so; in that case the decision was that there was no negligence (or was negligence); the facts in the present case are the same or stronger; therefore, the verdict in this case should be the same as the decision there.

Id. at 479, 153 S.E.2d at 81 (internal citations omitted).

66. G.S. 8C-1, Rule 408.

67. *Karriker*, 43 N.C. App. at 225–26, 258 S.E.2d at 474 (ordering new trial where defendant's counsel told jury, "This is a case that should not be here. The defendant made an effort to dispose of the matter, but plaintiff would not be reasonable.")

68. Fincher v. Rhyne, 266 N.C. 64, 68–70, 145 S.E.2d 316, 318–20 (1965); Scallon v. Hooper, 58 N.C. App. 551, 556–57, 293 S.E.2d 843, 845–46 (1982).

69. Cates v. Wilson, 321 N.C. 1, 11, 361 S.E.2d 734, 740 (1987) (ordering new trial where counsel made repeated reference to Medicaid payments); *see also* Fallis v. Watauga Med. Ctr., Inc., 132 N.C. App. 43, 52–54, 510

Unless directly relevant to a jury question,[70] the financial status of a party should not be discussed in a closing statement: "In a court of justice neither the wealth of one party nor the poverty of the other should be permitted to effect the administration of the law."[71] Nor should an argument appeal to the jury's own pecuniary interests[72] or ask the jurors to put themselves in the injured person's shoes.[73]

And, of course, it is improper for arguments to include inflammatory statements, abusive remarks, name-calling, religious arguments, and similar statements aimed at prejudicing the jury's decision rather than addressing the reasonable inferences to be drawn from the evidence.[74]

S.E.2d 199, 205–06 (1999) (comparing collateral source rule with argument regarding medical bills).

70. For example, in the punitive damages phase of a trial the jury may consider "[t]he defendant's ability to pay punitive damages, as evidenced by its revenues or net worth." G.S. 1D-35(2)i.

71. Watson v. White, 309 N.C. 498, 507, 308 S.E.2d 268, 273–74 (1983). In *Watson,* the trial court erred in overruling an objection to the following statement: "Can you imagine what a jury verdict, a low jury verdict, a little one, five thousand dollars, would do to that little family?" The remarks were "clearly improper, calculated to appeal to the sympathy of the jury" . . . and "injected extraneous considerations concerning defendants' financial situation so far as their capacity to respond to damages was concerned." *Id.* at 507, 308 S.E.2d at 273–74; *see also Scallon,* 58 N.C. App. at 556–57, 293 S.E.2d at 845–46 (improper to implore the jury to deal "cautiously and fairly with the estate and the property of [defendant]").

72. Smith v. Bohlen, 95 N.C. App. 347, 353, 382 S.E.2d 812, 816 (1989). In *Bohlen,* defendant's counsel argued, "If you were sitting around reading the newspaper and you saw something that upset them [*sic*] and you said 'Why don't they do something about it?' then this is your opportunity to be 'they.'" The Court of Appeals agreed that "counsel's remark can only be interpreted as a reference to publicity concerning lawsuits and their effect on the insurance industry. Thus, the remark was an improper appeal to the pecuniary interest of the jurors in that it implied that a verdict for defendant would help to hold down insurance costs." *Id.* at 353, 382 S.E.2d at 816.

73. Fox-Kirk v. Hannon, 142 N.C. App. 267, 279, 542 S.E.2d 346, 355 (2001) (improper in a child injury case to argue, "What would you require us to pay you? Would you take $100 a day for it to live with that the rest of your life?").

74. Johnson v. Amethyst Corp., 120 N.C. App. 529, 536–37, 463 S.E.2d 397, 402 (1995); *see also* GEN. R. P. SUPER. & DIST. CTS. 12 ("Counsel are at

In general, a closing argument must be transcribed and included in

---

all times to conduct themselves with dignity and propriety. . . . Abusive language or offensive personal references are prohibited."). In *Amethyst Corp.*, plaintiff sued a hospital for alleged sexual assault by a hospital employee. In his closing, the hospital's attorney made the following statements:

- "And about the same time in April of 1991 a law professor from Oklahoma State University [Anita Hill] accused a man who was nominated to be a Supreme Court Justice of the United States of sexual harassment and sexual impropriety. What was in it for her?" *Id.* at 536, 463 S.E.2d at 402.
- "In a plea arrangement orchestrated by the attorneys for the four women who were making the charges . . . for the purpose of bringing legal claims within two days after they came forward with these allegations. How plausible is it that in response to these charges, descriptions of the conduct like [plaintiff] has told you, that Judge Jane Harper—a female judge—would give [the alleged assailant] no active time if there was believable evidence that any of this were true?" *Id.*

Ordering a new trial, the Court of Appeals found counsel's Anita Hill argument to be "prejudicially infirm to the sense of fairness and justice in our legal system" and stated,

> The clear import of counsel's argument was to appeal to the passion and prejudice of the jurors that stem from that unrelated sexual harassment matter. We expressly reject the use of this type of inflammatory comparison which seeks only to . . . transfer the jurors' feelings from an unrelated matter to the case at hand.

And regarding the "shockingly inappropriate" plea arrangement argument, the court noted that

> most egregious are counsel's disparaging statements that because District Court Judge Jane Harper is a female judge, she would not have accepted a plea bargain giving [the alleged assailant] 'no active time if there was believable evidence that any of the [allegations] were true.' This argument is not only insulting to the judicial system as a whole, it further calls into question the fairness of female judges who preside over trials involving sexual misconduct. It is no more than a blatant attack on the integrity of judges who may share diverse qualities with a particular litigant.

Id. at 537, 463 S.E.2d at 402; *see also* Corwin v. Dickey, 91 N.C. App. 725, 728–29, 373 S.E.2d 149, 151 (1988) (new trial ordered where counsel argued that the case was "all for money" for the lawyers, was un-Christian, and would bring about a "reckoning on Judgment Day."); Clemons v. Lewis, 23

the record to be reviewed on appeal as grounds for a new trial.[75] In the absence of a transcript, the courts may still allow review if the relevant statements have been reconstructed in a sufficiently reliable form. In *Corwin v. Dickey*, for example, the Court of Appeals accepted a reconstruction of the narrative created during settlement of the record pursuant to North Carolina Rule of Appellate Procedure 9(c).[76] In a more recent case, on the other hand, the court found that although plaintiff had attempted to narrate the closing argument pursuant to Rule 9(c), there was no evidence that the narration 'accurately reflect[ed] the true sense of . . . [the] statements made[.]'"[77]

Improper Conduct of Witness or Third Party

Judges and attorneys are not the only players whose conduct may create prejudicial irregularities in the proceedings. Actions by witnesses and third parties, such as tampering with a jury,[78] attempting to influence a jury,[79] failing to disclose close relationships with the parties (or other sources of bias) at *voir dire*,[80] and failure to reveal relevant facts when properly sought during discovery,[81] are potential grounds for new trial. But they must have a materially prejudicial effect, and trial courts historically have been reluctant to order new trials for these reasons. Witness perjury is another potential basis for a new trial, and "whether

---

N.C. App. 488, 489–90, 209 S.E.2d 291, 292 (1974) (improper to comment that plaintiff had been in jail the night before the alleged incident).

75. Joines v. Moffitt, 226 N.C. App. 61, 68, 739 S.E.2d 177, 183 (2013) (citing Heatherly v. Indus. Health Council, 130 N.C. App. 616, 624, 504 S.E.2d 102, 108 (1998)).

76. 91 N.C. App. 725, 728, 373 S.E.2d 149, 151 (1988).

77. *Joines*, 226 N.C. App. at 67, 739 S.E.2d at 183; *cf.* Watson v. White, 309 N.C. 498, 508, 308 S.E.2d 268, 274 (1983) (refusing to grant new trial where record failed to provide context of alleged improper statement).

78. Love v. Moody, 68 N.C. 200 (1873) (affirming new trial where trial court found that counsel had spoken about the case to one of the jurors).

79. Keener v. Beal, 246 N.C. 247, 98 S.E.2d 19 (1957).

80. *See, e.g.*, Radford v. Young, 194 N.C. 747, 748, 140 S.E.2d 806, 807 (1927) (no prejudice created by distant relationship between jurors and plaintiff).

81. Horne v. Trivette, 58 N.C. App. 77, 82, 293 S.E.2d 290, 293 (1982).

this type of falsity warrants a new trial is discretionary."[82] It was within the court's discretion to order a new trial in a car accident case when a witness admitted to an investigator that he had lied on the stand about a material fact to ingratiate himself to one of the defendants.[83] But in a separate case, the judge did not abuse his discretion in denying a new trial where a key witness appeared to have lied on the stand about seeing defendants in North Carolina on a particular day; because opposing counsel did not depose the witness nor impeach him on cross-examination with available contradictory evidence, the testimony did not create a substantial miscarriage of justice.[84]

Lack of Proper Notice

Notice of a proceeding is adequate if it is "reasonably calculated, under all the circumstances, to apprise interested parties of the pendency of the action and afford them an opportunity to present their objections."[85] As the Supreme Court has stated, "Notice and an opportunity to be heard prior to depriving a person of his property are essential elements of due process of law which is guaranteed by the Fourteenth Amendment of the United States Constitution and Article I, section 17, of the North Carolina Constitution."[86] In general, parties to an action have "constructive notice of all orders and motions made during a regularly scheduled court date,"[87] but "this rule can bend when necessary to embrace common sense and fundamental

---

82. Krantz v. Owens, 168 N.C. App. 384, 387, 607 S.E.2d 337, 340 (2005).

83. McGinnis v. Robinson, 43 N.C. App. 1, 9–10, 258 S.E.2d 84, 89–90 (1979).

84. *Krantz*, 168 N.C. App. at 387–88, 607 S.E.2d at 340.

85. City of Randleman v. Hinshaw, 267 N.C. 136, 140, 147 S.E.2d 902, 905 (1966); Dalgewicz v. Dalgewicz, 167 N.C. App. 412, 418–19, 606 S.E.2d 164, 168 (2004).

86. McDonald's Corp. v. Dwyer, 338 N.C. 445, 448, 450 S.E.2d 888, 891 (1994).

87. Wood v. Wood, 297 N.C. 1, 6, 252 S.E.2d 799, 802 (1979); Trivette v. Trivette, 162 N.C. App. 55, 59, 590 S.E.2d 298, 302 (2004); *see generally* GEN. R. P. SUPER. & DIST. CTS. 2.

fairness."[88] Lack of adequate notice is a question of law reviewed *de novo* by appellate courts.[89] An actual lack of adequate notice that is not due to neglect or inattention of the movant, therefore, may constitute an irregularity in the proceedings requiring new trial. In *Brown v. Ellis*,[90] the defendant in an alienation of affection and criminal conversation action tried in Guilford County, North Carolina, was a resident of Orange County, California.[91] After representing defendant for over a year, defendant's counsel was allowed to withdraw. Both her motion to withdraw and the court's order, however, were mailed to defendant at the wrong address. The court thereafter mailed defendant an administrative order setting the trial, and later a trial calendar, to the same incorrect address. The trial was set for a Monday morning, but not until the prior Friday afternoon—when plaintiff's private investigator personally served defendant notice in California—did defendant receive any notice of the trial date. At that point defendant attempted to contact his counsel and only then learned that she had been allowed to withdraw. Trial proceeded three days later in defendant's absence, where the jury awarded plaintiff $600,000. The trial court denied defendant's motion for new trial.[92] The Court of Appeals, reversing, determined that defendant was never properly notified of his trial date "through no fault of [his] own" and thus was entitled to a new trial.[93]

The question of lack of notice has more frequently arisen in the context of Rule 60(b) motions where the movant has not discovered

---

88. *Trivette*, 162 N.C. App. at 59, 590 S.E.2d at 302 (citing Hagins v. Redevelopment Comm'n of Greensboro, 275 N.C. 90, 98, 165 S.E.2d 490, 495 (1969)) (internal quotations omitted).

89. Brown v. Ellis, 206 N.C. App. 93, 696 S.E.2d 813 (2010) (citing Swanson v. Herschel, 174 N.C. App. 803, 805, 622 S.E.2d 159, 160 (2005)); *Trivette*, 162 N.C. App. at 58, 590 S.E.2d at 302.

90. 206 N.C. App. 93, 696 S.E.2d 813 (2010).

91. *Brown*, 206 N.C. App. at 101, 696 S.E.2d at 820.

92. *Id.* at 102–03, 696 S.E.2d at 820–21.

93. *Id.* at 108–09, 696 S.E.2d at 824 (examining LaRoque v. LaRoque, 46 N.C. App. 578, 265 S.E.2d 444 (1980)).

the court's action within the ten days required by Rule 59. These cases are discussed in Part II.

Misrecording of Jury Verdict

The Court of Appeals has recognized as a potential basis for a new trial that "an error has occurred in the recording of the jury verdict."[94] The trial court must, however, "exercise great caution" when considering such a motion, and "should in no event grant such motion unless . . . the verdict as announced or delivered is different—and *all* of the jurors agree that it is different—from the verdict as assented to in the jury room at the time of voting[.]"[95] Evidence by only two of the jurors presented within ten days of judgment was, as a matter of law, insufficient to permit a new trial.[96] The evidentiary rule preventing jurors from impeaching their own verdict[97] does not prevent the court from considering evidence from jurors that a clerical error was made in recording the jury's verdict.[98]

Change in the Law

In *Hunnicut v. Griffin*,[99] a new trial was required where a change in law occurred in the midst of trial and the judge and counsel had little chance of learning of the change. The court charged the jury on February 3, 1984. The jury found in favor of defendant. Within ten days of judgment, plaintiffs moved for a new trial after having discovered that a Supreme Court decision handed down on February 2, the day of the charge conference, rendered the trial court's jury instructions erroneous.[100] Rejecting the argument that plaintiffs should

---

94. Chandler v. U-Line Corp., 91 N.C. App. 315, 325, 371 S.E.2d 717, 723 (1988). Note that in *Chandler* this motion was brought under Rule 59(a)(9) dealing with "any other reasons" for granting a new trial.

95. *Id.*

96. *Id.* at 326, 371 S.E.2d at 723.

97. *See infra* section titled "Misconduct of the Jury."

98. Handex of the Carolinas, Inc. v. Cty. of Haywood, 168 N.C. App. 1, 22, 607 S.E.2d 25, 38 (2005).

99. 76 N.C. App. 259, 332 S.E.2d 525 (1985).

100. *Id.* at 260, 332 S.E.2d at 525–26.

have learned of the change and objected at the charge conference, the Court of Appeals stated,

> Both court and counsel were understandably unaware that the law had changed: it would be unreasonable to expect either to be informed of such changes in the law when they occurred only hours before the jury was charged. . . . Both counsel and court lacked a realistic opportunity to apprise themselves of the holding in [the new] case. Under these circumstances, although plaintiffs did not object to the jury instructions, it was not error for the trial court to grant a new trial on the grounds that the jury had been erroneously charged.[101]

Misconduct of the Jury or Prevailing Party—Rule 59(a)(2)

As discussed above, courts have long characterized improper conduct of the court, counsel, witnesses and third parties as irregularities under Rule 59(a)(1). Rule 59(a)(2) specifically sets out "misconduct of the jury or prevailing party" as a separate discretionary basis for a new trial.

Misconduct of the Jury

Like the judge, attorneys, and other court officials, jurors in a civil case have a duty to maintain the fairness of the proceedings. They are instructed, among other things, to avoid all pre-deliberation communications about the case (including electronic communications) with each other, with family and friends, and with anyone else; to avoid all communication during the case with the attorneys, parties, and witnesses; to report to the bailiff attempts by anyone to talk with them about the case; to refrain from reading or listening to any media reports about the case; to refrain from consulting the scene of the incident or conducting any outside research related to the issues in the case; and to base their decisions solely on the evidence presented at trial.[102] When jurors fail to comply with these or other requirements,

---

101. *Id.* at 264–65, 332 S.E.2d at 528.

102. *See* N.C.P.I. (Civil) 100.20 (Recesses) and 100.21 (Recesses). For North Carolina criminal matters, cautionary instructions to this effect are

a party prejudiced by their actions may be entitled to a new trial. The decision to award a new trial "rests in the sound discretion of the trial judge, [whose] ruling will be upheld on appeal unless it is clearly erroneous."[103] In the case of a car accident that happened shortly after dark, for example, one of the jurors at evening recess conducted experiments viewing vehicles on the highway thirty minutes after sunset. The trial judge declined to grant a new trial. The Court of Appeals concluded that the judge had reviewed the matter with care and had not abused his discretion in deciding that the impropriety of the juror's conduct had not affected the verdict.[104] And in a motorcycle accident case, a trial judge acted within his discretion when awarding a new trial because four jurors were seen looking at a composite drawing of the alleged driver that had been left sitting out on the defense table after the trial court refused to allow it into evidence.[105] At least one pre-

---

set out in G.S. 15A-1236, as reflected in North Carolina Pattern Instruction (Criminal) 100.31 (Admonitions to Jurors at Recesses) and 100.33 (Recesses). No such similar statute exists for North Carolina civil deliberations. The website for the North Carolina Administrative Office of the Courts also provides a publicly available tutorial for potential jurors that summarizes many of these same cautionary instructions. *See* www.nccourts.org/Citizens/JDuty/JDutyvideo.asp.

103. O'Berry v. Perry, 266 N.C. App. 77, 81, 145 S.E.2d 321, 325 (1965); *see also* Wright v. Holt, 18 N.C. App. 661, 662–63, 197 S.E.2d 811, 812 (1973) (no abuse of discretion in determining no prejudice was caused by juror who overheard defendant in the restroom talking about the facts of the case); *see, e.g.*, Muse v. Charter Hosp. of Winston-Salem, 117 N.C. App. 468, 481, 452 S.E.2d 589, 599 (affirming denial of new trial where juror failed to disclose facts on *voir dire* but counsel had enough information to be on notice of problems), *aff'd per curiam*, 342 N.C. 403, 464 S.E.2d 44 (1995).

104. Brown v. Boren Clay Prods. Co., 5 N.C. App. 418, 421, 168 S.E.2d 452, 454 (1969).

105. Elks v. Hannan, 68 N.C. App. 757, 759–60, 315 S.E.2d 553, 554–55 (1984). The judge did not make any affirmative findings of actual prejudice but instead noted on the record that for a juror viewing it, "that picture was, for all intents and purposes, put in evidence." Since the effect of the picture on the jury could not be known, the judge chose to err on the side of caution and not "punish that plaintiff by reason of something that [defense counsel] did."

rules case warns that, when parties or counsel observe or are told of potential misconduct, they should bring the information to the court's attention as soon as practical or risk waiving an objection.[106]

The reach of Rule 59(a)(2) is limited by the evidentiary rule that prohibits using certain juror testimony to invalidate a judgment based on juror misconduct. This rule is codified as Rule of Evidence 606(b), which provides:

> Upon an inquiry into the validity of a verdict or indictment, a juror may not testify as to any matter or statement occurring during the course of the jury's deliberations or to the effect of anything upon his or any other juror's mind or emotions as influencing him to assent to or dissent from the verdict or indictment or concerning his mental processes in connection therewith, except that a juror may testify on the question whether extraneous prejudicial information was improperly brought to the jury's attention or whether any outside influence was improperly brought to bear upon any juror. Nor may his affidavit or evidence of any statement by him concerning a matter about which he would be precluded from testifying be received for these purposes.[107]

Evidence of jury misconduct must, in short, "come from a source other than the jury,"[108] unless it is testimony that the jury was subjected to extraneous prejudicial information or an outside influence. Allowing

---

106. *See, e.g.,* Bowman v. Howard, 182 N.C. 662, 666–67, 110 S.E. 98, 100–01 (1921) (no error to deny new trial where counsel, while jury deliberated, delayed four hours before informing court that jury had improperly viewed the property in question the night before).

107. G.S. 8C-1, Rule 606(b) (hereinafter Rule 606(b)). This rule became effective July 1, 1984.

108. Cummings v. Ortega, 365 N.C. 262, 272, 716 S.E.2d 235, 242 (2011) (citing State v. M'Leod, 8 N.C. (1 Hawks) 344, 346 (1821)); *see also* Winston-Salem Joint Venture v. City of Winston-Salem, 65 N.C. App. 532, 538, 310 S.E.2d 58, 62 (1983) ("It is firmly established in this State that jurors will not be allowed to attack or overthrow their verdicts, nor will evidence from them be received for such purpose.").

a juror to testify regarding the "internal processes of the jury"[109] after the verdict is rendered would "undermine full and frank discussion in the jury room, [the] jurors' willingness to return an unpopular verdict, and the community's trust in a system that relies on the decisions of laypeople."[110] A jury's internal influences generally are characterized as "information coming from the jurors themselves" and include such factors as "a juror not assenting to the verdict, a juror misunderstanding the instructions of the court, a juror being unduly influenced by the statements of his fellow-jurors, or a juror being mistaken in his calculations or judgments."[111] Extraneous information, on the other hand, is

> information dealing with the defendant or the case which is being tried, which . . . reaches a juror without being introduced into evidence. It does not include information which a juror has gained in his experience which does not deal with the defendant or the case being tried.[112]

In *McClain v. Otis Elevator Co., Inc.*, for example, it was proper for the trial court to deny a new trial based on affidavits of two jurors stating that the jury based its verdict on a consideration that was contrary to the court's instructions.[113] And in *Fenz v. Davis*,[114] a case involving an

---

109. *Cummings*, 365 N.C. at 268, 716 S.E.2d at 239.

110. *Id.* at 268, 716 S.E.2d at 239 (quoting Tanner v. United States, 483 U.S. 107, 120–21, 107 S. Ct. 2739, 2748, 97 L. Ed.2d 90, 106 (1987)) (citations omitted).

111. *Cummings*, 365 N.C. at 269, 716 S.E.2d at 240.

112. State v. Rosier, 322 N.C. 826, 832–33, 370 S.E.2d 359, 363 (1988).

113. 106 N.C. App. 45, 50, 415 S.E.2d 78, 80–81 (1992); *see also* Smith v. White, 213 N.C. App. 189, 195–96, 712 S.E.2d 717, 721 (2011) (juror statements after trial indicating jury had made compromise verdict were not admissible to "impeach, attack, or overthrow" the verdict in a motorcycle accident case); Lindsey v. Boddie Noel Enters., Inc., 355 N.C. 487, 562 S.E.2d 420 (2002), *rev'g per curiam*, 147 N.C. App. 166, 555 S.E.2d 369 (2001) (dictionary definitions not "extraneous prejudicial information"); Berrier v. Thrift, 107 N.C. App. 356, 362–63, 420 S.E.2d 206, 210 (1992) (declining to award new trial based on affidavits that jury foreman had told jurors that punitive damages were merely symbolic and not collectable).

114. 128 N.C. App. 621, 495 S.E.2d 748 (1998).

injured child, plaintiffs sought a new trial after a juror stated that the verdict, contrary to court instructions, was based partly on the conduct of the child's parents. Declining to consider the juror's affidavit, the Court of Appeals explained,

> The juror's affidavit in this case does not disclose that any extraneous information about the parties or the case was brought to the attention of the jurors. Information concerning the manner in which the child and her mother were seated in the van was put in evidence by plaintiffs; the effect of that evidence upon the minds, emotions, or mental processes of the jurors, based on their life experiences, is not a proper subject for juror testimony under G.S. § 8C-1, Rule 606(b).[115]

The restriction on juror testimony is not confined to misconduct during deliberations. The plaintiff in *Cummings v. Ortega,* a medical malpractice action, presented juror affidavits stating that a fellow juror had announced that his mind was made up, that the evidence would not change it, and that "the other jurors could agree with him or they would sit there through the rest of the year."[116] Plaintiff argued that these affidavits were not excluded under Rule 606(b) because the misconduct in question allegedly occurred before the jury's deliberations began. The Supreme Court disagreed, holding that Rule 606(b) "bars jurors from testifying during consideration of post-verdict motions seeking relief from an order or judgment about alleged predeliberation misconduct by their colleagues."[117] In explaining the policy behind a broad interpretation of the rule, the court explained that "allowing consideration of affidavits like those at issue could encourage dissatisfied litigants to annoy, embarrass, and harass jurors until some evidence of juror misconduct is uncovered in the hopes of delaying or perhaps undermining implementation of a verdict."[118]

---

115. *Id.* at 625, 495 S.E.2d at 751.

116. 365 N.C. at 262–63, 716 S.E.2d at 236.

117. *Id.* at 270, 716 S.E.2d at 241.

118. *Id.* at 272, 716 S.E.2d at 242. For further discussion of Rule 606(b), see Henry Brandis & Kenneth S. Broun, Brandis and Broun on

Even when a juror's testimony properly relates to an external influence, that influence will not justify a new trial unless it materially prejudiced the movant's case. In *Pinckney v. Van Damme*, plaintiff sued the famous martial arts action star Jean-Claude Van Damme for injuries to his eye received while filming a fight scene for the movie *Cyborg* in Wilmington, North Carolina.[119] After the jury returned a verdict for plaintiff, Van Damme moved for a new trial based on allegations that, during the trial, Juror 12 had visited a karate school to research the "crescent kick" that had injured plaintiff and that the juror was told that a martial artist with Van Damme's training "should have been able to stop on a dime."[120] Juror 4 testified that Juror 12 told the other jurors what she had learned.[121] After conducting a thorough examination of every juror, the trial court determined that the jury was not prejudicially influenced by any alleged extraneous information received by Juror 12. The Court of Appeals, finding no manifest abuse of discretion, affirmed the denial of a new trial.[122]

Misconduct of the Prevailing Party

A prevailing party's improper conduct that prejudicially affects the jury's determination is another basis for a new trial under Rule 59(a)(3). Our courts have acknowledged the potential impact of improper contact with jurors[123] or other attempts at unfairly influencing the jury,[124]

North Carolina Evidence § 148 at 479–82 (6th ed. 2004). Note that Rule 606(b) does not prevent the court from considering evidence from jurors that a clerical error was made in recording the jury's verdict. Handex of the Carolinas, Inc. v. Cty. of Haywood, 168 N.C. App. 1, 22, 607 S.E.2d 25, 38 (2005).

119. 116 N.C. App. 139, 141–42, 447 S.E.2d 825, 827 (1994).

120. *Id.* at 147–50, 447 S.E.2d at 830–32.

121. *Id.* at 150, 447 S.E.2d at 832.

122. *Id.* at 150–52, 447 S.E.2d at 832–33.

123. *See* O'Berry v. Perry, 266 N.C. App. 77, 81, 145 S.E.2d 321, 325 (1965) (opposing party and witness had friendly conversation with juror en route to lunch but did not discuss the case, so trial court did not abuse its discretion in denying new trial).

124. *See, e.g.*, Strickland v. Jacobs, 88 N.C. App. 397, 400, 363 S.E.2d 229, 230 (1988) (no abuse of discretion to order new trial where defendant cried

but modern case examples analyzing such misconduct are few. Perjury by a party on the stand also is a potential argument for a new trial, but courts historically have been reluctant to grant new trials for perjury, and a judge's decision in this regard is reviewed for abuse of discretion.[125]

Accident or Surprise—Rule 59(a)(3)

The third basis for a new trial is "accident or surprise which ordinary prudence could not have guarded against."[126] A common basis for "surprise" is the sudden appearance of a witness, exhibit, or other evidence that the other party had not disclosed in discovery or listed in a pretrial order. The courts have acknowledged that a party's surprise by such an unexpected event is a potential basis for mistrial or a new trial.[127] But the admission of such evidence is not necessarily error; the moving party must demonstrate that the surprise was not reasonably avoidable and was, of course, materially prejudicial. In a challenge to a will ("will caveat"), for example, caveators presented testimony and an exhibit that did not appear on the pretrial order. Propounders moved for a three-week continuance. The judge denied such a long continuance but advised propounders that "if you needed some time to respond to it if it were admitted, that would be reasonable" and later again offered to give them extra time.[128] The record showed, however, that propounders made no attempt to take advantage of the court's offer of extra

---

during much of the proceedings and judge was concerned about impact on jury).

125. Krantz v. Owens, 168 N.C. App. 384, 387, 607 S.E.2d 337, 340 (2005). It also may be noted that there is no civil cause of action for either perjury or subornation of perjury in North Carolina. Gilmore v. Gilmore, 748 S.E.2d 42, 46–47 (N.C. Ct. App. 2013); Strickland v. Hedrick, 194 N.C. App. 1, 19, 669 S.E.2d 61, 74 (2008).

126. Rule 59(a)(3). Note that discovery of new evidence is a type of "surprise," but it is given a category of its own, as discussed in the next section.

127. *In re* Will of Maynard, 64 N.C. App. 211, 221, 307 S.E.2d 416, 424 (1983) (citing State v. Hoffman, 281 N.C. 727, 735, 190 S.E.2d 842, 848 (1972)).

128. *Maynard*, 64 N.C. App at 220–21, 307 S.E.2d at 424.

time, and given this failure to mitigate, no new trial was required.[129] Also, in *Yorke v. Novant Health, Inc.*, a tort action in which plaintiff alleged improper use of a blood pressure machine, defendants initially denied during discovery that they could identify the type of machine used on defendant.[130] At trial, however, one of defendant's witnesses stated that the machine was a "Hewlett-Packard."[131] The trial judge properly denied plaintiff's motion for new trial, finding that, later in the discovery process, defendants' counsel had in fact sent a letter to plaintiff's counsel identifying the machine and making it available for plaintiff's inspection.[132]

Our courts also have addressed unfair surprise when the movant's attorney withdraws from representation shortly before trial and the court declines to continue the matter. Assuming the attorney's withdrawal is made pursuant to the rules of court,[133] withdrawal on the eve of a civil trial is not in and of itself grounds for a continuance.[134] Whether to grant a continuance is in the trial court's discretion once the judge "has determined from the facts and circumstances of a particular case whether immediate trial or continuance will best serve

---

129. *Id.* at 222, 307 S.E.2d at 424.

130. 192 N.C. App. 340, 357–59, 666 S.E.2d 127, 139 (2008).

131. *Id.* at 358, 666 S.E.2d at 139.

132. *Id.* at 358, 666 S.E.2d at 139–40; *see also* Hudgins v. Wagoner, 204 N.C. App. 480, 497, 694 S.E.2d 436, 449 (2010) (no new trial where defendants failed to "reference any discovery conducted to avoid or mitigate their purported surprise"); Spivey & Self, Inc. v. Highview Farms, Inc. 110 N.C. App. 719, 728–29, 431 S.E.2d 535, 540–41 (1993) (no basis for new trial where discovery responses did not create undue surprise when further related evidence was presented at trial); Perry-Griffin Found. v. Proctor, 107 N.C. App. 528, 535, 421 S.E.2d 186, 190–91 (1992) (abuse of discretion to order a new trial based on surprise where testimony was not outside limitations the trial court had previously set); Horne v. Trivette, 58 N.C. App. 77, 82, 293 S.E.2d 290, 293 (1982) (information witness failed to disclose in deposition was merely cumulative of other evidence and discrepancies could have been challenged on cross-examination).

133. *See* Gen. R. P. Super. & Dist. Cts. 16 (Withdrawal of Appearance).

134. Shankle v. Shankle, 289 N.C. 473, 484, 223 S.E.2d 380, 387 (1976).

the ends of justice."[135] A new trial may be required if the attorney misinformed the former client about the status of the case and the trial court denied a continuance. For example, in *Benton v. Mintz*,[136] a complex boundary dispute, defense counsel moved to withdraw, and defendant attended the hearing at which the court granted the withdrawal motion. The court then called the matter for immediate trial. Defendant informed the judge he did not know that the hearing that day would involve anything other than the motion to withdraw, and he repeatedly asked for more time to gather his witnesses. The judge denied any continuance, defendant was forced to proceed unrepresented, and after a trial involving complicated legal issues, judgment was awarded in favor of plaintiff. The judge denied defendant's new trial motion.[137] The Court of Appeals reversed, noting that the record supported defendant's position:

> [Defense counsel] notified the defendant that the hearing of 3 October 1988 would be "for the purpose of determining whether [he] will be permitted to withdraw . . . ." This notice fails to mention that trial was also scheduled for that date. The defendant's 30 September letter makes evident the defendant's lack of knowledge that the case was scheduled for trial. . . . [Defendant's counsel] verified that he had likely misled his client as to the nature of the 3 October proceedings. The record contains no indication that the defendant knew or should have known of the trial. Furthermore, the defendant made a notable layman's attempt to keep informed as of the trial date. On 17 May 1988, shortly after learning of his counsel's desire to withdraw, the defendant filed with the superior court clerk a request to be personally

135. *Id.* at 485, 223 S.E.2d at 387. Motions to continue are governed by North Carolina Rule of Civil Procedure 40(b), which provides, in part, "No continuance shall be granted except upon application to the court. A continuance may be granted only for good cause shown and upon such terms and conditions as justice may require." G.S. 1A-1, Rule 40(b).

136. 97 N.C. App. 583, 389 S.E.2d 410 (1990).

137. *Id.* at 585–86, 389 S.E.2d at 411–12.

> informed should his case be scheduled on a court calendar. Under these circumstances, the counsel's apparent failure to inform the defendant of the pending trial should not be attributable to the defendant.

The court concluded that the "few hours" of time defendant had to prepare his case was clearly insufficient to satisfy due process, and a new trial was required.[138] Under similar facts, a trial court abused its discretion in refusing to grant a new trial to plaintiff in a custody case. In *Ruth v. Ruth*,[139] counsel for a mother with custody of her children withdrew thirty minutes before the hearing. Plaintiff proceeded to represent herself in what she believed would be a hearing not to address custody, but instead to modify her ex-husband's visitation. As soon as she "realized that the trial had moved into a direction she was unprepared to defend," she moved for a continuance, which was denied. The judge then awarded custody to her former husband.[140] Reversing and remanding for new trial, the Court of Appeals noted that plaintiff had not sought to delay or evade the trial and that the record revealed she was likely unaware or misled by her attorney about the true nature of the trial.[141]

Newly Discovered Evidence—Rule 59(a)(4)

The fourth basis for a new trial is where there is "newly discovered evidence material for the party making the motion which he could not, with reasonable diligence, have discovered and produced at the trial[.]"[142] This rule is a remedy in the unusual event that a party discovers—before the expiration of its ten-day deadline for a new trial motion expires—that there is new evidence that is likely to alter the fact finder's decision. For later discoveries, Rule 60(b) provides a similar remedy.[143] Evidence is newly discovered if it existed at the time of

---

138. *Id.* at 589, 389 S.E.2d at 414.
139. 158 N.C. App. 293, 296–99, 580 S.E.2d 383, 384–86 (2003).
140. *Id.* at 295–96, 580 S.E.2d at 384.
141. *Id.* at 299, 580 S.E.2d at 386.
142. Rule 59(a)(4).
143. See Part II.

trial but could not have been discovered by the moving party through reasonable diligence.[144] The rationale for limiting the range of what can be considered "new" is that, if evidence arising *after* trial qualified as newly discovered, "litigation would never come to an end."[145] In *Broadbent v. Allison*,[146] a county airport, defending against a nuisance claim, argued that plaintiffs' post-trial purchase of adjacent land contradicted plaintiffs' testimony that they "were in constant fear for their lives living next to the airport."[147] The Court of Appeals explained that the purchase of additional property could not be a basis for relief because it occurred after the trial ended.[148] In a child custody matter, the mother was not entitled to a new trial in light of evidence that, after the custody hearing, the father left his steady job, stopped cooperating with the mother on child-rearing matters, and introduced the children to his girlfriend, with whom the children were not close.[149] Each alleged action occurred after the trial, so none could qualify as newly discovered.[150]

A party's diligence in obtaining *existing* evidence is an equally important requirement. In *Coleman v. Town of Hillsborough*, for exam-

---

144. Broadbent v. Allison, 176 N.C. App. 359, 364, 626 S.E.2d 758, 763 (2006) (citing Parks v. Green, 153 N.C. App. 405, 412, 571 S.E.2d 14, 19 (2002)). In *Gardner v. Harriss*, 122 N.C. App. 697, 471 S.E.2d 447 (1996), for example, defendants discovered on the first day of trial that plaintiff had failed to produce information about her prior back injuries. Finding that the discovery violation seriously compromised defendant's ability to challenge causation, the Court of Appeals held that defendant's motion for new trial should have been granted on the basis of newly discovered evidence. *Id.* at 699–700, 471 S.E.2d at 449–50.

145. Cole v. Cole, 90 N.C. App. 724, 728, 370 S.E.2d 272, 274 (1988).

146. 176 N.C. App. 359, 626 S.E.2d 758 (2006).

147. *Id.* at 364, 626 S.E.2d at 762.

148. *Id.* at 364, 626 S.E.2d at 763.

149. Faulkenberry v. Faulkenberry, 169 N.C. App. 428, 432, 610 S.E.2d 237, 240 (2005).

150. *Id.*; *see also Cole*, 90 N.C. App. at 728–29, 370 S.E.2d at 274–75 (in a paternity action, evidence that defendant fathered another child over a year after trial was not newly discovered evidence to prove that defendant's sterilization procedure had reversed itself).

ple, defendant could not base a new trial motion on an affidavit with "new information" where the underlying facts were "readily available to the Town at trial through the exercise of reasonable diligence."[151] In *Health Management Associates, Inc. v. Yerby*,[152] plaintiffs did not meet the diligence requirement where they argued that an affidavit revealing defendants' negligence qualified as newly discovered evidence. The affidavit had been served upon plaintiffs' counsel and filed in a related court file prior to an earlier summary judgment hearing.[153]

Even if the evidence is indeed newly discovered, it also must be likely to materially affect the outcome at retrial: "Evidence which is merely corroborative or cumulative of evidence offered at trial or which contradicts evidence of the opposing party is insufficient to warrant granting a new trial."[154] The airport defendant in *Broadbent* (discussed above) argued that, even though plaintiffs purchased the adjacent property after trial, they *intended* to purchase it before trial, and the intent itself was newly discovered evidence. The court held that even if plaintiffs' intent could be considered competent and admissible, it did not clearly contradict plaintiffs' trial testimony: "Since plaintiffs made the decision to live on the property in spite of the adjoining airport, it is not surprising that they would purchase additional land if such purchase would make their property more useful and enjoyable."[155] It is not enough that new evidence merely impeaches credibility; it should

---

151. 173 N.C. App. 560, 568–69, 619 S.E.2d 555, 561 (2005).

152. 215 N.C. App. 124, 715 S.E.2d 513 (2011).

153. *Id.* at 133, 715 S.E.2d at 520.

154. Horne v. Trivette, 58 N.C. App. 77, 82, 293 S.E.2d 290, 293 (1982); *see also* Lamm v. Lorbacher, 235 N.C. 728, 732–33, 71 S.E.2d 49, 52–53 (1952) (new testimony contradicting and impeaching defense witness as to only one issue not sufficiently likely to affect verdict); Mrozek v. Mrozek, 129 N.C. App. 43, 50, 496 S.E.2d 836, 841 (1998) (post-trial valuation of a marital home "irrelevant"); Yelton v. McKinney, 203 N.C. 785, 788, 167 S.E. 70, 72 (1933) (no new trial where new evidence merely cumulative); Tubiolo v. Abundant Life Church, Inc., 180 N.C. App. 238, 636 S.E.2d 341 (2006) (unpublished) (affidavits corroborating testimony given by plaintiff at trial were cumulative and thus did not provide basis for new trial).

155. Broadbent v. Allison, 176 N.C. App. 359, 365, 626 S.E.2d 758, 763 (2006).

create or allow a substantial new inference for the fact finder's serious consideration.[156] The trial court's decision to grant a new trial for newly discovered evidence is reviewed only for abuse of discretion,[157] but a judge should closely scrutinize the movant's argument prior to doing so. The North Carolina Supreme Court stated over a century ago that retrials based on new evidence should not be granted "for light causes and considerations" but, instead, "only in cases where it is very probable that substantial injustice has been done by reason of the unavoidable failure to produce the evidence . . . , and . . . it is probable that upon a new trial a different result will be reached and the right will prevail.[158]

---

156. *See, e.g.*, Ar-Con Constr. Co. v. Anderson, 5 N.C. App. 12, 20, 168 S.E.2d 18, 24 (1969) (evidence that plaintiff knew of defendant's unlicensed status not sufficiently likely to alter outcome of construction contract case).

157. *See, e.g.*, Poole v. Harvey Motor Co., 255 N.C. 563, 122 S.E.2d 414 (1961) ("No one could possibly be so well advised as to the justice and propriety of granting or refusing a motion for a new trial for newly discovered evidence as the judge who has just heard the facts developed in the trial.")

158. Warwick v. Taylor, 163 N.C. 68, 68, 79 S.E. 286, 287 (1913). Long before the Rules of Civil Procedure, the North Carolina Supreme Court articulated a series of requirements for granting a new trial based on new evidence. Although these specific strictures are not found within Rule 59 itself, they remain a foundation for the principles stated in more modern case law.

> [I]t shall appear by the affidavit: (1) That the witness will give the newly discovered evidence; (2) that it is probably true; (3) that it is competent, material, and relevant; (4) that due diligence has been used and the means employed, or that there has been no laches, in procuring the testimony at the trial; (5) that it is not merely cumulative; (6) that it does not tend only to contradict a former witness or to impeach or discredit him; (7) that it is of such a nature as to show that on another trial a different result will probably be reached and that the right will prevail.

Johnson v. Seaboard Air Line Ry. Co., 163 N.C. 431, 79 S.E. 690, 699 (1913).

Jury Disregard of Instructions—Rule 59(a)(5)

Jurors are charged with following the court's instructions whether they agree with them or not.[159] Rule 59(a)(5) provides a potential remedy where there is "manifest disregard by the jury of the instructions of the court." The jury's failure often stems from mistake or lack of understanding, but sometimes it is intentional or an attempt to reach a compromise verdict[160] and at times may lead to an insufficient or excessive damages figure.[161] Whatever the cause, if the result is unjust, a new trial may be appropriate.

---

159. The following instruction is included in North Carolina's pattern instructions to jurors: "It is absolutely necessary that you understand and apply the law as I give it to you, and not as you thought it was or as you might like it to be." N.C.P.I. (CIVIL) 101.05 (Function of the Jury).

160. A compromise verdict is one "reached only by the surrender of conscientious convictions on one material issue by some jurors in return for a relinquishment of matter in their like settled opinion on another issue, and the result is one which does not hold the approval of the entire [jury]." *Compromise Verdict*, BLACK'S LAW DICTIONARY (10th ed. 2014). Our Court of Appeals has further defined a compromise verdict as "one in which the jury answers the issues without regard to the pleadings, evidence, contentions of the parties or instructions of the court." Smith v. White, 213 N.C. App. 189, 195, 712 S.E.2d 717, 721 (2011). "The dollar amount of the verdict alone is insufficient to set aside the verdict as being an unlawful compromise" (*id.*), and the fact that a jury's verdict approximates an average of the damages valuations in evidence is not sufficient to establish a compromise verdict. Piedmont Triad Reg'l. Water Auth. v. Lamb, 150 N.C. App. 594, 597–98, 564 S.E.2d 71, 74 (2002).

Another manifestation of juror compromise is a "quotient" verdict—one in which the jury agrees in advance to be bound by the average of the amount each submits as damages. Gram v. Davis, 128 N.C. App. 484, 490, 495 S.E.2d 384, 388 (1998). Quotient verdicts do indeed provide grounds for a new trial, but they also are difficult to demonstrate. In *Seaman v. McQueen*, 51 N.C. App. 500, 506, 277 S.E.2d 118, 121 (1981), the Court of Appeals reversed the grant of a new trial where bailiff had found twelve pieces of paper in jury room which, averaged together, totaled the verdict. The court held that the papers provided no evidence that the jurors agreed *in advance* to accept the average.

161. *See infra* section titled "Excessive or Inadequate Damages—Rule 59(a)(6)."

The verdict sheet itself may show the jury's deviation from the instructions. For example, in a challenge to a will's validity ("will caveat"), the jury was instructed that if it answered "yes" to whether the document was executed according to law (issue one), it must also answer "yes" to whether the document was decedent's last will and testament (issue two). Instead, the jury answered "yes" to issue one and "no" to issue two.[162] The court held that the jury's manifest disregard of the court's instruction was evident, and a new trial was appropriate.[163] In *Industrial Circuits Co. v. Terminal Communications, Inc.*,[164] a breach of contract action, the jury was instructed not to consider certain "bill back" figures in its calculation of damages.[165] On the verdict sheet, the damages award plainly factored in the exact amount of the "bill back" figure, and the court concluded that there was no other way the jury could have arrived at its verdict. Because of its disregard of the court's instruction, a new trial was required.[166]

The jury's disregard also may be inferred by the nature of the verdict, but the inference must be quite clear. That a jury gave a surprisingly large damages verdict may not be enough to show that it disregarded the court's instructions.[167] But a verdict may reflect that the jury simply ignored the court's instructions to apply the law to the evidence. In *Roary v. Bolton*, the evidence of defendant's negligence and plaintiff's injuries in a motorcycle accident was essentially uncontroverted; the jury's refusal to award plaintiff any damages, therefore, showed a plain disregard for the court's instructions.[168] Similarly, in *Daum v. Lorick Enterprises, Inc.*, the court instructed that, in the event the jury found defendant liable, the plaintiff was entitled to all damages "past, pres-

---

162. *In re* Will of Leonard, 71 N.C. App. 714, 715, 323 S.E.2d 377, 378 (1984).

163. *Id.* at 719, 323 S.E.2d at 380.

164. 26 N.C. App. 536, 216 S.E.2d 919 (1975).

165. *Id.* at 539, 216 S.E.2d at 922.

166. *Id.* at 540, 216 S.E.2d at 922.

167. *See, e.g.*, Everhart v. O'Charley's, Inc., 200 N.C. App. 142, 160–61, 683 S.E.2d 728, 742 (2009) (the size of the jury's punitive damages verdict was not enough to indicate that the jury ignored instructions).

168. 150 N.C. App. 193, 195–96, 563 S.E.2d 21, 22–23 (2002).

ent, and prospective" resulting from defendant's harassment.[169] The jury found the employer liable but awarded plaintiff only her past medical bills in the sum of $1,300 despite uncontroverted evidence of her severe emotional distress and post-traumatic stress disorder. The Court of Appeals held that the jury "arbitrarily ignored the evidence," thereby entitling plaintiff to a new trial as to damages.[170] As the North Carolina Supreme Court has explained, "When it is apparent that a jury by its verdict holds the defendant responsible for a whole loaf of bread, it may not then neglectfully, indifferently, or capriciously cut off a portion of that loaf as it hands it to the plaintiff."[171] For the three-year-old plaintiff in *Marsh v. Trotman*, a $4,500 verdict contravened the court's instructions as a matter of law where her stipulated medical bills were $4,727.58 and it was uncontroverted that she suffered severe bleeding, a lacerated spleen, a severe cut and scarring on her forehead, and spent four days in the hospital, two in intensive care.[172]

By contrast, in a car accident case where the defendant challenged plaintiff's pain and suffering evidence and the damages verdict appeared to include a small recovery for pain and suffering, the trial court properly declined to find that the jury had disregarded its instructions.[173] In a similar scenario, plaintiff's evidence of her injuries was "not unequivocal" and involved several credibility issues. Because the jury was at liberty to disbelieve plaintiff's evidence, there was no

---

169. 105 N.C. App. 428, 430, 413 S.E.2d 559, 560–61 (1992).

170. *Id.* at 431–32, 413 S.E.2d at 561; *see also* Maness v. Bullins, 27 N.C. App. 214, 216–17, 218 S.E.2d 507, 509 (1975) (ordering new trial where jury found defendant liable to minor plaintiff but failed to award child damages despite no dispute as to his injuries).

171. Robertson v. Stanley, 285 N.C. 561, 567, 206 S.E.2d 190, 194 (1974) (citations omitted).

172. 96 N.C. App. 578, 582, 386 S.E.2d 447, 449 (1989); *see also* Wilkinson v. Cruz, 328 N.C. 568, 568, 402 S.E.2d 408, 409 (1991) (holding plaintiff entitled to new trial where damages of $4,000 were grossly inadequate given uncontradicted evidence of pain and suffering and other loss), *rev'g for reason stated in the dissent*, 100 N.C. App. 420, 396 S.E.2d 811 (1990).

173. Smith v. White, 213 N.C. App. 189, 196, 712 S.E.2d 717, 722 (2011).

evidence that it disregarded the court's instructions in awarding plaintiff no damages.[174]

Even a clear disregard for the court's instructions, however, may not warrant a new trial if the result was not inconsistent or unjust. In *D.G. II, LLC v. Nix*, the jury returned with a zero dollar verdict, disregarding the court's instruction to award at least nominal damages; a difference of a few dollars was no cause for a new trial.[175] In a breach of contract action, the jury was instructed to answer issues five through eight only if they found in favor of defendant on the first four issues. The jury instead returned the verdict sheet with all eight issues answered, but it found in favor of defendant as to all of them. The failure to follow instructions did not, therefore, create an inconsistent verdict, and a new trial was properly denied.[176] Likewise, in *Johnson & Laughlin, Inc. v. Hostetler*, the jury failed to follow the steps the court instructed it to follow in determining the issues; the resulting cumulative damages figure was, however, in line with the law and the evidence, so the trial court did not err in denying defendant's new trial motion.[177]

Excessive or Inadequate Damages—Rule 59(a)(6)

Any of several Rule 59 bases may be appropriate to challenge a low or high damages figure—the trial court's error and a jury's failure to follow instructions have been cited in cases discussed in other sections of this chapter. Rule 59(a)(6), however, specifically allows a challenge for "excessive or inadequate damages appearing to have been given under the influence of passion or prejudice." Under this standard, a party is not required to show any particular error or other irregularity in the proceedings—if the damages figure appears to be a result of

174. Horne v. Vassey, 157 N.C. App. 681, 687–88, 579 S.E.2d 924, 928–29 (2003).

175. 213 N.C. App. 220, 234–35, 713 S.E.2d 140, 150–51 (2011).

176. Strum v. Greenville Timberline, LLC, 186 N.C. App. 662, 666, 652 S.E.2d 307, 309–310 (2007).

177. 101 N.C. App. 543, 545–46, 400 S.E.2d 80, 81–82 (1991).

something other than the evidence, relief may be appropriate.[178] The trial court's discretion to grant or deny a new trial under this standard is very broad. Our courts have established a "high threshold for appellate intervention" in the trial court's discretionary rulings,[179] and appellate review "is strictly limited to the determination of whether the record affirmatively demonstrates a manifest abuse of discretion by the judge."[180] A "manifest abuse of discretion must be made to appear from the record as a whole with the party alleging the existence of an abuse bearing that heavy burden of proof."[181] In addition, "an appellate

---

178. In illustration of this point, the North Carolina Pattern Jury Instructions state

> Now, members of the jury, you have heard the evidence and the arguments of the attorneys. It is your duty to consider all of the evidence, all contentions arising from that evidence, and the arguments and positions of the attorneys. You must weigh all of these in light of your common sense and determine the truth of this matter. You are to perform this duty fairly and objectively, and without bias, sympathy, or partiality toward any party. N.C.P.I. (Civil) 150.10 (Jury Should Consider All Contentions)
>
> You should not be swayed by pity, sympathy, partiality or public opinion. You must not consider the effect of a verdict on the plaintiff or defendant (or on any other party), or concern yourself as to whether it pleases the Court. Both the plaintiff and the defendant (as well as the other parties) (as well as the public) expect that you will carefully and fairly consider all the evidence in the case, follow the law as given to you by the Court and reach a just verdict, regardless of the consequences.

N.C.P.I. (Civil) 150.12 (Jury Should Render Verdict Based on Facts, Not Consequences).

179. Campbell v. Pitt Cty. Mem'l Hosp., Inc., 321 N.C. 260, 264–65, 362 S.E.2d 273, 276 (1987).

180. Worthington v. Bynum, 305 N.C. 478, 482, 290 S.E.2d 599, 602 (1982); *see also* Callicutt v. Smith, 267 N.C. 252, 252, 148 S.E.2d 9, 9 (1966); Pelzer v. United Parcel Serv., Inc., 126 N.C. App. 305, 311, 484 S.E.2d 849, 853 (1997); Chaney v. Young, 122 N.C. App. 260, 264–65, 468 S.E.2d 837, 840 (1996).

181. *Worthington*, 305 N.C. at 484–85, 290 S.E.2d at 604.

court should not disturb a discretionary Rule 59 order unless it is reasonably convinced by the cold record that the trial judge's ruling probably amounted to a substantial miscarriage of justice."[182] When a judge determines that a new trial is appropriate under this section, the judge may order new trial solely as to the damages issue if damages can be thoroughly evaluated apart from the other issues.[183] Such partial new trials are discussed in greater detail below.[184]

Inadequate Damages

A party is not entitled to a new trial simply because the jury awarded lower compensatory damages than that party's evidence reflected. If the evidence of damages leaves fact issues or credibility questions for the jury—which typically is the case—a trial court's decision to deny a new trial will be affirmed.[185] In *Fenz v. Davis*,[186] for example, a minor was alleged to have permanent brain impairment, emotional and developmental difficulties, loss of sleep, depression, and similar conditions resulting from a car accident. The jury awarded the stipulated sum of her medical bills but only $1,500 for her personal injuries. The Court of Appeals found no manifest abuse of discretion in the trial court's denial of a new trial, explaining,

---

182. *Id.* at 487, 290 S.E.2d at 605. In *Page v. Boyles*, the trial court ordered a new trial on the basis of inadequate damages but specifically struck from the order a finding that the verdict "appears to have been awarded under passion or prejudice." 139 N.C. App. 809, 810, 535 S.E.2d 561, 562 (2000). Because the trial court intentionally omitted a key portion of this basis for new trial, the order was an abuse of its discretion. *Id.* at 810–11, 535 S.E.2d 562–63.

183. Kornegay v. Aspen Asset Grp., LLC, 204 N.C. App. 213, 235, 693 S.E.2d 723, 739 (2010) (citations omitted).

184. See *infra* section titled "Ordering Partial New Trial."

185. DiFrega v. Pugliese, 164 N.C. App. 499, 511, 596 S.E.2d 456, 464–65 (2004) (where credibility of damages evidence in a contract action was question for the jury, no error to deny new trial); McFarland v. Cromer, 117 N.C. App. 678, 682, 453 S.E.2d 527, 529 (1995) ("The evidence of damages was conflicting, and the jury was free to believe or disbelieve plaintiff's evidence.").

186. 128 N.C. App. 621, 495 S.E.2d 748 (1998).

> Although plaintiff's neuropsychologist opined that the effects of the injury were permanent, his testimony was vigorously cross-examined and he acknowledged that he had seen her only twice and that some of the indicia of permanent injury present upon his first examination had disappeared by the time of the second examination. The jury was free to accept or reject plaintiff's evidence regarding the severity or permanency of [her] injuries.[187]

Even a damages award of $1 has been undisturbed where plaintiff's evidence of emotional distress after unwanted sexual contact was "very much in conflict."[188] On the flip side, however, a trial judge has wide discretion to set aside such a verdict if he or she views it as inadequate under the circumstances.[189]

In some cases, plaintiffs have argued that a damages verdict was insufficient as a matter of law—thus requiring a new trial—because it did not even cover plaintiff's medical bills. This argument generally has succeeded on appeal only where the medical expenses were stipulated and causation and credibility were otherwise unchallenged.[190]

---

187. *Id.* at 625, 495 S.E.2d at 751–52; *see also* Pelzer v. United Parcel Serv., Inc., 126 N.C. App. 305, 311–12, 484 S.E.2d 849, 853 (1997) (verdict of $9,000 not too low where there were no stipulations as to damages and evidence showed plaintiff exaggerated symptoms, was able to work, and had previous injuries to same shoulder).

188. Hughes v. Rivera-Ortiz, 187 N.C. App. 214, 219–20, 653 S.E.2d 165, 169–70 (2007); *see also* Anderson v. Hollifield, 345 N.C. 480, 483–84, 480 S.E.2d 661, 664 (1997) (trial court did not err in refusing to set aside $1 verdict where defendant had contested both the existence of plaintiff's injuries and causation).

189. *See, e.g.*, Loy v. Martin, 156 N.C. App. 622, 625–26, 577 S.E.2d 407, 409–10 (2003) (trial court did not err in granting new trial where injured party had $13,118.75 in medical bills and jury awarded only $1).

190. *See, e.g.*, Daum v. Lorick Enters., Inc., 105 N.C. App. 428, 431–32, 413 S.E.2d 559, 561 (1992); Marsh v. Trotman, 96 N.C. App. 578, 582, 386 S.E.2d 447, 449 (1989), *cf.* Robertson v. Stanley, 285 N.C. 561, 569, 206 S.E.2d 190, 195–96 (1974). Even in a case where the parties stipulated that plaintiff incurred medical bills of $8,716.79, the trial court did not err in refusing to set aside a verdict of $3,215.59 because the stipulation "did not

In *Beaver v. Hampton*,[191] a car accident victim alleged a ruptured disc and presented medical bills of $69,440.54 as well as $38,000.00 in lost wages related to the accident. The jury nevertheless awarded him only $30,000.00. The trial court's denial of his new trial motion was affirmed, with the appellate court noting that "the proximate cause of [plaintiff's] injuries was hotly contested at trial. . . . [T]here was evidence that [his] ruptured disc could have occurred on several other occasions, and may not have been caused by the subject accident."[192] The evidence showed three other potential sources of his injury, and his own expert agreed there was "no way to know" whether the disc rupture resulted from the accident or another event.[193] In a similar scenario, in *Moon v. Bostian Heights Volunteer Fire Department*,[194] plaintiff showed medical expenses of $4,900 for surgery to his knee after a fall. The trial court denied a new trial after the jury awarded only $2,500. The trial court's decision was affirmed because there was evidence that some of the surgery was to relieve arthritis unrelated to the accident.[195]

---

state that such medical bills were incurred by plaintiff in the treatment of injuries resulting from defendant's negligence," and there was evidence plaintiff was treated for medical issues not related to defendant's actions. Coletrane v. Lamb, 42 N.C. App. 654, 657, 257 S.E.2d 445, 447 (1979). In most cases, however, damages stipulations are much more specific.

191. 106 N.C. App. 172, 416 S.E.2d 8, *vacated in part on other grounds*, 333 N.C. 455, 427 S.E.2d 317 (1993).

192. *Id.* at 178, 416 S.E.2d at 12.

193. *Id.* (further noting that "where there is no stipulation of damages, the testimony of witnesses becomes evidence for the sole province of the jury to consider"); *see also* Dafford v. JP Steakhouse, LLC, 210 N.C. App. 678, 687, 709 S.E.2d 402, 409 (2011) (denying new trial in a slip-and-fall case where the damages and causation were questions for the jury); Warren v. Gen. Motors Corp., 142 N.C. App. 316, 320, 542 S.E.2d 317, 319 (2001) (affirming denial of new trial where evidence showed other potential causes for some of plaintiff's injuries); Lusk v. Case, 94 N.C. App. 215, 216–17, 379 S.E.2d 651, 652 (1989) (damages verdict not too low where evidence supported contention that accident merely "aggravated" a disc condition).

194. 97 N.C. App. 110, 387 S.E.2d 225 (1990).

195. *Id.* at 113, 387 S.E.2d 227; *see also* Albrecht v. Dorsett, 131 N.C. App. 502, 503–05, 508 S.E.2d 319, 322 (1998) (refusing new trial where the

A defendant is not necessarily required to put on evidence in order to challenge—or "controvert"—plaintiff's damages. Typically cross-examination alone will suffice if it yields contradictions, inconsistencies, or credibility questions about plaintiff's evidence.[196] In addition, all evidence in the trial record is subject to review on appeal. In a car accident case, plaintiffs argued that the pain, suffering, and permanent injury damages awarded to three minors were unreasonably low, and the trial court granted a new trial based on four specific pieces of testimony.[197] On appeal, defendant argued that the trial court could not properly consider such testimony because plaintiffs had not objected to it at trial. The Court of Appeals disagreed, explaining that

> the trial court must consider the testimony and evidence presented at trial. Just because a party did not object to specific testimony does not prevent the trial court from considering it when ruling on a motion for new trial pursuant to [Rule] 59(a)(6). . . . [The rule] requires the trial court to find an award of damages to have been influenced by "passion or prejudice." Such a determination requires a consideration of the entire record.[198]

Excessive Damages

The Court of Appeals has shown considerable deference to the trial judge's decision either to grant or deny a new trial for excessive damages. In the relatively few opinions assessing a trial court's decision to

---

evidence of damages was "not unequivocal").

196. *Albrecht,* 131 N.C. App. at 506, 508 S.E.2d at 322; *see also* DiFrega v. Pugliese, 164 N.C. App. 499, 511, 596 S.E.2d 456, 465 (2004) ("It is well within the jury's power to minimize or wholly disregard even the testimony given by a party's expert witness.").

197. Guox v. Satterly, 164 N.C. App. 578, 581, 596 S.E.2d 452, 454 (2004). *See also* Hughes v. Rivera-Ortiz, 187 N.C. App. 214, 219, 653 S.E.2d 165, 169 (2007) (defendant put on no evidence but subjected plaintiff to lengthy cross-examination).

198. *Guox,* 164 N.C. App. at 581–82, 596 S.E.2d at 454–55. Note that the court contrasted Rule 59(a)(6) with 59(a)(8), which is based only on errors "objected to by the party making the motion." *Id.* at 582, 596 S.E.2d at 455.

set aside a verdict, the courts have declined to change the result.[199] In the leading case of *Worthington v. Bynum*,[200] the jury returned a verdict of $175,000 and $150,000 for the two plaintiffs, respectively, for injuries sustained in a car accident. Citing his belief that the trial had been an "extremely volatile situation" and that the jury had disregarded his instructions, had acted with passion or prejudice, and had returned a verdict contrary to the evidence, the trial judge, in his "considered discretion," granted defendant a new trial.[201] Discussing at length the trial court's broad authority to order a new trial, the Supreme Court, reversing the Court of Appeals, held that the trial judge did not abuse his discretion. While the plaintiffs' injuries were substantial and the evidence "surely warranted a large recovery," the evidence also suggested that the combined award was too high in light of plaintiffs' relatively modest medical bills, no loss of income from work, ability to continue the same work, and plaintiffs' relatively minor continuing disability.[202] The court explained,

> Due to their active participation in the trial, their first-hand acquaintance with the evidence presented, their observances of the parties, the witnesses, the jurors and the attorneys involved, and their knowledge of various other attendant circumstances, presiding judges have the superior advantage in best determining what justice requires in a certain case.[203]

---

199. *See, e.g.*, Worthington v. Bynum, 305 N.C. 478, 482, 290 S.E.2d 599, 602 (1982); Burgess v. Vestal, 99 N.C. App. 545, 393 S.E.2d 324 (1990) (no error to set aside $300,000 verdict in auto accident case); Campbell v. Pitt Cty. Mem'l Hosp., Inc., 321 N.C. 260, 264–65, 362 S.E.2d 273, 276 (1987) (refusing to disturb grant of new trial where jury awarded $4.85 million for injuries sustained during breech birth), Scott v. Trogdon, 268 N.C. 574, 574, 151 S.E.2d 18, 18 (1966) (summarily affirming grant of new trial on $10,000 personal injury verdict), Samons v. Meymandi, 9 N.C. App. 490, 496, 177 S.E.2d 209, 212 (1970) (stating deferential standard in affirming grant of new trial in false imprisonment case).

200. 305 N.C. 478, 290 S.E.2d 599 (1982).

201. *Id.* at 480–81, 290 S.E.2d at 601–02.

202. *Id.* at 486, 290 S.E.2d at 605.

203. *Id.* at 488, 290 S.E.2d at 605. In reversing the decision of the Court of Appeals, the Supreme Court overruled *Howard v. Mercer* (36 N.C. App.

More commonly, our trial courts have denied new trial motions made on the basis of excessive damages, and time and again their decisions have been upheld.[204] The breadth of appellate deference to a trial court's decision is well reflected in *Lovell v. Nationwide Mutual Insurance Co.*,[205] a suit against an insurer for bad-faith refusal to settle a claim. After their daughter died in a car accident, the parents sought

---

67, 243 S.E.2d 168 (1978)) to the extent that opinion attempted to narrow the range of a trial court's discretion and, in particular, rejected the suggestion that a trial court should not grant a new trial if verdict is within the "maximum limits of a reasonable range." *Worthington*, 305 N.C. at 485, 290 S.E.2d at 604.

204. *See, e.g.*, Beasley v. McLamb, 247 N.C. 179, 184–85, 100 S.E.2d 387, 390 (1957) (no error to deny new trial where jury awarded more than plaintiff's own valuation of services); White v. Thompson, 196 N.C. App. 568, 575–76, 676 S.E.2d 104, 110 (2009) (no error to deny new trial where evidence of damages for breach of fiduciary duty involved complicated accounting evidence); Greene v. Royster, 187 N.C. App. 71, 80–81, 652 S.E.2d 277, 283–84 (2007) (in fraud case, large punitive damages award not shown to be product of passion or prejudice merely because jury deliberated only twenty minutes); WRI/Raleigh, L.P. v. Shaikh, 183 N.C. App. 249, 256–57, 644 S.E.2d 245, 249 (2007) (in breach of lease, no abuse of discretion to deny new trial where it was not clear that jury failed to reduce damages to present value); City of Charlotte v. Whippoorwill Lake, Inc., 150 N.C. App. 579, 583, 563 S.E.2d 297, 300 (2002) (evidence sufficient to support damages verdict in condemnation action); Hawley v. Cash, 155 N.C. App. 580, 584–85, 574 S.E.2d 684, 687–88 (2002) (no abuse of discretion to deny relief from $2.5 million punitive damages verdict); Hutelmyer v. Cox, 133 N.C. App. 364, 373, 514 S.E.2d 554, 561 (1999) (no abuse in refusing to set aside $500,000 in compensatory and $500,000 in punitive damages for criminal conversation); Kremer v. Food Lion, Inc., 102 N.C. App. 291, 296–97, 401 S.E.2d 837, 840 (1991) ($90,000 for fractured hip in slip-and-fall case not shown to be excessive); Jones v. Hughes, 110 N.C. App. 262, 266–67, 429 S.E.2d 399, 402–02 (1993) (no error to deny new trial where jury awarded $100,000 for dental injuries); Reed v. Abrahamson, 108 N.C. App. 301, 307–08, 423 S.E.2d 491, 494–95 (1992) (no error to deny new trial where jury awarded $50,000 for 5 percent permanent partial disability to spine); Griffin v. Griffin, 45 N.C. App. 531, 532, 263 S.E.2d 39, 40 (1980) (no error to deny new trial in car accident case after jury returned $175,000 verdict for various injuries, including permanent reduced vision).

205. 108 N.C. App. 416, 424 S.E.2d 181, *aff'd*, 334 N.C. 682, 435 S.E.2d 71 (1993).

the full $250,000 of body injury coverage under the applicable insurance policy. In the midst of discussion, trial, and eventual settlement of this claim for $200,000, the insurer failed to pay the parents a related $2,000 in policy coverage for medical payments. The mother later sued the insurer for the $2,000.[206] Despite the fact that the mother asked the court for only $15,000 in punitive damages, and that there was evidence the parents had never actually made a formal claim with the insurer for the $2,000 payment, the jury awarded the mother $250,000 in punitive damages. Affirming the trial court's refusal to order a new trial, the Court of Appeals noted that the amount sought was "a factor, but . . . not determinative as to whether the verdict was excessive" and noted that "damages in this state are governed by the evidence presented, rather than the claim made for relief . . . ."[207] Although the evidence of the insurer's potential aggravated conduct related more to the bodily injury claim than to the medical payments coverage, the court found that the evidence overall was sufficient to support the jury's punitive damages verdict.[208]

Even in the context of a breach of contract action—in which damages are more susceptible to proof in hard numbers—the Court of Appeals has declined to second-guess the trial judge. In *Decker v. Homes, Inc./Construction Management & Financial Group*, the plaintiffs' own evidence of their home's construction defects showed damages between $85,000 and $185,692.40.[209] The jury nevertheless awarded more than $270,000, and the trial judge declined to order a new trial. The Court of Appeals affirmed, stating that "the trial judge . . . was clearly in a much better position than this Court to determine whether the award was excessive."[210]

---

206. *Id.* at 418–19, 424 S.E.2d at 183–84.

207. *Id.* at 427, 424 S.E.2d at 188.

208. *Id.*

209. 187 N.C. App. 658, 665, 654 S.E.2d 495, 500–01 (2007).

210. *Id. But see* Munie v. Tangle Oaks Corp., 109 N.C. App. 336, 343–44, 427 S.E.2d 149, 153 (1993) ($125,000 award and subsequent remittitur to $60,000 bore no relationship to evidence of $45,000 in damages for breach of contract).

Remittitur and Additur

As an alternative to granting a new trial, trial courts may order remittitur (reduction) or additur (increase) in the amount of a verdict.[211] Authority for remittitur exists only if the party in whose favor the verdict was rendered consents to the alteration.[212] Likewise, authority for additur exists only with the defending party's consent.[213] Even where the proper party consents, however, the trial court may, in its discretion, order a new trial instead.[214]

It should be noted, however, that remittitur or additur may not be a sure fix for a damages verdict gone wrong. Even if the damages sum is altered by the court, it may still be challenged by the opposing party on appeal if the adjusted amount itself has no basis in the evidence. In *Munie v. Tangle Oaks Corp.*,[215] for example, a jury returned a verdict

---

211. Redevelopment Comm'n of Durham v. Holman, 30 N.C. App. 395, 397, 226 S.E.2d 848, 849–50 (1976) (remittitur); Caudle v. Swanson, 248 N.C. 249, 261, 103 S.E.2d 357, 366 (1958) (additur). Authority for additur and remittitur long pre-dates enactment of Rule 59, and both remain permissible under the Rules of Civil Procedure. *Holman*, 30 N.C. App. at 397, 226 S.E.2d at 849.

212. Pittman v. Nationwide Mut. Fire Ins. Co., 79 N.C. App. 431, 434, 332 S.E.2d 441, 444 (1986). *See, e.g.*, S. Furn. Hardware, Inc. v. Branch Banking & Trust Co., 136 N.C. App. 695, 705, 526 S.E.2d 197, 202–03 (2000) (error to condition the outcome of a new trial motion on the parties' acceptance of a remittitur); Gardner v. Harriss, 122 N.C. App. 697, 699–700, 471 S.E.2d 447, 449–50 (1996) (error to order remittitur instead of new trial where plaintiff's discovery violations led to defendant's inability to challenge key causation and damages allegations); Jorgensen v. Seeman, 95 N.C. App. 767, 770, 383 S.E.2d 702, 704 (1989) (court erred in unilaterally reducing verdict); Leary v. Nantahala Power & Light Co., 76 N.C. App. 165, 178, 332 S.E.2d 703, 712 (1985) (trial court erred in reducing the verdict by $10,000 over the plaintiff's objection); Indus. Circuits Co. v. Terminal Commc'ns, Inc., 26 N.C. App. 536, 540, 216 S.E.2d 919, 922 (1975) (trial court erred in reducing a verdict on its own and without consent).

213. *Caudle*, 248 N.C. at 261, 103 S.E.2d at 366; Overton v. Purvis, 162 N.C. App. 241, 245, 591 S.E.2d 18, 22 (2004) (noting that defendant had given consent to the motion).

214. Lazenby v. Godwin, 40 N.C. App. 487, 493–94, 253 S.E.2d 489, 496 (1979).

215. 109 N.C. App. 336, 427 S.E.2d 149 (1993).

of $125,000 for breach of contract related to the construction of a boat slip. The trial court found this damages figure unjustifiable, remarking that "the maximum amount of damages that could have been available under the evidence presented was $45,000."[216] With plaintiff's consent, the court reduced the award to $60,000. The Court of Appeals found that the $60,000 reduced award was still excessive and remanded for a new damages trial.[217]

Insufficiency of the Evidence to Justify Verdict; Verdict Contrary to Law—Rule 59(a)(7)

Insufficiency of the Evidence to Justify Verdict

Perhaps the broadest area of discretion is under Rule 59(a)(7), which allows a court to grant a new trial if it determines that the evidence weighs against the verdict. This analysis is not the same as the standard for granting JNOV under Rule 50(b), where the court may grant judgment in favor of the moving party only if the evidence was insufficient *as a matter of law* to support the jury's decision; that is, that there was not more than a scintilla of evidence to support the verdict.[218] Rule 59(a)(7) authorizes the less sweeping remedy of a new trial where the court decides that the evidence—though legally sufficient to support a verdict under Rule 50—nevertheless weighed against the jury's decision.[219]

Consider this hypothetical example: In a trade secrets misappropriation trial, defendant moves for a directed verdict at the close of the evidence. The judge believes at that time that the evidence is insufficient as a matter of law to support a verdict for plaintiff but, believing the jury will find for defendant, reluctantly denies the directed verdict motion. The jury instead finds for plaintiff. On defendant's combined motion for JNOV and new trial,[220] the judge reassesses the evidence

---

216. *Id.* at 343–44, 427 S.E.2d at 153.

217. *Id.*

218. *See* Chapter 1.

219. *In re* Will of Buck, 350 N.C. 621, 624, 516 S.E.2d 858, 860 (1999).

220. *See infra* section titled "Combined Motions for JNOV and New Trial."

and decides the JNOV motion is a very close call. Ultimately, the judge determines that *some* competent evidence existed to support the jury's decision and thus denies the JNOV, as she must. However, because she believes the evidence weighed in favor of the movant, rather than the prevailing party, and that the verdict is probably unjust, in her discretion she orders a new trial under Rule 59(a)(7). The court's decision to deny the JNOV motion will be reviewed *de novo* as a question of law. If it is affirmed, the decision to grant a new trial will be reviewed as a matter of the trial court's discretion. The chart in Figure 1 (page 94) illustrates the distinctions between authority to grant JNOV under Rule 50 and a new trial under Rule 59.

In the context of Rule 59, the term "insufficiency of the evidence" means that the verdict is, in the court's opinion, against the greater weight of the evidence.[221] The trial court "in essence . . . determine[s] whether the verdict, because it is against the weight of the credible evidence, will result in an injustice if it is allowed to stand."[222] The court's authority to grant a new trial for insufficiency of the evidence is very broad and will not be reversed on appeal absent an abuse of discretion.[223] The Supreme Court has stated that "an appellate court

---

221. *Buck*, 350 N.C. at 624, 516 S.E.2d at 860 (citing Nationwide Mut. Ins. Co. v. Chantos, 298 N.C. 246, 252, 258 S.E.2d 334, 338 (1979)). While "greater weight" is the most common term used to explain this basis, the Supreme Court has explained that arguments over precise terminology—specifically whether the term "great" or "greater" weight applies—create a distinction without a difference:

> In determining whether to grant a new trial because the verdict is against the weight of the credible evidence, the primary focus of the trial court must be upon whether the verdict represents an injustice, not upon refined semantical distinctions between the "great" and "greater" weight of the evidence. . . . We conclude that any distinction between the "great" and "greater" weight standards is like twenty-four carat gold, too refined for practical usefulness in this context.

Buck, 350 N.C. at 628, 516 S.E.2d at 862–63.

222. *Id.* at 628, 516 S.E.2d at 863.

223. Nytco Leasing, Inc. v. Se. Motels, Inc., 40 N.C. App. 120, 132, 252 S.E.2d 826, 834 (1979) (citing Dixon v. Shelton, 9 N.C. App. 392, 176 S.E.2d

should not disturb a discretionary Rule 59 order unless it is reasonably convinced by the cold record that the trial judge's ruling probably amounted to a substantial miscarriage of justice."[224]

This broad authority is a matter of long-standing tradition in common law,[225] which was "not diminished by the adoption of the Rules of Civil Procedure."[226] Trial courts should exercise this authority "with *great care and exceeding reluctance*" because setting aside a verdict "will always have some tendency to diminish the fundamental right to trial by jury in civil cases which is guaranteed by our Constitution."[227] Appellate courts, however,

> should place great faith and confidence in the ability of our trial judges to make the right decision, fairly and without partiality, regarding the necessity of a new trial. Due to their active participation in the trial, their first-hand acquaintance with the evidence presented, their observations of

---

390 (1970)).

224. *Buck*, 350 N.C. at 625, 516 S.E.2d at 861 (quoting Anderson v. Hollifield, 345 N.C. 480, 483, 480 S.E.2d 661, 663 (1997)); *see also* Kor Xiong v. Marks, 193 N.C. App. 644, 654, 668 S.E.2d 594, 601 (2008) ("In ruling on a Rule 59(a)(7) motion, the trial court should 'set aside a jury verdict only in those exceptional situations where the verdict will result in a miscarriage of justice[.]'").

225. *See, e.g.*, Carolina Coach Co. v. Cent. Motor Lines, 229 N.C. 650, 653, 50 S.E.2d 909, 911 (1948) ("[A] motion to set aside a verdict as not in conformity with the evidence is addressed to the discretion of the trial judge[.]"); Edwards v. Upchurch, 212 N.C. 249, 249, 193 S.E. 19, 19 (1937) ("The trial judge has the power to set aside a verdict and order a new trial, when in his opinion the verdict is not supported by the evidence or is against the weight of the evidence."); Mfrs.' Fin. Acceptance Corp. v. Jones, 203 N.C. 523, 526, 166 S.E. 504, 506 (1932) (stating that a court's authority to set aside a verdict as against the weight of evidence is "so well settled that it is not debatable"); Goodman v. Goodman, 201 N.C. 808, 809–10, 161 S.E. 686, 687 (1931) ("No principle is more fully settled than that this court will not interfere with the discretion of a trial judge in setting aside the verdict, as being against the weight of evidence[.]").

226. *Buck*, 350 N.C. at 625, 516 S.E.2d at 861 (citing Britt v. Allen, 291 N.C. 630, 635, 231 S.E.2d 607, 612 (1977)).

227. *Buck*, 350 N.C. at 626, 516 S.E.2d at 861; Hines v. Wal-Mart Stores E., L.P., 191 N.C. App. 390, 393, 663 S.E.2d 337, 339 (2008).

> the parties, the witnesses, the jurors and the attorneys involved, and their knowledge of various other attendant circumstances, presiding judges have the superior advantage in best determining what justice requires in a certain case.[228]

In various contexts, appellate courts have declined to disturb trial court decisions both denying[229] and granting[230] new trials for insufficiency of evidence under Rule 59(a)(7). In a case challenging the validity of a will, a judge had the discretion to grant new trial even where "both parties presented substantial evidence in support of their theories."[231] The record showed that the trial court made a "painstaking appraisal of the evidence"; whether that evidence weighed in one

---

228. *Buck*, 350 N.C. at 626, 516 S.E.2d at 861.

229. *See, e.g.*, *Kor Xiong*, 193 N.C. App. at 655, 668 S.E.2d at 601–02 (no abuse of discretion to deny new trial where plaintiff's expert witness's testimony was not unequivocal); Strum v. Greenville Timberline, LLC, 186 N.C. App. 662, 667, 652 S.E.2d 307, 310 (2007) (no abuse of discretion to deny new trial where competent evidence existed to support verdict on unpaid commission); Beroth Oil Co. v. Whiteheart, 173 N.C. App. 89, 95–97, 618 S.E.2d 739, 744–45 (2005) (no abuse of discretion to deny new trial where evidence supported damages verdict related to unfair trade practices); Whaley v. White Consol. Indus., 144 N.C. App. 88, 93, 548 S.E.2d 177, 181 (2001) (no abuse of discretion to refuse new trial where jury awarded over $2 million in punitive damages against project owner in favor of injured worker); Yeargin v. Spurr, 78 N.C. App. 243, 246, 336 S.E.2d 680, 681–82 (1985) (no abuse of discretion to refuse new trial on counterclaim for conversion).

230. *See, e.g.*, Loy v. Martin, 156 N.C. App. 622, 625–26, 577 S.E.2d 407, 409–410 (2003) (no error to grant new trial where injured party had $13,118.75 in medical bills and jury awarded only $1); Burgess v. Vestal, 99 N.C. App. 545, 549, 393 S.E.2d 324, 327 (1990) (affirming grant of new trial on jury's $300,000 damages verdict in car accident case); Williams v. Randolph, 94 N.C. App. 413, 423–24, 380 S.E.2d 553, 560 (1989) (affirming new trial for attorney in suit alleging breach of fiduciary duty based on unreasonable legal fees); Fisher v. Thompson, 50 N.C. App. 724, 735, 275 S.E.2d 507, 515 (1981) (no error in denying new trial in auto negligence action where evidence was disputed).

231. *Buck*, 350 N.C. at 630, 516 S.E.2d at 863.

Figure 1. Post-Judgment Motions Decision Chart

Court's Conclusion	Evidence insufficient as a matter of law to support a verdict for plaintiff.	Greater weight of evidence favors defendant, but some evidence for plaintiff.	Evidence does not clearly weigh in favor of either party.	Greater weight of evidence favors plaintiff, but some evidence for defendant.	Evidence for plaintiff is uncontroverted (met burden as a matter of law).
Court's Action	Court should grant JNOV for defendant if verdict is for plaintiff.	Court should deny JNOV motions.* May grant new trial for defendant if verdict is for plaintiff.	Court should deny JNOV motion.	Court should deny JNOV motion. May grant new trial for plaintiff if verdict is for defendant.	Court should grant JNOV for plaintiff if verdict is for defendant.**

* This diagram assumes a jury trial. In a non-jury trial, the court, as finder of fact, may grant a Rule 41(b) dismissal for defendant at close of plaintiff's evidence even where the plaintiff has presented evidence that would be sufficient to take to a jury.

** A court should take extra caution when granting JNOV for the party with the burden of proof.

direction or another was, for purposes of Rule 59(a)(7), the judge's decision to make.[232]

Given this highly deferential review standard, successfully challenging a decision under Rule 59(a)(7) is an uphill climb indeed. In two recent cases, however, new trials under this basis have been undone by the crafting of the court's written findings of fact and conclusions of law.[233] In the first, *Langwell v. Albemarle Family Practice, PLLC,*[234] a medical negligence action involving care by a nurse practitioner, the jury returned a verdict in favor of defendants. The trial court granted

232. *Id.* at 630, 516 S.E.2d at 864.

233. *See infra* section titled "Written Findings of Fact and Conclusions of Law."

234. 203 N.C. App. 666, 668–69, 692 S.E.2d 476, 479 (2010).

a new trial and, at defendants' request, made a written order with findings of fact.[235] Eleven findings of fact regarded the plaintiff's evidence in a light favorable to plaintiff; only one mentioned defendants' evidence; and omitted completely was any mention of the "critical expert testimony" of the practitioner herself. The Court of Appeals concluded that "the order on its face reveals that the trial court failed to consider all the competent and relevant evidence presented at trial."[236] In addition, although the findings did not explain how defendants' evidence was unreliable or otherwise incompetent, the new trial order concluded, "It is the opinion of the Court and in the Court's discretion that the jury has been misled by unreliable testimony on the part of the defense and that in the opinion of the Court and its discretion a jury has returned an erroneous verdict."[237] Because this conclusion had no support in the findings, the order "probably amounted to a substantial miscarriage of justice" and was reversed.[238] Surely the outcome in *Langwell* would have been different if the trial court had not been asked to make written findings of fact, leaving the appellate court to presume that the judge weighed all the competent evidence.[239] A lesson from *Langwell* is that, where the court makes writing findings of fact, those findings should reflect a measured assessment of the record and a conclusion pointedly invoking the judge's very broad discretion to weigh the evidence against the verdict.

In the second opinion, *Hines v. Wal-Mart Stores East, L.P.*,[240] a slip-and-fall case, the trial court granted a new trial to plaintiff after the

235. *Id.*

236. *Id.* at 672–73, 692 S.E.2d at 481–82.

237. *Id.* at 674, 692 S.E.2d at 482.

238. *Id.*

239. Indeed, before the request for findings of fact was made, the trial court noted simply that "the reason for the granting of the motion for new trial is in the [c]ourt's discretion[.]" *Id.* at 669, 692 S.E.2d at 479; *see also* Selph v. Selph, 267 N.C. 635, 638–39, 148 S.E.2d 574, 577 (1966) (recognizing that if the trial judge had simply, in his discretion, found that justice required a new trial, "his order would have been unassailable on appeal.").

240. 191 N.C. App. 390, 663 S.E.2d 337 (2008).

jury declined to find defendant negligent. In a written order, the trial court made findings that included the following:

1. No evidence was produced to show that the defendant had complied with its policies and/or practices of performing "zone defense" and "safety sweeps" prior to the plaintiff's fall in the location of the plaintiff's fall.
2. The defendant was not able to identify any employee and/or persons responsible for performing the "zone defense" and "safety sweeps" in the location that the plaintiff fell at or near the time the plaintiff fell.
3. The plaintiff testified that the employee and/or agent of the defendant . . . told the plaintiff after the plaintiff fell that she was sorry but the defendants had not had time to clean up the spill on the floor because the store was so busy.
4. [A witness] testified that she heard [defendant's agent] say that she was sorry but the employees of the store did not have time to clean up the spill . . . because the store was so busy.[241]

These findings revealed that the judge improperly shifted the burden of proof to defendant by "requiring defendant to produce evidence that defendant had been acting in a non-negligent manner at the time of plaintiff's fall."[242] The Court of Appeals acknowledged the breadth of a judge's discretion in weighing the evidence under Rule 59(a)(7) but concluded that weighing the evidence while misallocating the burden of proof was an abuse of discretion.[243]

241. *Id.* at 392, 663 S.E.2d at 339.
242. *Id.* at 394, 663 S.E.2d at 340.
243. *Id.* at 393, 663 S.E.2d at 339–40.

Verdict Contrary to Law

Rule 59(a)(7) also provides for relief where the "verdict is contrary to law." This section is intended to address problems inherent in the jury's verdict other than errors of law by the court, which are covered in subsection (a)(8) and are subject to a *de novo* review standard.[244]

Before enactment of the rules, this basis was typically used to address inconsistencies in the jury's verdict,[245] and this remains an appropriate modern use.[246] It is more common, however, to see inconsistent verdicts challenged in terms of a jury's disregard of court instructions, as discussed above.[247]

Error in Law—Rule 59(a)(8)

Rule 59(a)(8) allows the trial court to grant a new trial for an "error in law occurring at the trial and objected to by the party making the motion." Unlike Rule 59(a)'s eight discretionary grounds, a grant or denial of new trial based on an error of law is reviewed *de novo*.[248] If a

---

244. See next section; *see also In re* Brown, 23 N.C. App. 109, 110–11, 208 S.E.2d 282, 283 (1974) (argument that court's judgment was "contrary to law" could not substitute for appeal of court's legal determinations).

245. *See, e.g.*, Benbow v. W. Union Tel. Co., 261 N.C. 404, 406, 134 S.E.2d 652, 654 (1964) (analyzing an argument that a verdict finding neither party negligent was necessarily contrary to law).

246. *See* Harris v. Bridges, 46 N.C. App. 207, 213, 264 S.E.2d 804, 807 (1980) (affirming a partial new trial due to court's determination that inconsistent verdict was contrary to law).

247. *See supra* section titled "Jury Disregard of Instructions—Rule 59(a)(5)"; Robertson v. Stanley, 285 N.C. 561, 206 S.E.2d 190 (1974).

248. Automotive Grp., LLC v. A-1 Auto Charlotte, LLC, 750 S.E.2d 562, 565 (N.C. Ct. App. 2013); Kinsey v. Spann, 139 N.C. App. 370, 373, 533 S.E.2d 487, 490 (2000); Chiltoski v. Drum, 121 N.C. App. 161, 164, 464 S.E. 2d 701, 703 (1995) ("Appellate courts . . . must utilize the 'abuse of discretion' standard only in those instances where there is no question of 'law or legal inference.'"); Seaman v. McQueen, 51 N.C. App. 500, 505, 277 S.E.2d 118, 121 (1981); *see also* Sockwell & Assocs., Inc. v. Sykes Enters. Inc., 127 N.C. App. 139, 142, 487 S.E.2d 795, 797 (1997) (reversing new trial granted on basis of misapprehension of law); Schall v. Jennings, 99 N.C. App. 343, 346, 393 S.E.2d 130, 132 (1990) (reversal required where trial court granted new trial based on error in determining it lacked subject matter

party seeks a new trial based on a legal error, the appropriate remedy is either to make a timely motion for relief under Rule 59(a)(8) or to raise the error on appeal.[249] When a trial court grants a new trial under this subsection, it must specify the errors of law upon which the ruling is based. Otherwise, proper appellate court review would be a guessing game.[250] Where a judge's order simply cited "errors committed by the Court," the Court of Appeals declined to "embark on a voyage of discovery through an unchartered record to find the errors of law referred to in the order."[251] This specificity requirement applies also when the new trial order is on the court's own motion[252] and when it is a conditional ruling following the grant of JNOV under Rule 50(c).[253] The Court of Appeals has stated that when the trial court fails to specify its error, "the general course is to reverse and remand for reinstatement of the verdict."[254] Any type of prejudicial legal error

---

jurisdiction); Harrell v. Sagebrush of N.C., LLC, 191 N.C. App. 381, 385, 663 S.E.2d 444, 446–47 (2008) (reversal required where trial court granted new trial based on erroneous conclusion regarding exclusion of evidence).

249. Hagwood v. Odom, 88 N.C. App. 513, 519, 364 S.E.2d 190, 193 (1988).

250. Bryant v. Nationwide Mut. Fire Ins. Co., 313 N.C. 362, 381–82, 329 S.E.2d 333, 344–45 (1985) ("Specificity in the trial judge's order pursuant to Rule 59(a)(8) is mandatory if the trial judge's decision is to be completely reviewable."). In *Burgess v. Vestal,* however, the court's failure to specify its errors of law did not require reversal because the court also granted a new trial in its broad discretion under Rule 59(a)(7). 99 N.C. App. 545, 549, 393 S.E.2d 324, 327 (1990) (holding that failure to specify detracted "not one whit" from the discretionary new trial order).

251. Barnett v. Security Ins. Co. of Hartford, 84 N.C. App. 376, 380, 352 S.E.2d 855, 858 (1987) (quoting *In re* Will of Herring, 19 N.C. App. 357, 360, 198 S.E.2d 737, 740 (1973)).

252. Rule 59(d) (discussed *infra* in the section titled "Motions by the Court"); *Herring,* 19 N.C. App. at 360, 198 S.E.2d at 740.

253. *Barnett,* 84 N.C. App. at 380, 352 S.E.2d at 858. Rule 50(c)(1) requires the trial court to "specify the grounds for granting or denying a motion a new trial" when making a conditional ruling on a motion made under *any* of the nine subsections of Rule 59.

254. *Barnett,* 84 N.C. App. at 380, 352 S.E.2d at 858. Presumably the Court of Appeals could remand for the trial court to specify the error. This may be impractical if the matter cannot be remanded to the same judge

may be cited as a basis for relief under this subsection.[255] The most common categories by far, however, are erroneous admissions and exclusions of evidence and submission of faulty jury instructions and issues.

Erroneous Admission or Exclusion of Evidence

In the course of a trial, a judge makes numerous rulings on admission of testimony, documents, and other evidence. If a party wishes to base a new trial motion on one of these rulings, it must first have lodged a proper objection during trial.[256] In addition, when the alleged error is

---

who presided over the trial, but the fact that the same trial judge is not a resident of or assigned to the same district at the time of remand should not prohibit him or her from making additional findings. *See* Andrews v. Peters, 89 N.C. App. 315, 317–18, 365 S.E.2d 709, 711 (1988). For a discussion of who may rule on a Rule 59 motion, *see infra* section titled "Who May Rule."

255. *See, e.g.*, Gardner v. Harriss, 122 N.C. App. 697, 700, 471 S.E.2d 447, 450 (1996) (in case decided prior to G.S. 1-181.2, error to admit exhibits into jury room without consent); Willoughby v. Wilkins, 65 N.C. App. 626, 637, 310 S.E.2d 90, 97 (1983) (failure to allow discovery of physician's prior psychiatric treatment impaired plaintiff's action in suit against hospital). Rule 59(a)(8) also may be invoked pursuant to Rule 59(e) as a remedy in a non-jury context for relief from errors of law appearing in the trial court's order. Elrod v. Elrod, 125 N.C. App. 407, 410, 481 S.E.2d 108, 110 (1997) (relief from errors in custody order).

Although prejudicial legal errors typically entitle a movant to new trial, the Court of Appeals has held that "where the trial court's ruling is correct upon any theory of law, the judgment of the lower court stands." Jones v. Patience, 121 N.C. App. 434, 443, 466 S.E.2d 720, 725 (1996) (citing Payne v. Buffalo Reinsurance Co., 69 N.C. App. 551, 555, 317 S.E.2d 408, 411 (1984)).

256. Rule 59(a)(8). *See, e.g.*, State *ex rel.* Everett v. Hardy, 65 N.C. App. 350, 354, 309 S.E.2d 280, 283 (1983) (argument that testimony was improperly allowed waived by failure to object at trial to earlier identical testimony); Fisher v. Thompson, 50 N.C. App. 724, 731, 275 S.E.2d 507, 513 (1981) (error in admitting evidence that violated collateral source rule waived by failing to object and by stipulating to the same facts). Note that Rule 46 limits the requirement for objections (or repeated objections) in certain lines of questioning where the witness's competency or qualification has been challenged; when an objection to specific evidence has already

the *exclusion* of evidence, "an offer of proof is required to constitute a sufficient objection under Rule 59(a)(8)[.]"[257] The error must also be prejudicial. Rule of Civil Procedure 61 provides as follows:

> No error in either the admission or exclusion of evidence . . . is ground for granting a new trial or for setting aside a verdict or for vacating, modifying, or otherwise disturbing a judgment or order, unless refusal to take such action amounts to the denial of a substantial right.[258]

To show denial of a substantial right under Rule 61, the movant must show that "a different result would have likely ensued had the error not occurred."[259] Put differently, there must be "a reasonable prospect of placing the party who asks for a new trial in a better position than the one which he occupies by the verdict."[260] If an evidentiary ruling

---

been overruled or sustained; and when the court or a juror propounds questions. *See* G.S. 1A-1, Rule 46.

257. Kor Xiong v. Marks, 193 N.C. App. 644, 656, 668 S.E.2d 594, 602 (2008) (stating this rule and declining to review exclusion of evidence where no offer of proof was made at trial). In civil cases, offers of proof of excluded evidence are governed by Rule of Civil Procedure 43(c), which provides,

> In an action tried before a jury, if an objection to a question propounded to a witness is sustained by the court, the court on request of the examining attorney shall order a record made of the answer the witness would have given. The court may add such other or further statement as clearly shows the character of the evidence, the form in which it was offered, the objection made and the ruling thereon. In actions tried without a jury the same procedure may be followed, except that the court upon request shall take and report the evidence in full, unless it clearly appears that the evidence is not admissible on any grounds or that the witness is privileged.

G.S. 1A-1, Rule 43(c).

258. G.S. 1A-1, Rule 61.

259. Suarez v. Wotring, 155 N.C. App. 20, 30, 573 S.E.2d 746, 752 (2002).

260. Lockett v. Sister-2-Sister Sols., Inc., 209 N.C. App. 60, 69, 704 S.E.2d 299, 305 (2011); O'Mara v. Wake Forest Univ. Health Scis., 184 N.C. App. 428, 440–41, 646 S.E.2d 400, 407 (2007) (admission of evidence not basis for new trial where movants failed to articulate how excluding it would likely have changed outcome).

materially impaired that party's right to prosecute or defend its case, a new trial is required.[261] But if excluded evidence was cumulative of other evidence, merely corroborated other evidence, or was substantially presented to the jury by other sufficiently reliable means, a new trial may not be appropriate.[262]

Erroneous, Incomplete, or Otherwise Improper Instructions or Jury Issues

It is the court's duty to explain the law with respect to all material features of the case arising from the evidence.[263] Instructions to the jury may fail to meet this standard in various ways, and when such failure is prejudicial, a new trial is required. As with other errors of law, however,

---

261. *See, e.g.*, Smith v. White, 213 N.C. App. 189, 193–94, 712 S.E.2d 717, 720 (2011) (new trial properly granted based on exclusion of evidence of repairs to establish diminution in value); Decker v. Homes, Inc./Constr. Mgmt & Fin. Grp., 187 N.C. App. 658, 667, 654 S.E.2d 495, 501–02 (2007) (new trial required where defendant not permitted to present evidence pursuant to G.S. 1D-35 before issue of punitive damages submitted to jury); Marley v. Gantt, 72 N.C. App. 200, 201, 323 S.E.2d 725, 725–26 (1984) (error in allowing certain cross-examination did deny plaintiff a substantial right); Willoughby v. Wilkins, 65 N.C. App. 626, 637–38, 310 S.E.2d 90, 97–98 (1983) (prejudicial error to refuse admission of evidence of prior lawsuits against expert witness necessary to impeach his credibility); *see also In re* Gamble, 244 N.C. 149, 157, 93 S.E.2d 66, 71–72 (1956) (prejudicial error to refuse inspection of sealed document for purpose of reasonably cross-examining key witness).

262. Harrell v. Sagebrush of N.C., LLC, 191 N.C. App. 381, 385, 663 S.E.2d 444, 446–47 (2008); *see, e.g.*, *Suarez*, 155 N.C. App. at 30, 573 S.E.2d at 753 (admission of deposition testimony of expert witness not prejudicial because it merely corroborated competent evidence already in the record); Warren v. City of Asheville, 74 N.C. App. 402, 409–10, 328 S.E.2d 859, 864 (1985) (no prejudice in reading deposition to jury in violation of Rule 32 because it was cumulative of other evidence already properly admitted); Fisher v. Thompson, 50 N.C. App. 724, 728–29, 275 S.E.2d 507, 511–12 (1981) (in negligence case, failure to admit accident report not prejudicial because critical portions of the report admitted through other means).

263. Foy v. Spinks, 105 N.C. App. 534, 541, 414 S.E.2d 87, 90 (1992) (citing Owens v. Harnett Transfer, Inc., 42 N.C. App. 532, 540, 257 S.E.2d 136, 141 (1979)).

the aggrieved party must first object in order to move for a new trial.[264] Objection also is required to preserve the issue for appeal.[265]

New trials often are warranted when the jury instructions include a materially incorrect statement of the law. In a car accident case, for example, a new trial was required due to an instruction that mischaracterized the law by extending the family purpose doctrine to cover company-owned vehicles and removing the basic element of family

---

264. Rule 59(a)(8); Davis v. Davis, 360 N.C. 518, 522, 631 S.E.2d 114, 118 (2006). When a party moves for a new trial based on an error of law to which it has already objected, that party will to have to engage—perhaps somewhat awkwardly—in re-arguing the same issue to the same judge. This type of re-argument is not the type of "improper purpose" contemplated by Rule of Civil Procedure 11. A trial judge erred in imposing Rule 11 sanctions against a defendant for re-arguing to the judge the issue of *res judicata* pursuant to a Rule 59(a)(8) motion. Automotive Grp., LLC v. A-1 Auto Charlotte, LLC, 750 S.E.2d 562, 567 (N.C. Ct. App. 2013).

265. The North Carolina Rules of Appellate Procedure provide as follows:

> A party may not make any portion of the jury charge or omission therefrom the basis of an issue presented on appeal unless the party objects thereto before the jury retires to consider its verdict, stating distinctly that to which objection is made and the grounds for the objection; provided that an opportunity was given to the party to make the objection out of the hearing of the jury, and, on request of any party, out of the presence of the jury.

N.C. R. App. P. 10(a)(2). "The obvious purpose behind the requirement of a timely objection is to avoid the need to completely retry a case when a judge could merely correct the instructions." Hanna v. Brady, 73 N.C. App. 521, 528, 327 S.E.2d 22, 26 (1985); *see also* Steele v. Bowden, 768 S.E.2d 47, 59–60 (N.C. Ct. App. 2014) (jury instructions not reviewed where defendant failed to object at trial); Powell v. Omli, 110 N.C. App. 336, 346, 429 S.E.2d 774, 778 (1993) (appellant waived argument by failing to object); Tatum v. Tatum, 79 N.C. App. 605, 609–10, 339 S.E.2d 817, 819–20, *aff'd as modified*, 318 N.C. 407, 348 S.E.2d 813 (1986) (jury instructions as to contributory negligence not reviewed where no objection at trial).

use.[266] An instruction misallocating the burden of proof in a contract case also required new trial.[267]

An instruction on a matter or submission of an issue not supported by the evidence is further grounds for new trial.[268] New trials have been granted, for example, based on a contributory negligence instruction where such negligence could be inferred only from the fact of injury,[269] on an instruction on the sudden emergency doctrine where the evidence showed no situation compelling instant action,[270] and on submission of unfair and deceptive trade practices where the evidence failed to support damages from this claim.[271] It is also error for an instruction to coerce a jury into arriving at a unanimous verdict by suggesting that failure to do so would waste judicial resources.[272]

If a court presents an instruction or issue that is misleading, convoluted, or confusing, and therefore impairs the jury's ability to understand the law or decide the issues, a new trial may be required. Generally, "the form and number of issues submitted is within the

---

266. Jackson v. Carland, 192 N.C. App. 432, 443–44, 665 S.E.2d 553, 560–61 (2008); *see also* Edwards v. Hardy, 126 N.C. App. 69, 73, 483 S.E.2d 724, 726–27 (1997) (erroneous instruction as to amount of lien was prejudicial error); Kinney v. Goley, 4 N.C. App. 325, 332, 167 S.E.2d 97, 102 (1969) (erroneous instruction that failure to give turn signal was negligence per se required new trial).

267. Heart of the Valley Motel, Inc. v. Edwards, 111 N.C. App. 896, 898–99, 433 S.E.2d 466, 467–68 (1993).

268. Pinckney v. Baker, 130 N.C. App. 670, 674, 504 S.E.2d 99, 102 (1998); Giles v. Smith, 112 N.C. App. 508, 512, 435 S.E.2d 832, 834 (1993).

269. Stacy v. Jedco Constr., Inc., 119 N.C. App. 115, 122, 457 S.E.2d 875, 880 (1995).

270. Sobczak v. Vorholt, 181 N.C. App. 629, 640–41, 640 S.E.2d 805, 813 (2007); *see also Pinckney*, 130 N.C. App. at 674, 504 S.E.2d at 102 (sudden emergency doctrine instruction not warranted by the evidence).

271. Decker v. Homes, Inc./Constr. Mgmt. & Fin. Grp., 187 N.C. App. 658, 666, 654 S.E.2d 495, 501 (2007).

272. Cty. of Lenoir *ex rel.* Dudley v. Dawson, 60 N.C. App. 122, 126–28, 298 S.E.2d 418, 420–21 (1982) (extending to civil cases the policy behind G.S. 15A-1235 and State v. Lamb, 44 N.C. App. 252, 261 S.E.2d 130 (1979)). *See also* N.C.P.I. (Civil) 150.50 (Failure of Jury to Reach Verdict), which includes no such coercive statements.

court's discretion,"[273] but they should be formatted to allow the jury to consider independent issues separately.[274] In a personal injury action involving a construction site, the issues as submitted did not permit the jury to consider separately defendant's own alleged contributory negligence and the alleged contributory negligence imputed to him through his employees.[275] In ordering a new trial, the Court of Appeals reiterated that "it is misleading to embody in one issue two propositions as to which the jury might give different responses."[276] And in the recent case of *Fortner v. Hornbuckle*,[277] the Court of Appeals ordered a new trial due to the trial court's "simultaneous and condensed" discussions of two distinct legal doctrines—completed gifts and retained interests.[278] In addition, the two issues were "not formatted on the verdict sheet in a manner that would allow the jury to assess them separately and rendered the appellate court unable to determine the precise basis for the jury's verdict."[279]

It is the court's duty to submit to the jury the material, disputed issues raised by the pleadings and supported by the trial record.[280] To object, however, to the court's failure to present an "issue of fact raised

---

273. *Stacy*, 119 N.C. App. at 122, 457 S.E.2d at 880 (quoting Wilson v. Pearce, 105 N.C. App. 107, 112, 412 S.E.2d 148, 150 (1992)).

274. Edwards v. Hardin, 113 N.C. App. 613, 616, 439 S.E.2d 808, 810 (1994) (citing Edge v. Feldspar Corp., 212 N.C. 246, 247, 193 S.E. 2, 2 (1937)).

275. *Stacy*, 119 N.C. App. at 123, 457 S.E.2d at 880 ("These questions were propositions to which the jury might give separate answers, allowing the jury to answer the issue without reaching a unanimous verdict as to either proposition.").

276. *Id.* at 122, 457 S.E.2d at 880 (quoting Foy v. Spinks, 105 N.C. App. 534, 538, 414 S.E.2d 87, 88 (1992)).

277. 761 S.E.2d 683 (N.C. Ct. App. 2014).

278. *Id.* at 691–92 (holding that the framing of these issues was insufficient to allow the jurors to "understand these concepts and properly apply them to the facts of the case.").

279. *Id.* at 692. *See also generally* Rule of Civil Procedure 49(b) ("Issues shall be framed in concise and direct terms, and prolixity and confusion must be avoided by not having too many issues.").

280. Winston-Salem Joint Venture v. City of Winston-Salem, 65 N.C. App. 532, 537, 310 S.E.2d 58, 62 (1983).

by the pleadings and evidence," a party must first demand submission of the issue before the jury retires to deliberate.[281]

In addition, the court's instructions on the applicable law also must cover all material aspects of the case arising from the evidence.[282] When a party seeks a "special instruction," however, that party must make the request in compliance with Rule of Civil Procedure 51(b), which provides,

> Requests for special instructions must be in writing, entitled in the cause, and signed by the counsel or party submitting them. Such requests for special instructions must be submitted to the judge before the judge's charge to the jury is begun . . . . Written requests for special instructions shall, after their submission to the judge, be filed with the clerk as a part of the record.[283]

A "special instruction" is an instruction that targets a particular point or elaborates on a specific issue not covered by the North Carolina Pattern Jury Instructions[284] or not otherwise included in the court's

---

281. G.S. 1A-1, Rule 49(c). The rule provides,

> If, in submitting the issues to the jury, the judge omits any issue of fact raised by the pleadings or by the evidence, each party waives his right to a trial by jury of the issue so omitted unless before the jury retires he demands its submission to the jury. As to an issue omitted without such demand the judge may make a finding; or, if he fails to do so, he shall be deemed to have made a finding in accord with the judgment entered.

See also Barnett v. Security Ins. Co. of Hartford, 84 N.C. App. 376, 380, 381–82, 352 S.E.2d 855, 858, 858–60 (1987) (objection to issue not preserved when demand not made under Rule 49(c)).

282. Bare v. Barrington, 97 N.C. App. 282, 285, 388 S.E.2d 166, 167 (1990).

283. G.S. 1A-1, Rule 51(b); *see also* G.S. 1-181 (same requirements).

284. The Pattern Jury Instructions "are intended to provide a useful starting point for lawyers and judges in developing jury instructions for a specific case." N.C.P.I. (Civil) (Introduction). Given the tremendous scope of these instructions (currently constituting seven large binders covering civil, criminal, and motor vehicle cases), this description is an

proposed instructions.[285] If the party does not comply with Rule 51(b), the trial court has discretion to deny the requested special instruction.[286] In several cases the Court of Appeals has declined to review a failure to include a particular instruction because the requesting party failed to submit the instruction in writing as required by the rule.[287] Rule 51(b) also provides, however, that "the [trial] judge may, in his discretion, consider [special instruction] requests regardless of the time they are made."[288] To that end, the Court of Appeals has granted a new trial where the judge considered an untimely request but then denied it after erroneously concluding that the proposed instruction did not accurately reflect the law.[289] A proper special instruction request under Rule 51(b) constitutes a valid objection to the omission of that instruction, and the submitting party "need not object to the instructions as

---

understatement indeed. *See* State v. Walston, 367 N.C. 721, 730–31, 766 S.E.2d 312, 318–19 (2014) (noting the significance of these instructions). Nevertheless, it is certainly true that no compilation could possibly contemplate every potential instruction necessary to cover the issues in every case. For this reason, parties and their counsel have a vital role in framing instructions to fit each matter.

285. Hanks v. Nationwide Mut. Fire Ins. Co., 47 N.C. App. 393, 404, 267 S.E.2d 409, 415 (1980) ("It is the duty of the party desiring instructions on a subordinate feature of the case or greater elaboration on a particular point to aptly tender request for special instructions."). Typically, the charge conference required by the General Rules of Practice provides the parties ample opportunity, outside the jury's presence, to discuss and object to proposed instructions and to request additional instructions. *See* Gen. R. P. Super. & Dist. Cts. 21.

286. Swink v. Weintraub, 195 N.C. App. 133, 155, 672 S.E.2d 53, 68 (2009).

287. *See, e.g., id.* at 155, 672 S.E.2d at 67–68 (failure to include informed consent instruction); Beroth Oil Co. v. Whiteheart, 173 N.C. App. 89, 98, 618 S.E.2d 739, 746 (2005) (no error in refusal to append additional language to special instruction where language not submitted in writing); Hanna v. Brady, 73 N.C. App. 521, 526, 327 S.E.2d 22, 25 (1985) (failure to provide limiting instruction regarding certain damages).

288. Rule 51(b).

289. Erie Ins. Exch. v. Bledsoe, 141 N.C. App. 331, 338, 540 S.E.2d 57, 63 (2000).

read" to preserve the issue on appeal.[290] If a party's properly requested special instruction is a correct statement of law and is supported by the evidence, the court is required to give it.[291] The court is not required to give the instruction exactly as requested, but must at least provide it in substance.[292] If a court's failure to give a requested instruction materially prejudices the requesting party's case, a new trial is warranted.[293]

---

290. Foy v. Spinks, 105 N.C. App. 534, 540, 414 S.E.2d 87, 89 (1992) (citing State v. Smith, 311 N.C. 287, 290, 316 S.E.2d 73, 75 (1984)); *see also* Roberts v. Young, 120 N.C. App. 720, 726, 464 S.E.2d 78, 83 (1995) ("[T]he policy of [N.C. R. App. P. 10(a)(2)] is met when a request to alter an instruction has been submitted to the court at the charge conference."). The Court of Appeals showed some leniency in *Kinsey v. Spann* by allowing review of an omitted instruction where the party submitted the request to the trial court in writing under Rule 51(b) but failed to include counsel's signature. The court concluded that, despite the lack of signature, "plaintiff has acted sufficiently in order to preserve her objection to the instructions on appeal[.]" 139 N.C. App. 370, 373, 533 S.E.2d 487, 490 (2000); *see also* King v. Brooks, 224 N.C. App. 315, 319, 736 S.E.2d 788, 792 (2012) (citing *Kinsey* in stating that the court may review *de novo* a failure to include an instruction even in the absence of strict compliance with Rule 51(b)).

291. Sobczak v. Vorholt, 181 N.C. App. 629, 640–41, 640 S.E.2d 805, 813 (2007) (failure to include requested instruction on statutory violation that constituted negligence per se required new trial); Ellison v. Gambill Oil Co., Inc., 186 N.C. App. 167, 169, 650 S.E.2d 819, 821 (2007) (remanding a hazardous substances contamination case for failure to instruct on third-party exception to strict liability); Maglione v. Aegis Family Health Ctrs., 168 N.C. App. 49, 57–58, 607 S.E.2d 286, 291–92 (2005) (new trial warranted based on exclusion of requested instruction on good faith and fair dealing). *Cf.* Cobb *ex rel.* Knight v. Town of Blowing Rock, 213 N.C. App. 88, 94, 713 S.E.2d 732, 736 (2011) (affirming trial court's refusal to instruct on landowner's higher duty of care owed to a child because it was an incorrect statement of law), *rev'd on other grounds*, 365 N.C. 414, 722 S.E.2d 479 (2012).

292. Walker v. Town of Stoneville, 211 N.C. App. 24, 40, 712 S.E.2d 239, 250 (2011); *Sobczak*, 181 N.C. App. at 636, 640 S.E.2d at 810; Faeber v. E.C.T. Corp., 16 N.C. App. 429, 430, 192 S.E.2d 1, 2 (1972).

293. Outlaw v. Johnson, 190 N.C. App. 233, 243, 660 S.E.2d 550, 559 (2008) (citing Carrington v. Emory, 179 N.C. App. 827, 832, 635 S.E.2d 532, 535 (2006)).

"Any Other Reason"—Rule 59(a)(9)

The final basis for relief permits a new trial for "any other reason heretofore recognized as grounds for new trial." A trial court's discretion to set aside a verdict "has always been inherent,"[294] and the adoption of Rule 59 of the Rules of Civil Procedure "did not diminish the trial judge's traditional discretionary authority" but instead merely formalized it into nine specific grounds.[295] This section is, therefore, a catch-all for any basis not already captured by the other eight grounds.[296] As with the other discretionary bases, decisions under Rule 59(a)(9) are not reversible absent manifest abuse of discretion.[297]

The rationale typically cited under this rule is that the ends of justice will be met by a new trial. Recognizing general justice as a traditional discretionary basis, the Court of Appeals in *Sizemore v. Raxter* declined to find an abuse of discretion when the trial court granted a new negligence trial for this reason.[298] And in a dispute between a county and a property owner, the Court of Appeals refused to disturb a new trial order invoking Rule 59(a)(9) where the trial judge concluded that "justice and equity require that this court consider any additional evidence" concerning the location of the disputed property.[299] The scope of a court's ability to evaluate justice and equity appears to be

---

294. Britt v. Allen, 291 N.C. 630, 634, 231 S.E.2d 607, 611 (1977) (quoting Bird v. Bradburn, 131 N.C. 488, 42 S.E. 936 (1902)); Selph v. Selph, 267 N.C. 635, 638, 148 S.E.2d 574, 577 (1966).

295. *Britt*, 291 N.C. at 635, 231 S.E.2d at 611–12.

296. *Id.*

297. *Id.* at 635, 231 S.E.2d at 611; Sizemore v. Raxter, 58 N.C. App. 236, 237, 293 S.E.2d 294, 294 (1982).

298. 58 N.C. App. 236, 236–37, 293 S.E.2d 294, 294 (1982) (citing Walston v. Greene, 246 N.C. 617, 99 S.E.2d 805 (1957)); *see also* Jackson v. Culbreth, 199 N.C. App. 531, 539, 681 S.E.2d 813, 818 (2009) ("[Our Supreme Court has approved a new trial . . . when equity and justice so require."). For pre-rules examples of the use of justice and equity as bases for a new trial, *see generally*, Goldston v. Chambers, 272 N.C. 53, 157 S.E.2d 676 (1967) and Bundy v. Sutton, 207 N.C. 422, 177 S.E. 420 (1934).

299. Guilford Cty. Planning & Dev. Dept. v. Simmons, 115 N.C. App. 87, 91, 443 S.E.2d 765, 768 (1994) ("It is well established that a court may set aside a verdict under Rule 59(a)(9) in the interests of justice and equity.").

very broad. A useful example is the recent case of *Boykin v. Wilson Medical Center.*[300] In *Boykin,* the trial court compressed a medical negligence trial into the four-day week preceding a Friday Fourth of July holiday. As a result, the jury endured twelve-hour days of evidence ("approximately 46 hours over four days"). They then began deliberations at 10:00 P.M. the night before the holiday and returned a verdict at 10:45.[301] In ordering a new trial under Rule 59(a)(9) due to the "marathon trial schedule," the judge made several findings of fact regarding his assessment of the exhausted jury, including the following:

> [I]n retrospect, the choice the Court put to the tired jurors whether to begin deliberations and finish up that night or to return on the Fourth of July put a burden on them to depart from a process of calm, fair, and unhurried deliberation to which the parties were entitled. Instead, the choice very likely pushed the jurors to a hurried verdict driven by a desire to finish with the case so that they could enjoy the three day Fourth of July weekend.[302]

Emphasizing the scope of a trial judge's discretion under Rule 59(a)(9), the Court of Appeals declined to second-guess the judge's findings and affirmed the new trial order. Even acknowledging that his findings may have been "somewhat based on speculation,"[303] the court explained that the judge

> was in a far better position to determine whether his ill-advised trial schedule resulted in "a palpable miscarriage of justice" than can we based upon a cold record. The trial court was able to personally observe the level of fatigue in the attorneys and jurors, and to gauge the level of attentiveness

300. 201 N.C. App. 559, 686 S.E.2d 913 (2009).

301. *Id.* at 560, 686 S.E.2d at 914.

302. *Id.* at 562, 686 S.E.2d at 915.

303. *Id.* at 565, 686 S.E.2d at 917. The Court of Appeals rejected the argument that, because the trial record showed specific documentation of only one complaint of juror fatigue, the judge's findings of fact were unsupported. *Id.*

> of the jurors. These things clearly weighed heavily in [his] decision to grant a new trial, but are intangible factors which an appellate court cannot possibly evaluate.[304]

The "intangible factors" affecting justice and equity are not limited to court processes but may include such matters as excessive prejudice in the community affecting the tone of the trial, undue imbalances in the parties' representation leading to an unjust verdict,[305] or a jury gone astray in ways not addressed through the other Rule 59 bases.[306] In short, while a trial judge must respect the jury's role as fact-finder and the parties' interest in finality, there may be times when the court's discretion under Rule 59(a)(9) can be "brought to bear to secure the administration of exact justice."[307]

The case law discussing Rule 59(a)(9) certainly depicts the court's discretion under this "catch-all" as extremely broad. It seems, however, as a practical matter, that a trial judge may go too far if he or she invokes this basis in a manner that obviously circumvents the limitations that apply to the other eight enumerated bases.

---

304. *Id.* at 564, 686 S.E.2d 916–17.

305. *See* Bird v. Bradburn, 131 N.C. 488, 489, 42 S.E. 936, 937 (1902).

306. *See, e.g.*, Garrison v. Garrison, 87 N.C. App. 591, 593, 361 S.E.2d 921, 923 (1987) (no error in finding verdict of no liability unjust where judge observed, in part, that the jury included a lawyer and liability insurance agent).

307. *Bird*, 131 N.C. at 489, 42 S.E. at 937 (quoted in Worthington v. Bynum, 305 N.C. 478, 483, 290 S.E.2d 599, 603 (1982)).

Procedure and Jurisdiction

The Motion

Time Requirements

A "motion for a new trial shall be served not later than 10 days after entry of the judgment."[308] Note that the movant's deadline under Rule 59 is to *serve* the motion, not file it.[309] A motion that was served on the tenth day after judgment but not filed until the eleventh day was timely under this rule.[310] Timely service of a new trial motion not only determines whether the trial court may rule on it, but, as discussed in the next section, also dictates the deadline for appeal.

The trial court has no authority under Rule of Civil Procedure 6(b) to extend the time for service of a new trial motion.[311] Nor may the parties agree to extend the deadline by stipulation or otherwise.[312] If a party cannot, however, obtain any necessary supporting affidavits in time to serve them with the new trial motion under Rule 59(c), Rule 6(b) may be used to seek an extension of time to serve such affidavits.[313]

---

308. Rule 59(b); Fallis v. Watauga Med. Ctr., Inc., 132 N.C. App. 43, 54–55, 510 S.E.2d 199, 207 (1999); Garrison *ex rel.* Chavis v. Barnes, 117 N.C. App. 206, 210, 450 S.E.2d 554, 557 (1994). Oral motions made before entry of judgment are discussed later in this section.

309. Rule 59(b); *see also* State *ex rel.* Moore Cty. Bd. of Educ. v. Pelletier, 168 N.C. App. 218, 221, 606 S.E.2d 907, 909 (2005) ("[T]he relevant action the movant must make within ten days of entry of judgment under Rule 59(a) is service, not filing."). Service of a motion for new trial is governed by Rule 5. *See* G.S. 1A-1, Rule 5. While Rule 59 itself does not specifically require *filing* of a written new trial motion, filing is implicit in Rule 7, and Rule 5(d) requires filing of all papers that must be served. *See* G.S. 1A-1, Rule 5(d). In practical terms, the motion must be filed in order for the court to take action on it.

310. *Pelletier*, 168 N.C. App. at 220, 606 S.E.2d at 909.

311. Rule 6(b) gives the trial court broad discretion to extend deadlines established in the Rules of Civil Procedure, but it explicitly excludes most significant post-trial motions for relief: "[N]either the court nor the parties may extend the time for taking any action under Rules 50(b), 52, 59(b), (d), (e), 60(b), except to the extent and under the conditions stated in them." Rule 59(b) includes no extension provisions of its own.

312. Rule 6(b).

313. Extensions of time under Rule 6(b) are, however, in the court's discretion; the movant takes a risk in failing to serve affidavits with the motion

Whatever the status of the movant's supporting materials, the new trial motion itself, to be valid, *must* be timely served.

The ten-day service requirement for a new trial motion begins with entry of judgment. "Entry," in this context, has a specific statutory meaning. Under Rule of Civil Procedure 58, "a judgment is entered when it is reduced to writing, signed by the judge, and filed with the clerk of court."[314] Neither the rendering of the verdict nor the reading of the verdict is entry of judgment.[315] Nor is a trial court's announcement of a judgment in open court.[316] If the court's judgment is served by one of the parties by mail, the movant's time to serve a motion for new trial is extended by three days.[317] If a party is not timely served the judgment as required by Rule 58, the time limit for filing a new trial

---

itself. Parties should make all reasonable efforts to obtain supporting materials within the ten days after judgment.

314. G.S. 1A-1, Rule 58.

315. Griffith v. N.C. Dep't of Corr., 210 N.C. App. 544, 549, 709 S.E.2d 412, 416–17 (2011); Olson v. McMillian, 144 N.C. App. 615, 619, 548 S.E.2d 571, 574 (2001); Sheehan v. Harper Builders, Inc. v. Hazelwood Constr. Co., Inc., 83 N.C. App. 630, 631, 351 S.E.2d 114, 115 (1986).

316. *Griffith*, 210 N.C. App. at 549, 709 S.E.2d at 417 (citing Worsham v. Richbourg's Sales & Rentals, 124 N.C. App. 782, 784, 478 S.E.2d 649, 650 (1996)); Muse v. Charter Hosp. of Winston-Salem, 117 N.C. App. 468, 480–81, 452 S.E.2d 589, 598, *aff'd per curiam*, 342 N.C. 403, 464 S.E.2d 44 (1995).

317. The rule states,

> The party designated by the judge or, if the judge does not otherwise designate, the party who prepares the judgment, shall serve a copy of the judgment upon all other parties within three days after the judgment is entered. Service and proof of service shall be in accordance with Rule 5. If service is by mail, three days shall be added to the time periods prescribed by Rule 50(b), Rule 52(b), and Rule 59.

G.S. 1A-1, Rule 58; *see also* D.G. II, LLC v. Nix, 213 N.C. App. 220, 225, 713 S.E.2d 140, 145 (2011) (noting that service by mail of the judgment gives the movant a "total of thirteen days from the date judgment is entered to serve by mail a motion for new trial[.]"); Stem v. Richardson, 350 N.C. 76, 78, 511 S.E.2d 1, 2 (1999) ("According to the clear language of Rule 58, the moving party is entitled to three additional days [for] . . . a motion for a new trial pursuant to Rule 59 if service of the judgment was made by mail.").

motion "shall be tolled for the duration of any period of noncompliance with this service requirement" but not "longer than 90 days from the date the judgment is entered."[318] Service of a new trial motion is not required on a party who has defaulted for failure to appear.[319]

It is not unusual for a party to move for new trial orally in open court soon after the verdict is read—often on the basis that the evidence is insufficient to support the verdict.[320] With opposing counsel (or unrepresented party) present, service of a written motion is not necessary.[321] Within ten days after judgment is later entered, however, that party may serve a second—this time written—motion for new trial if the party discovers or develops additional grounds under Rule 59(a).[322] The Court of Appeals has explained, "It is clear from a reading of Rule 59(a) that the grounds set forth there contemplate situations or circumstances which may arise or become known *after* a party has made the usually perfunctory motions for a new trial at the end of the trial."[323]

The outside time limit for serving a new trial motion is well settled. But what is the *earliest* time a valid new trial motion can be made? As noted above, our courts have recognized the practice of making new trial motions orally, in open court, well before formal entry of judgment. No doubt many such motions have been ruled on nearly as quickly as they were made. But is such a summary disposition premature? As for written motions served outside of open court, but still prior to entry of judgment, are such pre-judgment motions valid, and may the court rule on them? In *Watson v. Dixon*, the Court of Appeals stated in apparent dicta that "Rules 50 and 59 . . . implicitly

---

318. *Stem*, 350 N.C. at 78, 511 S.E.2d at 2; *see also Nix*, 213 N.C. App. at 226, 713 S.E.2d at 146 (applying this rule where defendant, ordered to prepare the judgment, failed to serve it on plaintiff in accordance with Rule 58).

319. Hennessee v. Cogburn, 39 N.C. App. 627, 629, 251 S.E.2d 623, 624 (1979) (construing Rule 59(b) and Rule 5(a)).

320. Sherrod v. Nash Gen. Hosp., Inc., 348 N.C. 526, 531, 500 S.E.2d 708, 711 (1998).

321. *Id.*

322. *Id.*

323. *Id.*

provide that these post-trial motions cannot be filed until after entry of judgment."[324] Thus, the oral motions at issue "were not properly before the trial court as post-trial motions under Rules 50 and 59."[325] A year later, in *Stevens v. Guzman*,[326] the Court of Appeals found itself bound by the language in *Watson* and invalidated a new trial motion because it was made prior to entry of judgment.[327] In 2008, however, in *Kor Xiong v. Marks*, the Court of Appeals stated that the validity of a pre-judgment motion for new trial appeared to be an issue of first impression in this state.[328] Finding that the *Watson* language was dicta, the court followed numerous federal opinions and held that motions for a new trial may indeed properly be made prior to entry of judgment.[329] The trial court, however, "does *not* have jurisdiction to hear and determine the motion until *after* entry of judgment."[330] Thus, it appears that a motion for new trial may be served prior to entry of judgment, but—whether the motion is oral or written—the trial court must wait until after entry of judgment to properly dispose of it. In any event, a movant can help a trial judge avoid this jurisdictional pitfall by awaiting entry of judgment before serving a new trial motion.

Motions by the Court

If the trial judge identifies the need for a new trial for any reason permitted under Rule 59(a), the judge need not await a party's motion. Rule 59 authorizes the court to order a new trial "of its own initiative."[331] The court must give notice to the parties and conduct

---

324. 130 N.C. App. 47, 51, 502 S.E.2d 15, 19 (1998).

325. *Id.*

326. 140 N.C. App. 780, 538 S.E.2d 590 (2000).

327. *Id.* at 782, 538 S.E.2d 592. The result was that the movant's pre-judgment new trial motion did not toll the time limit to file an appeal, and her appeal was dismissed. See discussion of appeal tolling in the section *infra* titled "Effect on Appeal Deadlines."

328. 193 N.C. App. 644, 652, 668 S.E.2d 594, 599 (2008).

329. *Id.* at 652–53, 668 S.E.2d at 599. The court (apparently inadvertently) refers to the time limit for *service* of a new trial motion as a time limit for "filing."

330. *Id.* at 653, 668 S.E.2d at 600 (emphasis added).

331. Rule 59(d).

a hearing.[332] The court's *order*—not just its notice of hearing—must then be made no later than ten days after entry of judgment.[333] The order also must specify the grounds for granting a new trial.[334] This requirement applies whether or not a party requests that the court specify the grounds.[335] Although Rule 59 does not so state, the Court of Appeals has held that the trial court may amend, on its own motion, a judgment made after a non-jury trial.[336]

Effect on Appeal Deadlines

The general deadline for filing and service of a written notice of appeal of a civil judgment is thirty days after entry of judgment.[337] If, however, a party has made a timely motion for relief under Rule 59, the "thirty day period for taking appeal is tolled as to all parties until entry of an

---

332. *Id.*

333. *Id.*; Jones v. S. Gen. Ins. Co., 222 N.C. App. 435, 436–37, 731 S.E.2d 508, 509 (2012). In *Jones*, the court reversed an order for a new trial entered more than ten days after judgment, stating "We find no ambiguity in the language of Rule 59(d). . . . [T]he trial court may order a new trial on its own initiative '[n]ot later than 10 days after entry of judgment[.]'"

Note that Federal Rule of Civil Procedure 59(d) was amended in 2009 to allow a 28-day period after entry of judgment for a federal court to order a new trial. Fed. R. Civ. P. 59(d). North Carolina's Rule 59(d) has not been amended to allow this longer time period.

334. Rule 59(d).

335. In *Chiltoski v. Drum*, the Court of Appeals explained that "[w]hen the judge acts of his own initiative he must set out the grounds in his order. Otherwise, the purpose of the Rule will not be accomplished; the record will not reveal the basis upon which the order is made or permit intelligent review by an appellate court." 121 N.C. App. 161, 162, 464 S.E.2d 701, 702 (1995) (citing *In re* Will of Herring, 19 N.C. App. 357, 360, 198 S.E.2d 737, 740 (1973)).

336. Fox v. Fox, 103 N.C. App. 13, 22, 404 S.E.2d 354, 359 (1991). See Chapter 3.

337. N.C. R. App. P. 3(c). The deadline is thirty days "after entry of judgment if the party has been served with a copy of the judgment within the three day period prescribed by Rule 58 of the Rules of Civil Procedure; or . . . within thirty days after service upon the party of a copy of the judgment if service was not made within that three day period[.]" N.C. R. App. P. 3(c)(1), (2). But see *Wilkins Family Medicine, P.A., v. WakeMed*, ___ S.E.2d ___ (N.C. Ct. App. Jan. 5, 2016), and *Magazian v. Creagh*, 759 S.E.2d 130,

order disposing of the motion[.]"[338] After a Rule 59 motion is served, the appeal period begins to run again from the date the trial court enters an order on the new trial motion (or from the date of untimely service of the order as directed by Rule of Appellate Procedure 3(c)).[339] If a party has made an initial oral motion for new trial in open court and then later—but within ten days after judgment—makes a written motion stating grounds that arose or became known after the initial motion, the motion is considered timely and the appeal period will be tolled under Rule 3(c)(3).[340] Once a party has made a Rule 59 motion, to preserve its appeal the party must wait for the trial court to dispose of the motion or, if it chooses not to wait, must appeal within the original appeal deadline. An appeal was dismissed where a party had made a

---

131 (N.C. Ct. App. 2014), for the effect of *actual notice* of a final order on the three-day service period.

338. N.C. R. App. P. 3(c)(3); G.S. 1-279.1.

339. N.C. R. App. P. 3(c)(3). *See* Scarvey v. First Fed. Savs. & Loan Ass'n of Charlotte, 146 N.C. App. 33, 36–37, 552 S.E.2d 655, 657 (2001) (motion to alter or amend judgment under Rule 59 citing errors of law tolled the appeal deadline under Rule 3(c)(3)).

340. Sherrod v. Nash Gen. Hosp., Inc., 348 N.C. 526, 531, 500 S.E.2d 708, 711 (1998). In *Sherrod,* plaintiff's first motion asserted that the verdict was contrary to the weight of the evidence. In her later motion, filed nine days after judgment, she also asserted a manifest disregard of the instructions of the court, errors of law, jury misconduct, and delays and disruptions at trial. *Id. But see* Oak Health Care Inv'rs of NC, Inc. v. Johnson, 209 N.C. App. 754, 710 S.E.2d 709 (2011) (unpublished) (*citing Sherrod* in holding that a subsequent motion did not toll the appeal period because "there was nothing prohibiting [movant] from raising the arguments" in his prior Rule 59 motion). In *Middleton v. Middleton,* 98 N.C. App. 217, 390 S.E.2d 453 (1990), movants made a subsequent written motion apparently asserting the same grounds as their initial oral motion that had been denied in open court. The Court of Appeals determined that, because this motion had been denied when asserted, the same motion submitted after entry of judgment did not toll the time for taking an appeal. *Id.* at 221, 390 S.E.2d at 455. The extent to which *Middleton* remains useful precedent is unclear, however, in light of the more recent Court of Appeals holding that a trial judge has no jurisdiction to rule on a new trial motion until after entry of judgment. *See* Kor Xiong v. Marks, 193 N.C. App. 644, 653, 668 S.E.2d 594, 600 (2008) (discussed *supra* in section titled "Time Requirements.").

timely motion under Rule 59 but then, after thirty days had passed from entry of judgment, filed an appeal of the underlying judgment before the trial court had ruled on the Rule 59 motion.[341]

The appeal period is not tolled under Rule of Appellate Procedure 3(c)(3) based on a motion brought under Rule 59 if Rule 59 is not a proper basis for relief. In a recent case, for example, the trial court granted summary judgment and default judgment against defendant. Defendant filed a motion to set aside these judgments pursuant to Rule 59(a)(8) and (9), which the trial court denied. The Court of Appeals noted that the filing of a Rule 59 motion after summary judgment did not toll the time to appeal: "Because both Rule 59(a)(8) and (9) are properly made after a trial, and the case *sub judice* concluded at the summary judgment stage, [the] motion did not toll the appeal, permitting us to dismiss the appeal[.]"[342]

---

341. Lovallo v. Sabato, 216 N.C. App. 281, 284, 715 S.E.2d 909, 912 (2011). The Court of Appeals stated that Rule 3(c)(3) "clearly contemplates a ruling by the trial court on such motions in order for the tolling period to apply" and that "defendant is unable to utilize the tolling provisions in this case, as the trial court never ruled on her . . . motions." *Id.*; *see also* Reeder v. Carter, 226 N.C. App. 270, 273–74, 740 S.E.2d 913, 916–17 (2013) (applying the analysis from *Lovallo*).

342. Bodie Island Beach Club, Ass'n, Inc. v. Wray, 215 N.C. App. 283, 287–88, 716 S.E.2d 67, 72 (2011). The court nevertheless granted certiorari to review the order pursuant to N.C. R. App. P. 21. *Id.* In *Batlle v. Sabates*, by contrast, the court determined that the appeal period under Rule 3(c)(3) was tolled by a Rule 59(e) motion (based on 59(a)(7) grounds) challenging the dismissal of an action with prejudice as a sanction for failure to comply with discovery requests. 198 N.C. App. 407, 413, 681 S.E.2d 788, 793 (2009). The court noted, however, that

> no party to this proceeding has contended that a litigant is not entitled to seek relief from an order imposing sanctions pursuant to [Rule 37(d)], under [Rule 59], and we do not, for that reason, express an opinion on that issue here. However, we note in passing that the decision of this Court in *Smith v. Johnson,* 125 N.C. App. 603, 606, 481 S.E.2d 415, 417 (1997), *disc. review denied,* 346 N.C. 283, 487 S.E.2d 554 (1997), appears to assume that relief under [Rule 59], is, at least in theory, available to individuals who have been sanctioned for discovery violations.

The Court of Appeals also has held that appeal tolling does not apply where the movant failed to state the specific basis for relief under Rule 59.[343] In *North Carolina Alliance for Transportation Reform, Inc. v. North Carolina Department of Transportation*,[344] the trial court determined that a party's Rule 59(e) motion to alter or amend a judgment was not a proper Rule 59 motion because it failed to invoke any of the grounds under Rule 59(a). The Court of Appeals agreed that the movants had failed to "reveal[ ] the basis for the motion" and thus the "improper" Rule 59 motion did not toll the deadline for appeal.[345]

Stating a Specific Basis

Although Rule 59 does not itself require that a party's written motion state a specific basis for relief,[346] Rule of Civil Procedure 7(b)(1) requires that a civil motion "shall be made in writing, shall state with particularity the grounds therefor, and shall set forth the relief or order sought."[347] Pursuant to Rule 7, a trial court may deny a motion that does not adequately set forth a specific basis under Rule 59(a).[348] A party seeking alteration or amendment of a judgment under Rule 59(e)

Id. at n.1.

343. The requirement of a specific basis is discussed more generally in the next section, "*Stating a Specific Basis.*"

344. 183 N.C. App. 466, 469–70, 645 S.E.2d 105, 108 (2007).

345. *Id.*; Smith v. Johnson, 125 N.C. App. 603, 606–07, 481 S.E.2d 415, 417 (1997) (Rule 59 motion that cited two Rule 59(a) subsections but contained no allegations to support any such bases did not toll the appeal deadline); Dusenberry v. Dusenberry, 87 N.C. App. 490, 492, 361 S.E.2d 605, 606 (1987) ("[T]o suspend the running of the appeal clock, a Rule 59(e) motion must not only be timely served, it must also meet the demands of Rule 7(b).").

346. However, as discussed *supra* in the section titled "Motions by the Court," Rule 59(d) requires that motions *made by the trial court judge* must "specify the grounds therefor."

347. G.S. 1A-1, Rule 7(b)(1).

348. Meehan v. Cable, 135 N.C. App. 715, 721, 523 S.E.2d 419, 423 (1999).

should be particularly careful to state the basis for the motion to reflect the Rule 59(a) grounds being raised.[349]

Ideally a party serving a Rule 59 motion will (1) cite the appropriate subsection or subsections of Rule 59(a); *and* (2) note the substantive basis for seeking Rule 59 relief. But the most important task appears to be the latter: The Court of Appeals has held that "mere recitation of the rule number relied upon by the movant is not a statement of the grounds within the meaning of Rule 7(b)(1)."[350] In *Meehan v. Cable*, for example, defendants' motion for a new trial cited Rules 59(a)(5), (a)(7), and (a)(8) but did not "state any specific basis for granting a new trial" and thus was in violation of Rule 7.[351] At the same time, the failure to state a particular rule number should not doom the motion "so long as the substantive grounds and relief desired are apparent and the nonmovant is not prejudiced thereby."[352] Where the movants failed to identify a specific Rule 59 subsection, the Court of Appeals nevertheless reviewed the motion because the basis was clear to the court and opposing party.[353] The Court of Appeals also has declined to penalize

---

349. *Transportation Reform*, 183 N.C. App. at 469–70, 645 S.E.2d at 108; Clark v. Penland, 146 N.C. App. 288, 291, 552 S.E.2d 243, 245 (2001); *Dusenberry*, 87 N.C. App. at 492, 361 S.E.2d at 606 ("[W]here court and adverse party cannot comprehend the basis of a motion, they are rendered powerless to respond to it."). See Chapter 3 for a discussion of amendment of judgments under Rule 59.

350. Smith v. Johnson, 125 N.C. App. 603, 606, 481 S.E.2d 415, 417 (1997).

351. 135 N.C. App. 715, 721, 523 S.E.2d 419, 423 (1999).

352. Edwards v. Hardy, 126 N.C. App. 69, 71, 483 S.E.2d 724, 726 (1997) (citing Garrison v. Garrison, 87 N.C. App. 591, 596, 361 S.E.2d 921, 925 (1987); *see also Transportation Reform*, 183 N.C. App. at 470, 645 S.E.2d at 108 ("[W]hile failure to give the number of the rule under which a motion is made is not necessarily fatal, the grounds . . . and the relief sought must be consistent with the Rules of Civil Procedure").

353. *Edwards*, 126 N.C. App. at 71, 483 S.E.2d at 726; *see also* Elrod v. Elrod, 125 N.C. App. 407, 410, 481 S.E.2d 108, 110 (1997) (motion related to a custody order was reviewable despite failure to reference Rule 59 because motion clearly cited trial court's errors of law).

movants who have mistakenly cited the wrong rule or subsection but have otherwise adequately stated a basis for their Rule 59 motions.[354]

The failure to state a specific basis for a Rule 59 motion may also prevent tolling of the period for appeal.[355] Even where tolling is not at issue, however, the Court of Appeals has declined to review a court's ruling on a Rule 59 motion where the movant did not properly state grounds for relief.[356]

Affidavits and Other Support

If a Rule 59 motion calls for consideration of matters not already in the trial record, the moving party may need to present affidavits in support of its arguments. Affidavits are most likely to be necessary if the grounds are jury or prevailing party misconduct under subsection (a)(2);[357] accident or surprise under (a)(3), or newly discovered evidence under (a)(4).[358] And some irregularities under (a)(1), particularly if they

---

354. *See, e.g.*, Harrell v. Sagebrush of N.C., LLC, 191 N.C. App. 381, 384, 663 S.E.2d 444, 446 (2008) (where motion was based on errors of law but erroneously cited Rule 59(a)(1)(4) rather than (a)(8)); *Garrison*, 87 N.C. App. at 596, 361 S.E.2d at 925 (motion citing Rule 50(b) rather than 59(a) not fatally defective because basis for motion was clear); *see also* Rutherford Plantation, LLC v. Challenge Golf Grp. of the Carolinas, LLC, 225 N.C. App. 79, 83, 737 S.E.2d 409, 412 (2013) (a "scrivener's error" in specifying Rule 59(a)(8) rather than (a)(7) not prejudicial where relief requested was clear), *aff'd per curiam with equally divided panel*, 367 N.C. 197, 753 S.E.2d 152 (2014). Note also that the general rules of practice require parties to state the rule number or numbers on which their motions are based. GEN. R. P. SUPER. & DIST. CTS. 6. Lapses in complying with this rule, however, are treated with leniency where the court and parties are aware of the basis for the motion. Wood v. Wood, 297 N.C. 1, 6–7, 252 S.E.2d 799, 802 (1979).

355. *See supra* section titled "Effect on Appeal Deadlines."

356. *Meehan*, 135 N.C. App. at 721, 523 S.E.2d at 423.

357. *See supra* section titled "Misconduct of the Jury" regarding limitations on use of juror affidavits to impeach a verdict.

358. Under pre-rules case law, affidavits were required under this basis. *See* Johnson v. Seaboard Air Line Ry. Co., 163 N.C. 431, 79 S.E. 690, 699 (1913) (cited in Locklear v. Snow, 5 N.C. App. 434, 438, 168 S.E.2d 445, 448 (1969)).

become known after trial has ended, may need to be demonstrated through affidavits.[359]

Affidavits in support of the motion "shall be served with the motion."[360] Although the ten-day deadline for serving the new trial motion itself cannot be extended under Rule of Civil Procedure 6(b), a party may seek an extension of time to serve accompanying affidavits. Such extensions are, of course, at the court's discretion; to avoid the peril of having the motion denied, a party should seek an extension only if the delay is unavoidable. After the affidavits are served, the opposing party has ten days to serve opposing affidavits.[361] The court may extend the time period for opposing affidavits up to thirty days for good cause shown. The parties also may stipulate to an extension of up to thirty days.[362] In addition, the court may permit the moving party to serve affidavits in reply to the opposing party's affidavits.[363] The rule does not specify a time frame for service of reply affidavits. Although Rule 59 addresses only affidavits, the moving party is not prohibited from offering other materials in support of its argument—such as deposition excerpts and relevant documentary evidence—as necessary. It also may be appropriate to offer live testimony if the trial court permits a hearing on the motion.

---

359. *See, e.g.*, McGinnis v. Robinson, 43 N.C. App. 1, 3, 258 S.E.2d 84, 86 (1979) (affidavit presented with motion to establish witness perjury).

360. Rule 59(c). *See, e.g.*, Payne v. Payne, 91 N.C. App. 71, 76, 370 S.E.2d 428, 431 (1988) (trial court did not err in failing to consider movant's affidavit after motion was heard). As discussed earlier, our courts have recognized the practice of making new trial motions orally in court before the trial court enters judgment. Presumably if an affidavit is necessary to support such a motion, the moving party will ask the court's leave to serve the affidavit at a later time.

361. Rule 59(c). The rule does not impose a *requirement* of opposing affidavits but simply sets a time frame for service of such affidavits, if there are any.

362. *Id.*

363. *Id.*

Combined Motions for JNOV and New Trial

Rule 50 provides that a party moving for JNOV may combine the JNOV motion with a motion for new trial under Rule 59.[364] The party is not *required* to make a combined motion, however, and a motion for directed verdict or JNOV is not a prerequisite to a new trial motion.[365] The procedure for the court's disposition of a combined JNOV and new trial motion is discussed in the section titled "Conditional Rulings on Combined New Trial Motions" in Chapter 1.

Motion after Verdict Set Aside by JNOV

Rule 50 provides that a party whose verdict is set aside on an opposing party's JNOV motion may serve a new trial motion under Rule 59 no later than ten days after entry of the JNOV.[366] The moving party should observe all other relevant procedural requirements for new trial motions.

The Court's Order

Who May Rule

Only the trial judge who presided over the trial may rule on a new trial motion.[367] A second judge lacks jurisdiction to hear the matter even where the first judge has recused herself or himself. In *Sisk v. Sisk,* plaintiff filed a motion for a new trial and soon thereafter also requested that the trial judge recuse himself on the basis of partiality. After the judge acceded to the recusal request, the new trial motion was heard and granted by another trial judge.[368] The Court of Appeals

---

364. Rule 50(b)(1) ("A motion for a new trial may be joined with this motion, or a new trial may be prayed for in the alternative."). Motions for JNOV are discussed in Chapter 1.

365. Garrison v. Garrison, 87 N.C. App. 591, 595, 361 S.E.2d 921, 924 (1987) ("Rule 50(b) merely establishes a procedure whereby a movant may, *if he chooses,* join the new trial motion with one for judgment notwithstanding the verdict.").

366. Rule 50(c)(2).

367. Gemini Drilling & Found., LLC v. National Fire Ins. Co. of Hartford, 192 N.C. App. 376, 390, 665 S.E.2d 505, 514 (2008).

368. 221 N.C. App. 631, 632, 729 S.E.2d 68, 70 (2012).

reversed the new trial order, holding that the second judge had no jurisdiction to hear the new trial motion.[369] This rule arose in two cases where the trial judge erroneously failed to rule on a Rule 59 motion after ruling on a JNOV motion as required by Rule 50(c).[370] By the time the cases reached appellate disposition, the trial judge was no longer on the bench. Rather than remanding for hearing at the trial level, the Supreme Court determined that "[i]t would be inappropriate for another superior court judge who did not try the case to now pass upon plaintiffs' alternative motion for a new trial."[371] Instead, the appellate court itself should conduct the review of errors to determine if the party is entitled to a new trial.[372] In addition, Rule 63 does not provide authority for another judge to rule on a new trial motion when the judge who presided over the trial is unable to do so.[373]

Hearing

When the trial court orders a new trial under Rule 59 on its own motion, it is required to provide notice to the parties and conduct a hearing.[374] When a motion is by a party, however, Rule 59 contains no specific requirement that the court conduct a formal hearing before ruling on the motion. In general, hearings on such motions are customary, particularly if the arguments are complex, include multiple discretionary bases, or require consideration of matters outside the

---

369. *Id.* at 633, 729 S.E.2d at 70. The Court of Appeals went on to address the merits of the new trial motion and ultimately concluded that there was no basis for a new trial. *Id.* at 633–37, 729 S.E.2d at 71–73.

370. Graves v. Walston, 302 N.C. 332, 275 S.E.2d 485 (1981); Hoots v. Calaway, 282 N.C. 477, 193 S.E.2d 709 (1973).

371. *Graves*, 302 N.C. at 340, 275 S.E.2d at 489; *Hoots*, 282 N.C. at 490, 193 S.E.2d at 717.

372. *Graves*, 302 N.C. at 340, 275 S.E.2d at 489; *Hoots*, 282 N.C. at 490, 193 S.E.2d at 717.

373. *Gemini Drilling*, 192 N.C. App. at 390, 665 S.E.2d at 514 ("[t]he function of a substitute judge under this rule is ministerial rather than judicial"). *But see* Springs v. City of Charlotte, 222 N.C. App. 132, 135, 730 S.E.2d 803, 805 (2012) (holding that Rule 63 authorizes a substituted judge to submit an opinion under G.S. 1D-50).

374. Rule 59(d).

record. Such hearings may occur by operation of court practice if they are duly noticed by a party pursuant to Rule of Civil Procedure 6(d) or appear on a motions calendar pursuant to the applicable court calendaring rules or policy. But the Court of Appeals declined to find that the trial court abused its discretion by ruling on Rules 59 and 60 motions without a hearing where the movant argued that a hearing would have been her only opportunity to subpoena her supporting witness.[375] Before ruling on a written motion without a hearing, the court must allow the parties at least a reasonable opportunity to respond, including permitting the full allotted time to serve opposing affidavits under Rule 59(c), and should consider any requests by the movant to submit reply affidavits.[376]

If the court conducts a hearing on a Rule 59 motion, the parties must be given notice and an opportunity to respond.[377] In *Otto v. Certo*, for example, the trial court granted plaintiff's Rule 59 motion after conducting a hearing without defendants or their counsel present, and the record revealed no actual notice or attempted notice to defendants of the hearing date.[378] The Court of Appeals reversed and remanded for a new hearing, holding that the lack of notice deprived defendants of an opportunity to object in violation of their right to due process.[379] When hearing a new trial motion, the court may—in

---

375. Ollo v. Mills, 136 N.C. App. 618, 625, 525 S.E.2d 213, 217 (2000).

376. *See* Rule 59(c).

377. Rule of Civil Procedure 5(a) requires service of every written notice applicable to the action. *See* G.S. 1A-1, Rule 5(a). Rule 6(d) sets out the general timing requirements for notices of hearing. As noted in the same rule, however, these requirements are altered somewhat by the timing allowances for service of affidavits in Rule 59(c). *See* G.S. 1A-1, Rule 6(d). Many local court rules include preferred procedures and forms for requesting a hearing on a motion. *See, e.g.*, Local Rules for Civil Superior Court, Tenth Judicial District, North Carolina, Local Form 1, www.nccourts.org/Courts/CRS/Policies/LocalRules.

378. 210 N.C. App. 468, 472–73, 708 S.E.2d 183, 186 (2011).

379. *Id.* at 473, 708 S.E.2d at 186.

addition to considering the parties' affidavits—take live testimony or consider deposition testimony.[380]

Timing of Order and Stay of Execution

An order on the court's own initiative under Rule 59 must be made within ten days of entry of judgment.[381] When the motion is by a party, however, there is no specified time frame within which the court must enter an order.[382] The party's timely service of the motion tolls the period for appeal of the underlying judgment until the trial court enters an order on the Rule 59 motion, and the trial court may rule on the motion after the underlying appeal period (typically thirty days) has expired.[383] The court may also enter an order on a Rule 59 motion after the session of court in which the motion was heard has expired.[384] As with all orders, the court should dispose of post-trial motions as

---

380. *See* G.S. 1A-1, Rule 43(e). *See, e.g.*, Ruth v. Ruth, 158 N.C. App. 293, 296–97, 580 S.E.2d 383, 385 (2003) (court took live testimony of plaintiff after she moved for new trial due to lack of proper notice); McGinnis v. Robinson, 43 N.C. App. 1, 4, 258 S.E.2d 84, 86 (1979) (court heard live testimony of private investigator hired to interview witness accused of perjury); *see also* Pinckney v. Van Damme, 116 N.C. App. 139, 148–152, 447 S.E.2d. 825, 831–33 (1994) (court conducted examination of jurors immediately after verdict in response to new trial motion alleging juror misconduct).

381. Rule 59(d).

382. For a discussion of whether the court may enter an order prior to judgment, see *supra* section titled "Time Requirements."

383. N.C. R. App. P. 3(c)(3).

384. Rule of Civil Procedure 6(c) provides that

> [t]he period of time provided for the doing of any act or the taking of any proceeding is not affected or limited by the continued existence or expiration of a session of court. The continued existence or expiration of a session of court in no way affects the power of a court to do any act or take any proceeding, but no issue of fact shall be submitted to a jury out of session.

G.S. 1A-1, Rule 6(c); *see also* Housing, Inc. v. Weaver, 305 N.C. 428, 440, 290 S.E.2d 642, 649 (1982) (holding that court may amend judgment under Rule 59 "after the adjournment of the term during which the judgment was entered"). For a discussion of a court's ability to enter an order after a term or session of court has ended, see Michael Crowell, *Out-of-Term,*

soon as reasonably possible, bearing in mind basic fairness and judicial efficiency, the parties' need for finality, and the benefits of ruling on matters when they are fresh in the judge's mind. The filing of a Rule 59 motion does not automatically stay enforcement of the underlying judgment past the automatic (thirty-day) stay allowed in Rule 62(a).[385] The trial court, therefore, has discretion under Rule 62(b) to stay execution of proceedings to enforce the judgment while a Rule 59 motion is pending.[386]

Written Findings of Fact and Conclusions of Law

The North Carolina Supreme Court has stated that "it is almost always helpful to an appellate court in applying the abuse of discretion standard to a trial court's discretionary ruling, to have the trial court make whatever findings and conclusions it can muster in support of its ruling."[387] Nevertheless, in a Rule 59 order, the trial court is *not*

Out-of-Session, Out-of-County, ADMIN. OF JUST. BULL. 2008/05 (UNC School of Government, Nov. 2008).

385. *See* G.S. 1A-1, Rule 62(a).

386. See Rule 62(b), which states,

> In its discretion and on such conditions for the security of the adverse party as are proper, the court may stay the execution of or any proceedings to enforce a judgment pending the disposition of a motion for a new trial or to alter or amend a judgment made pursuant to Rule 59 . . . [.] If the time provided in the controlling statute or rule of appellate procedure for giving notice of appeal from the judgment had not expired before a stay under this subsection was entered, that time shall begin to run immediately upon the expiration of any stay under this section, and no execution shall issue nor shall proceedings be taken for enforcement of the judgment until the expiration of that time.

This rule applies also to motions for additional findings under Rule 52(b). *Id.* The authority to issue a stay applies also to Rule 50 and Rule 60 motions.

387. Andrews v. Peters, 318 N.C. 133, 138, 347 S.E.2d 409, 413 (1986). In the absence of findings and conclusions, the appellate court will review the ruling "on the cold record." *Id.*; *see also* Campbell v. Pitt Cty. Mem'l Hosp., Inc., 321 N.C. 260, 265, 362 S.E.2d 273, 276 (1987) (noting that the "cold record" did not reveal any manifest abuse of discretion).

required to include written findings of fact and conclusions of law unless a party specifically requests them.[388] When a party properly requests findings and conclusions, the court must include them for all discretionary bases.[389] If the basis upon which the court grants a new trial is an error of law—which is reviewed *de novo*—findings of fact are unnecessary even where a party requests them.[390] The trial court must, however, specify the error of law so that the appellate court may review it.[391]

A proper request for findings and conclusions is made pursuant to Rule 52(a)(2).[392] The party must make the request before the trial

---

388. Strickland v. Jacobs, 88 N.C. App. 397, 399, 363 S.E.2d 229, 230 (1988) ("Absent a specific request made pursuant to Rule 52(a)(2), a trial court is not required to either state the reasons for its decision or make findings of fact showing those reasons."); Edge v. Metro. Life Ins. Co., 78 N.C. App. 624, 626–27, 337 S.E.2d 672, 674 (1985).

If the order is made on the court's own motion, the court must "specify the grounds therefor" even if no party requests that it do so. Rule 59(d). *See supra* section titled "Motions by the Court." And the court must always "specify the grounds for granting or denying the motion for the new trial" when making a conditional new trial ruling after granting JNOV under Rule 50(c). Rule 50(c)(1).

Note also that in 2014 the General Assembly amended G.S. 7A-45.3 to require the presiding business court judge in a complex business case to "issue a written opinion in connection with any order granting or denying a motion under G.S. 1A-1, Rule . . . 59 or 60, . . . other than an order effecting a settlement agreement or jury verdict." This requirement does not depend on a request for written findings and conclusions pursuant to Rule 52(a). S.L. 2014-102 (S.B. 853), sec. 2.

389. Krantz v. Owens, 168 N.C. App. 384, 386, 607 S.E.2d 337, 339–40 (2005) (citing *Andrews*, 318 N.C. at 133, 347 S.E.2d at 409).

390. N.C. Indus. Capital, LLC v. Clayton, 185 N.C. App. 356, 371–72, 649 S.E.2d 14, 25 (2007). The Court of Appeals explained that for grounds that will receive *de novo* review, "findings of fact and conclusions of law will not aid our review and thus are not required." The court remanded the trial court's order, however, because there were no findings and conclusions regarding the court's discretionary decisions under Rules 59(a)(5), (a)(6), and (a)(9).

391. *See supra* section titled "Error in Law—Rule 59(a)(8)."

392. Rule 52(a)(2) provides that "[f]indings of fact and conclusions of law are necessary on decisions of any motion . . . only when requested by

court issues its ruling on the Rule 59 motion.[393] Findings of fact in a Rule 59 order are not intended to resolve the substantive factual disputes in the case (as they would in a non-jury trial judgment under Rule 52(a)(1)).[394] Instead, the task is to "facilitate meaningful appellate review" by setting out the facts and circumstances that led to the trial court's decision on the Rule 59 motion.[395] In *Andrews v. Peters,* the trial court granted a new trial based on inadequate damages and that the evidence was insufficient to justify the verdict.[396] The court's pertinent findings and conclusions were as follows:

> [3] That the court has thoroughly considered all of the evidence that was given during the course of this trial. That the court has reviewed its notes that were made during the course of the trial. That the court has a distinct recollection of the trial.
>
> [4] That the court in its considered discretion is of the opinion that the motion filed by the plaintiff in this cause should be allowed and that the plaintiff should be given a new trial as to the second issue presented to the jury.
>
> CONCLUSIONS OF LAW:
>
> Based upon the foregoing findings of fact, the court does hereby conclude that the court should in its considered discretion grant a new trial to the plaintiff as to the second issue presented to the jury[.][397]

---

a party[.]" Subsection (a)(3) further states that "[i]f an opinion or memorandum of decision is filed, it will be sufficient if the findings of fact and conclusions of law appear therein."

393. *Strickland,* 88 N.C. App. at 399, 363 S.E.2d at 230.

394. Rule 52(a)(1) provides, "In all actions tried upon the facts without a jury or with an advisory jury, the court shall find the facts specially and state separately its conclusions of law thereon and direct the entry of the appropriate judgment."

395. Andrews v. Peters, 318 N.C. 133, 139, 347 S.E.2d 409, 413 (1986).

396. *Id.* at 136, 347 S.E.2d at 412.

397. *Id.* at 137, 347 S.E.2d at 412.

The Supreme Court held that these findings and conclusions were not adequate to satisfy Rule 52(a)(2) and explained that

> [t]he trial judge in making his discretionary ruling on the adequacy of the damages should have made findings directed toward the state of the testimony before him and the jury on the subject of damages. The trial judge should have, through appropriate findings, made his view of the evidence on damages clear for the purpose of sustaining his ruling. . . . If the trial judge concluded there was no conflict in the damages testimony, he should nevertheless have found what he believed to be the extent of plaintiff's losses for the purpose, again, of supporting his ruling. These findings should have been made with the purpose of supporting a conclusion that the damages verdict appeared to have been made under the influence of passion or prejudice.[398]

The facts to be included in a Rule 59 order will, of course, vary depending on the discretionary basis at issue and the circumstances of each case. Whatever the situation, however, it is not enough to make general statements simply invoking the court's discretionary authority.

Ordering Partial New Trial

When the court orders a new trial, the case is put back on the docket for trial *de novo*. The parties generally are not affected by rulings made during the original trial and are not "bound by the evidence presented at the former trial."[399] In some circumstances, however, it is appropriate for the court to order a new trial as to only part of the case: "A new trial may be granted to all *or any* of the parties and on all *or part* of the issues[.]"[400] In *Belmany v. Overton*,[401] for example, the North Carolina

---

398. *Id.* at 140, 347 S.E.2d at 413–14.

399. Roary v. Bolton, 150 N.C. App. 193, 196, 563 S.E.2d 21, 23 (2002) (citing Burchette v. Lynch, 139 N.C. App. 756, 760–61, 535 S.E.2d 77, 80 (2000)); Reece v. Reece, 6 N.C. App. 606, 608, 170 S.E.2d 546, 548 (1969).

400. Rule 59(a) (emphasis added).

401. 270 N.C. 400, 154 S.E.2d 538 (1967).

Supreme Court remanded for retrial only as to whether a negligent driver was the agent of the car's owner. If on retrial the jury were to find an agency relationship, the trial court was required to enter judgment for the amount of damages the jury found in the first trial.[402] A decision to order a partial new trial is in the judge's discretion,[403] but the court should do so only when the issue to be retried is "entirely separable from the others, . . . it is perfectly clear that there is no danger of complication[,] and no possible injustice can be done to either party."[404]

Partial new trials most commonly address damages, leaving the underlying liability determinations intact.[405] Although potentially efficient, this approach should be exercised very cautiously. Retrials of damages alone are appropriate only "if the damage issue is sepa-

---

402. *Id.* at 406, 154 S.E.2d at 542; *see also* Mace v. Pyatt, 203 N.C. App. 245, 256–57, 691 S.E.2d 81, 89–91 (2010) (remanding for new trial as to compensatory but not punitive damages where punitive damages were supported by nominal compensatory damages). The court also may order a new trial as to fewer than all the parties involved in the earlier trial. Kesler v. Stokes, 264 N.C. 357, 358, 141 S.E.2d 489, 489–90 (1965); Sanders v. Yancey Trucking Co., 62 N.C. App. 602, 611–12, 303 S.E.2d 600, 605–06 (1983).

403. Loy v. Martin, 156 N.C. App. 622, 625–26, 577 S.E.2d 407, 409–10 (2003); Cicogna v. Holder, 345 N.C. 488, 489, 480 S.E.2d 636, 637 (1997). Likewise, even where retrial could be confined to damages, a court's decision to order retrial of all issues is reviewed for abuse of discretion. *See, e.g.*, Lazenby v. Godwin, 40 N.C. App. 487, 494, 253 S.E.2d 489, 496 (1979) (affirming grant of new trial on all issues "even though the error occurred in only one issue").

404. Robertson v. Stanley, 285 N.C. 561, 568, 206 S.E.2d 190, 195 (1974) (citations omitted).

405. *See, e.g.*, Fortune v. First Union Nat'l Bank, 323 N.C. 146, 151, 371 S.E.2d 483, 486 (1988) (retrial only as to damages to beneficiary from trustee's breach of fiduciary duty); Housing, Inc. v. Weaver, 305 N.C. 428, 443–44, 290 S.E.2d 642, 651 (1982) (holding it was appropriate for trial court to order new trial as to damages alone); Brown v. Neal, 283 N.C. 604, 616–17, 197 S.E.2d 505, 512 (1973) (same); Indus. Circuits Co. v. Terminal Commc'ns, Inc., 26 N.C. App. 536, 547–48, 216 S.E.2d 919, 926–27 (1975) (ordering new trial on damages where jury's calculation contravened the court's instruction).

rate and distinct from the other issues and the new trial can be had without danger of complication with other matters in the case. It must be clear that the error in assessing damages did not affect the entire verdict."[406] In *Handex of the Carolinas, Inc. v. County of Haywood*,[407] the jury returned a single damages figure, and it was not clear whether the figure was based on the four claims properly submitted to the jury or those submitted in error; the trial court was therefore required to grant a new trial as to both liability and damages for the four valid claims.[408] In a similar scenario, the jury in *Weyerhaeuser Co. v. Godwin Building Supply Co., Inc.*[409] found plaintiff liable on defendant's counterclaim for breach of contract and awarded a specific damages sum. The trial court's damages instruction was found erroneous, requiring a new trial. Examining whether partial retrial was appropriate, the Supreme Court found that the jury could have based liability on any of a number of theories, and it was impossible to tell which of them formed the basis for the damages figure.[410] Because damages were "so intertwined with the issue of liability," the court found that a new trial on damages alone "might well result in confusion and uncertainty and in injustice to one or more parties."[411] In a case where the contractual basis for a jury's liability determination was clear, however, and the jury appeared simply to have miscalculated allowable damages, the court was not required to order a retrial as to all issues.[412]

---

406. Kornegay v. Aspen Asset Grp., LLC, 204 N.C. App. 213, 235, 693 S.E.2d 723, 739 (2010) (citations omitted).

407. 168 N.C. App. 1, 607 S.E.2d 25 (2005).

408. *Id.* at 20, 607 S.E.2d at 37; *see also* Estridge v. Housecalls Healthcare Grp., Inc., 131 N.C. App. 744, 750–51, 509 S.E.2d 219, 223 (1998), *rev'd on other grounds*, 351 N.C. 183, 522 S.E.2d 581 (1999) (new trial where damages for two claims were "lumped together" on verdict sheet and court could not distinguish between them).

409. 292 N.C. 557, 234 S.E.2d 605 (1977).

410. *Id.* at 564, 234 S.E.2d at 609.

411. *Id.* at 566, 234 S.E.2d at 610.

412. *Kornegay*, 204 N.C. App. at 236–37, 693 S.E.2d at 739–40.

A retrial only as to damages also is prohibited if the jury appears to have returned a compromise verdict.[413] In *Robertson v. Stanley* the Supreme Court explained,

> Where it appears that the verdict was the result of a compromise, such error taints the entire verdict and requires a new trial as to all of the issues in the case. If the award of damages to the plaintiff is "grossly inadequate," so as to indicate that the jury was actuated by bias or prejudice, or that the verdict was a compromise, the court must set aside the verdict in its entirety and award a new trial on all issues.[414]

In *Robertson*, the court found it very likely that the jury awarded a compromise verdict where a boy was hit by a car while lying in the grass at a drive-in movie. The driver was found negligent, but the boy was awarded no damages for pain and suffering despite uncontroverted evidence of a severe injury to his shoulder requiring three hospitalizations and two operations and resulting in permanent scarring and pain. This inconsistent outcome, coupled with the fact that the boy's father was awarded the boy's medical expenses, strongly indicated that the jury compromised between finding the driver negligent and the boy contributorily negligent.[415] Because "the error in assessing damages tainted the entire verdict," it was unfair to order retrial as to damages alone.[416]

---

413. For a discussion of compromise verdict, see *supra* section titled "Jury Disregard of Instructions—Rule 59(a)(5)."

414. 285 N.C. 561, 569, 206 S.E.2d 190, 195–96 (1974).

415. *Robertson*, 285 N.C. at 568–70, 206 S.E.2d at 193–96.

416. *Id.* at 569, 206 S.E.2d at 196.

Conditional Rulings on New Trial Motions

A party moving for JNOV may combine that motion with a motion for new trial.[417] When the judge receives a combined motion and *grants* the JNOV motion, the judge also must make a conditional ruling on the new trial motion.[418]

Jurisdiction over New Trial Motions after Appeal

If the underlying judgment has been appealed, the trial court has no authority to rule on a Rule 59 motion.[419] As the Court of Appeals has stated, "The general rule is that an appeal takes the case out of the jurisdiction of the trial court. Thereafter, pending the appeal, the trial judge is *functus officio*."[420] This is the case even when the Rule 59 motion and the notice of appeal occur at the same time.[421] This general rule has "two exceptions and one qualification": the trial judge retains jurisdiction to make rulings in the case (1) during the session in which the judgment appealed from was entered and (2) for the purpose of settling the case on appeal; and the judge, after notice and a proper show-

---

417. Rule 50(b)(1).

418. Rule 50(c)(1); *In re* Will of Buck, 350 N.C. 621, 623, 516 S.E.2d 858, 860 (1999); Bryant v. Nationwide Mut. Fire Ins. Co., 313 N.C. 362, 379, 329 S.E.2d 333, 343 (1985); Graves v. Walston, 302 N.C. 332, 339, 275 S.E.2d 485, 489 (1981); Lyon v. May, 119 N.C. App. 704, 708, 459 S.E.2d 833, 836 (1995). This process is discussed in further detail in Chapter 1 in the section titled "Conditional Rulings on Combined New Trial Motions."

419. Estrada v. Jaques, 70 N.C. App. 627, 637–38, 321 S.E.2d 240, 247 (1984); Wiggins v. Bunch, 280 N.C. 106, 108, 184 S.E.2d 879, 880 (1971); Am. Aluminum Prods., Inc. v. Pollard, 97 N.C. App. 541, 545, 389 S.E.2d 589, 592 (1990); Jim Walter Homes, Inc. v. Peartree, 24 N.C. App. 579, 580, 211 S.E.2d 457, 458 (1975); *see also* G.S. 1-294 ("When an appeal is perfected . . . it stays all further proceedings in the court below upon the judgment appealed from, or upon the matter embraced therein[.]").

420. *Estrada*, 70 N.C. App. at 637, 321 S.E.2d at 247; *see also* Curry v. First Fed. Savs. & Loan Ass'n of Charlotte, 125 N.C. App. 108, 112, 479 S.E.2d 286, 289 (1997) (applying the rule to a purported Rule 59(e) motion).

421. *Pollard*, 97 N.C. App. at 545, 389 S.E.2d at 592; Seafare Corp. v. Trenor Corp., 88 N.C. App. 404, 411, 363 S.E.2d 643, 649 (1988).

ing, may determine that the appeal has been abandoned and thereby regain jurisdiction over the case.[422]

Appealability of New Trial Order

An order granting or denying a new trial under Rule 59 is immediately appealable to the Court of Appeals.[423] Our courts have held, however, that orders granting a *partial* new trial may not be immediately appealed absent proper certification of immediate appeal pursuant to Rule 54(b) or loss of a substantial right.[424] Orders granting partial new trial are discussed above in the section titled "Ordering Partial New Trial."

---

422. *Estrada*, 70 N.C. App. at 637–38, 321 S.E.2d at 247 (quoting Bowen v. Hodge Motor Co., 292 N.C. 633, 635–36, 234 S.E.2d 748, 749 (1977)); *Pollard*, 97 N.C. App. at 545, 389 S.E.2d at 592.

423. G.S. 1-277(a) ("An appeal may be taken from every judicial order or determination of a judge of a superior or district court [that] . . . grants or refuses a new trial.").

424. Land v. Land, 201 N.C. App. 672, 676–77, 687 S.E.2d 511, 515–16 (2010) (citing Unigard Ins. Co. v. Dickens, 41 N.C. App. 184, 254 S.E.2d 197 (1979)); LaFalce v. Wolcott, 76 N.C. App. 565, 568, 334 S.E.2d 236, 238 (1985); Johnson v. Garwood, 49 N.C. App. 462, 463, 271 S.E.2d 544, 544–45 (1980); *see also* Burgess v. Vestal, 99 N.C. App. 545, 548, 393 S.E.2d 324, 326 (1990) (noting that partial new trials are not appealable but holding that new trial order in that case was not partial). In *Land*, the court interpreted the version of G.S. 7A-27 that was in effect prior to amendments made by Session Law 2013-411. The pertinent statutory language regarding appeal of an "interlocutory order . . . that . . . grants or refuses new trial" remains substantively the same, however, so it appears that the current version of the statute would not affect the holding in *Land*.

Note that Session Law 2014-102 (S.B. 853) amended G.S. 7A-27 to make a final judgment in a mandatory or discretionary complex business case and an order of a Business Court Judge that "grants or refuses a new trial" appealable of right directly to the North Carolina Supreme Court. *See* S.L. 2014-102, sec. 1.

Chapter 3

Amendment of Judgments after Non-Jury Trials

Judge's Role

In a non-jury (or "bench") trial, the judge is the trier of fact.[1] Because there is no jury verdict, the procedural mechanisms of directed verdict and JNOV do not apply.[2] The proper means of seeking judgment at the close of the plaintiff's evidence in a non-jury trial is through involuntary dismissal under Rule of Civil Procedure 41(b).[3] Rule 41(b) provides as follows:

1. Chase Dev. Grp. v. Fisher, Clinard, & Cornwell, PLLC, 211 N.C. App. 295, 302, 710 S.E.2d 218, 223–24 (2011) ("[I]n a non-jury trial, the judge also assumes the role of the jury.") (citing Laughter v. Lambert, 11 N.C. App. 133, 136, 180 S.E.2d 450, 452 (1971)).

2. O'Grady v. First Union Nat'l Bank, 296 N.C. 212, 218, 250 S.E.2d 587, 592 (1978) ("A Rule 50(a) motion for directed verdict is appropriate only to a case tried before a jury."); Miles v. Carolina Forest Ass'n, 167 N.C. App. 28, 34, 604 S.E.2d 327, 332 (2004); Hill v. Lassiter, 135 N.C. App. 515, 517, 520 S.E.2d 797, 799–800 (1999) (citing Kelly v. Harvester Co., 278 N.C. 153, 159, 179 S.E.2d 396, 398 (1971)).

3. *Chase Delopment Group,* 211 N.C. App. at 300, 710 S.E.2d at 222; *Lassiter,* 135 N.C. App. at 517, 520 S.E.2d at 799–800.

> After the plaintiff, in an action tried by the court without a jury, has completed the presentation of his evidence, the defendant, without waiving his right to offer evidence in the event the motion is not granted, may move for a dismissal on the ground that upon the facts and the law the plaintiff has shown no right to relief.[4]

Under this rule, the judge may enter an order dismissing the claims subject to the motion if (1) the evidence was insufficient as a matter of law to support the claim (just as in a Rule 50 motion) or (2) the judge, as trier of fact, simply was not persuaded by the evidence.[5] Unlike in

---

4. Section 1A-1, Rule 41(b) (hereinafter Rule 41(b)), of the North Carolina General Statutes (hereinafter G.S.). While the rule says "plaintiff" and "defendant," it later makes clear that its provisions apply equally to counterclaims, crossclaims, and third-party claims. Rule 41(c).

Although a Rule 50 motion is inappropriate in a non-jury trial, the appellate courts often have held that such a motion may properly be treated as a Rule 41(b) motion. *O'Grady*, 296 N.C. at 218, 250 S.E.2d at 592; *Miles*, 167 N.C. App. at 34, 604 S.E.2d at 332; Greensboro Masonic Temple v. McMillan, 142 N.C. App. 379, 381–82, 542 S.E.2d 676, 677 (2001); *Lassiter*, 135 N.C. App. at 517, 520 S.E.2d at 800; Nw. Bank v. Rash, 74 N.C. App. 101, 102–03, 327 S.E.2d 302, 304 (1985). Likewise, in a jury trial, an improperly designated Rule 41(b) motion may properly be treated as a Rule 50 motion. Flack v. Garriss, 58 N.C. App. 573, 575, 293 S.E.2d 827, 828 (1982); Pergerson v. Williams, 9 N.C. App. 512, 516–17, 176 S.E.2d 885, 888 (1970).

5. *O'Grady*, 296 N.C. at 218, 250 S.E.2d at 592 ("[T]he judge can give judgment against the plaintiff, not only because his proof has failed to make out a case (as is permitted under Rule 50), but also on the basis of facts as the judge may then determine them."); *Greensboro Masonic Temple*, 142 N.C. App. at 381, 542 S.E.2d at 677; *Lassiter*, 135 N.C. App. at 517, 520 S.E.2d at 800. In *Lassiter*, the court explained that "dismissal under Rule 41(b) should be granted if the plaintiff has shown no right to relief or if the plaintiff has made out a colorable claim but the court nevertheless determines as the trier of fact that the defendant is entitled to judgment on the merits." *Id.* (citing Ayden Tractors v. Gaskins, 61 N.C. App. 654, 660, 301 S.E.2d 523, 527 (1983)). The rule states that "[t]he court as trier of the facts may then determine them and render judgment against the plaintiff or may decline to render any judgment until the close of all the evidence." Rule 41(b).

a jury trial, the judge is not required to view the evidence in the light most favorable to the plaintiff; instead, as finder of fact, the judge considers, weighs, and determines the inferences to be drawn from all competent evidence and assesses the credibility of the witnesses.[6] So, in a non-jury trial, even if the plaintiff "made out a prima facie case which would have precluded a directed verdict for the defendant in a jury case," the judge may dismiss the claim at the close of the plaintiff's evidence and dispense with hearing the defense.[7]

The judge also may choose to deny the Rule 41(b) motion at the close of plaintiff's evidence, hear defendant's case, and issue a judgment after all the evidence.[8] Whether the judge dismisses after plaintiff's evidence under Rule 41(b) or issues judgment after all the evidence, the judge *must* make written findings of fact and conclusions of law as provided in Rule of Civil Procedure 52(a).[9] Rule 52(a)(1) requires that "[i]n all actions tried upon the facts without a jury . . . the court shall find the facts specially and state separately its conclusions of law thereon and direct the entry of the appropriate judgment.[10]

---

6. *Chase Development Group*, 211 N.C. App. at 302, 710 S.E.2d at 223–24; Karger v. Wood, 174 N.C. App. 703, 706, 622 S.E.2d 197, 200 (2005); *Miles*, 167 N.C. App. at 34, 604 S.E.2d at 332 (citing Dealers Specialties, Inc. v. Hous. Servs., 305 N.C. 633, 636, 291 S.E.2d 137, 139 (1982)); *Lassiter*, 135 N.C. App. at 517, 520 S.E.2d at 800.

7. Lumbee River Elec. Membership Corp. v. City of Fayetteville, 309 N.C. 726, 741, 309 S.E.2d 209, 218 (1983) (citing Helms v. Rea, 282 N.C. 610, 194 S.E.2d 1 (1973)); Beck v. Beck, 175 N.C. App. 519, 523, 624 S.E.2d 411, 414 (2006).

8. Whitaker v. Earnhardt, 289 N.C. 260, 264, 221 S.E.2d 316, 319 (1976).

9. Rule 41(b); Rule 52(a); *O'Grady*, 296 N.C. at 218, 250 S.E.2d at 592; *Lassiter*, 135 N.C. App. at 517, 520 S.E.2d at 800 ("If the trial court grants a defendant's motion for involuntary dismissal, he must make findings of fact and failure to do so constitutes reversible error."). An exception to this finding of fact requirement exists when the plaintiff's evidence is insufficient as a matter of law; in that case, there is no dispute of material fact and thus nothing for the trial court to "find." Bauman v. Woodlake Partners, LLC, 199 N.C. App. 441, 454, 681 S.E.2d 819, 823–24 (2009); Harris v. N.C. Farm Bureau Mut. Ins. Co., 91 N.C. App. 147, 150, 370 S.E.2d 700, 702 (1988).

10. Rule 52(a)(2); *see, e.g.*, Tolbert v. Hiatt, 95 N.C. App. 380, 385, 382 S.E.2d 453, 456 (1989) (stating the requirement); Traber v. Crawford, 28 N.C. App. 694, 698–99, 222 S.E.2d 713, 715–16 (1976) (granting new trial

Amendment of Judgment after Non-Jury Trial

Rule 52(b)

The first avenue for seeking amendment or alteration of the court's findings of fact after a non-jury trial is through a motion for amendment of judgment. Rule 52(b) provides as follows:

> Upon motion of a party made not later than 10 days after entry of judgment the court may amend its findings or make additional findings and may amend the judgment accordingly.[11]

---

when findings did not cover all issues in the case); Littlejohn v. Hamrick, 15 N.C. App. 461, 465, 190 S.E.2d 299, 301 (1972) (remanding for new trial an order lacking sufficient findings and conclusions); Luther v. Hauser, 24 N.C. App. 71, 75, 210 S.E.2d 218, 220–21 (1974) (remanding case for findings of fact). Rule 52 goes on to state that "If an opinion or memorandum of decision is filed, it will be sufficient if the findings of fact and conclusions of law appear therein." Rule 52(a)(3).

11. Rule 52(b). The Court of Appeals, following federal precedent, has concluded that a trial court may amend both findings of fact and conclusions of law under this rule. *See, e.g.*, Spoon v. Spoon, 755 S.E.2d 66, 70 (N.C. Ct. App. 2014) (citing O'Neill v. S. Nat'l Bank of N.C., 40 N.C. App. 227, 231, 252 S.E.2d 231, 234 (1979)). The court has also stated that the

> primary purpose of a Rule 52(b) motion is to enable the appellate court to obtain a correct understanding of the factual issues determined by the trial court. If a trial court has omitted certain essential findings of fact, a motion under Rule 52(b) can correct this oversight and avoid remand by the appellate court for further findings.

Branch Banking & Trust Co. v. Home Fed. Savs. & Loan Ass'n of E. N.C., 85 N.C. App. 187, 198–99, 354 S.E.2d 541, 548 (1987).

This rule may not properly be used to seek amendment of an order in which findings of fact are not appropriate. Broughton v. McClatchy Newspapers, Inc., 161 N.C. App. 20, 33–34, 588 S.E.2d 20, 30 (2003) (motion not appropriate for relief from summary judgment because findings of fact not appropriate in summary judgment order).

Motions to amend judgment under Rule 52(b) must be made[12] not later than ten days after entry of judgment.[13] Pursuant to Rule of Civil Procedure 58, "a judgment is entered when it is reduced to writing, signed by the judge, and filed with the clerk of court."[14] The time for making the Rule 52(b) motion may not be extended by the court or the parties under Rule of Civil Procedure 6(b).[15]

Rule 52(b) also states that "[t]he motion may be made with a motion for a new trial pursuant to Rule 59." Because Rule 59 motions must be "served" within ten days of entry of judgment,[16] it appears that a motion to amend judgment under Rule 52(b) combined with a Rule 59 motion must be *served* within ten days of entry of judgment.

Rule 59

In addition, if a party seeks alteration or amendment of a judgment for any of the reasons that justify a new trial under Rule 59(a), the party also may move for amendment of the judgment under Rule 59. The closing paragraph of Rule 59(a) states,

> On a motion for a new trial in an action tried without a jury, the court may open the judgment if one has been entered, take additional testimony, amend findings of fact and conclusions of law or make new findings and conclusions, and direct the entry of a new judgment.[17]

---

12. Rule of Civil Procedure 7(b)(1) provides that

> an application to the court for an order shall be by motion which, unless made during a hearing or trial or at a session at which a cause is on the calendar for that session, shall be made in writing, shall state with particularity the grounds therefor, and shall set forth the relief or order sought. The requirement of writing is fulfilled if the motion is stated in a written notice of the hearing of the motion.

13. Rule 52(b).
14. G.S. 1A-1, Rule 58.
15. *See* Rule 6(b).
16. Rule 59(e).
17. Rule 59(a).

A motion to amend under this rule is a matter of the court's discretion.[18] The rule gives the trial judge wide authority to reopen the case to further evidence[19] and contemplates amendments to the judgment ranging anywhere from minor adjustments to findings of fact to a complete alteration of the outcome. Although Rule 59 does not so specify, the Court of Appeals has held that the trial judge may alter or amend the judgment on its own motion if done within the time allowed for a party's motion.[20] As stated in Rule 59(e), motions to alter or amend a judgment under Rule 59(a) must be served not later than ten days after entry of judgment.[21] Like Rule 52(b) motions, the time for making a Rule 59 motion may not be extended by the court or the parties under Rule of Civil Procedure 6(b).[22]

Motions to alter or amend a judgment after a non-jury trial must be based on one or more of the relevant grounds listed in Rule 59(a).[23] A party seeking alteration or amendment of a judgment pursuant to

---

18. Bartlett Milling Co., L.P. v. Walnut Grove Auction & Realty Co., Inc., 192 N.C. App. 74, 665 S.E.2d 478 (2008) (citing Strickland v. Jacobs, 88 N.C. App. 397, 399, 363 S.E.2d 229, 230 (1988)).

19. *See, e.g.,* Hoover v. Kleer-Pak of N.C., Inc., 33 N.C. App. 661, 665–66, 236 S.E.2d 386, 389 (1977) (noting judge's wide discretion to reopen non-jury trial "to have all the facts before him before reaching a final decision[.]"); Philco Fin. Corp. v. Mitchell, 26 N.C. App. 264, 267, 215 S.E.2d 823, 824–25 (1975) (affirming amendment of order after trial judge reopened trial to have additional evidence).

20. Fox v. Fox, 103 N.C. App. 13, 22, 404 S.E.2d 354, 359 (1991) ("The trial court has the power to amend its judgment within the ten-day period provided by Rule 59(e).") The precise procedure by which the court may do so has not been specified, so it is not clear that the court is required to give the parties notice and a hearing as it must, under Rule 59(d), when granting a new trial on its own motion. But prior notice would certainly seem to be the better practice.

21. Rule 59(e); Garrison *ex rel.* Chavis v. Barnes, 117 N.C. App. 206, 210, 450 S.E.2d 554, 557 (1994); Coats v. Coats, 79 N.C. App. 481, 482, 339 S.E.2d 676, 676 (1986).

22. *See* Rule 6(b).

23. Ice v. Ice, 136 N.C. App. 787, 790, 525 S.E.2d 843, 845 (2000) (motion based on purported post-trial error of law not based on Rule 59 grounds). See Chapter 2 for discussion of grounds for bringing a Rule 59 motion.

Rule 59(a) and (e) should be particularly careful to state the basis for the motion to reflect the Rule 59(a) grounds being raised.[24] If the party does not state a sufficient basis, the appellate court may determine that the motion did not toll the appeal deadline.[25]

Effect of Appeal; Appeal Tolling

An appeal of the underlying judgment divests the trial court of jurisdiction to rule on a new trial motion under Rule 59,[26] but the same is *not* true for motions to amend under Rule 52(b).[27] Timely motions to amend judgment under Rule 52(b) and Rule 59 toll the time for taking appeal of the underlying judgment. Pursuant to Rule of Appellate Procedure 3(c)(3), the period for filing and service of a notice of appeal is tolled until entry of an order disposing of the Rule 52(b) or Rule 59 motion (or its untimely service, as specified in the rule) and then begins to run as provided in that rule.[28]

---

24. N.C. Alliance for Transp. Reform, Inc. v. N.C. Dep't of Transp., 183 N.C. App. 466, 469–70, 645 S.E.2d 105, 108 (2007); Clark v. Penland, 146 N.C. App. 288, 291, 552 S.E.2d 243, 245 (2001); Dusenberry v. Dusenberry, 87 N.C. App. 490, 492, 361 S.E.2d 605, 606 (1987).

25. *Transportation Reform*, 183 N.C. App. at 469–70, 645 S.E.2d at 108; Smith v. Johnson, 125 N.C. App. 603, 606–07, 481 S.E.2d 415, 417 (1997); *Dusenberry*, 87 N.C. App. at 492, 361 S.E.2d at 606. *But see* Baker v. Tucker, 768 S.E.2d 874, 878–89 (N.C. Ct. App. 2015) (adequate basis stated where it was clear that movant argued for relief based on trial court's misapprehension of facts and misapplication of law).

26. See section titled "Jurisdiction over New Trial Motions after Appeal" in Chapter 2.

27. York v. Taylor, 79 N.C. App. 653, 654–55, 339 S.E.2d 830, 831 (1986) ("The trial court is not divested of jurisdiction to hear and rule on a Rule 52(b) motion even though notice of appeal has been given."); Parrish v. Cole, 38 N.C. App. 691, 695, 248 S.E.2d 878, 880 (1978) ("[A] timely motion, pursuant to Rule 52(b), will not be barred by an earlier notice of appeal.").

28. N.C. R. App. P. 3(c)(3). For the effect of *actual notice* on the service requirements under Rule 3(c) of the Rule of Appellate Procedure, see *Wilkins Family Medicine, P.A., v. WakeMed*, ___ S.E.2d ___ (N.C. Ct. App.

Appeal of Judgment after Non-Jury Trial

Rule 52(c) provides that, on appeal from judgment after a non-jury trial, a party may question the sufficiency of the evidence to support the judge's findings whether or not the party (1) objected to the findings in the trial court, (2) made a motion to amend the findings or a motion for judgment, or (3) requested specific findings.[29] When a party makes proper exceptions to the trial court's findings of fact on appeal,[30] the appeals court reviews only whether those findings were supported by competent evidence.[31] If the findings have evidentiary support, they will not be reversed even if the evidence would also support different findings.[32] Challenged conclusions of law are reviewed for whether they are supported by the findings of fact,[33] and if such support exists, absent errors of law they will be affirmed.[34]

Jan. 5, 2016), and *Magazian v. Creagh*, 759 S.E.2d 130, 131 (N.C. Ct. App. 2014).

29. Rule 52(c).

30. If the party fails to assign error on appeal to the objectionable findings, the findings are conclusive on appeal. *See* Sharpe v. Park Newspapers of Lumberton, Inc., 317 N.C. 579, 582, 347 S.E.2d 25, 28 (1986); Whitaker v. Earnhardt, 289 N.C. 260, 264, 221 S.E.2d 316, 319 (1976).

31. Chase Dev. Grp. v. Fisher, Clinard, & Cornwell, PLLC, 211 N.C. App. 295, 301, 710 S.E.2d 218, 223 (2011); Resort Realty of the Outer Banks, Inc. v. Brandt, 163 N.C. App. 114, 116, 593 S.E.2d 404, 407–08 (2004) (citing Sessler v. Marsh, 144 N.C. App. 623, 628, 551 S.E.2d 160, 163 (2001).

32. Williams v. Pilot Life Ins. Co., 288 N.C. 338, 342, 218 S.E.2d 368, 371 (1975) ("[T]he court's findings of fact have the force and effect of a verdict by a jury and are conclusive on appeal if there is evidence to support them, even though the evidence might sustain findings to the contrary."); *In re* Estate of Trogdon, 330 N.C. 143, 147, 409 S.E.2d 897, 900 (1991); Pulliam v. Smith, 348 N.C. 616, 625, 501 S.E.2d 898, 903 (1998); *Williams*, 288 N.C. at 342, 218 S.E.2d at 371; Praver v. Raus, 220 N.C. App. 88, 91, 725 S.E.2d 379, 382 (2012); Yurek v. Shaffer, 198 N.C. App. 67, 80, 678 S.E.2d 738, 747 (2009).

33. Everette v. Collins, 176 N.C. App. 168, 171, 625 S.E.2d 796, 798 (2006) ("The trial court's conclusions of law and orders will not be reversed if supported by the findings of fact."); *Brandt*, 163 N.C. App. at 116, 593 S.E.2d at 407–08; Bernard v. Cent. Carolina Truck Sales, Inc., 68 N.C. App. 228, 229, 314 S.E.2d 582, 583-84 (1984).

34. *Brandt*, 163 N.C. App. at 116, 593 S.E.2d at 408.

Part II Relief from Final Judgments and Orders under Rule 60(b)

Introduction

As discussed in Part I, there are two main methods of seeking relief from judgment at the trial court level in the immediate aftermath of a judgment: judgment notwithstanding the verdict (JNOV) under Rule 50 and new trial or amendment of judgment under Rules 59(a) and 52(b). For a broader range of court orders, Rule of Civil Procedure 60(b) allows a trial court to "relieve a party or his legal representative from a final judgment, order, or proceeding" for a number of specified reasons based in equity.[1] The six categories of grounds under Rule 60(b) are

(1) Mistake, inadvertence, surprise, or excusable neglect;

(2) Newly discovered evidence which by due diligence could not have been discovered in time to move for a new trial under Rule 59(b);

(3) Fraud (whether heretofore denominated intrinsic or extrinsic), misrepresentation, or other misconduct of an adverse party;

(4) The judgment is void;

(5) The judgment has been satisfied, released, or discharged, or a prior judgment upon which it is based has been reversed or otherwise vacated, or it is no longer equitable that the judgment should have prospective application; or

(6) Any other reason justifying relief from the operation of the judgment.[2]

The general time frame for seeking relief under this rule is a "reasonable time" with an outside limit of one year after judgment for the first three categories.[3] The rule has its foundation in many of the traditional, equitable bases for relief that pre-date enactment of the Rules of Civil

1. Section 1A-1, Rule 60(b) (hereinafter Rule 60(b)), of the North Carolina General Statutes (hereinafter G.S.).

2. *Id.*

3. *See infra* section titled "Time Limits."

Procedure.[4] In reaching a decision under this rule, therefore, a court should be guided by equitable principles, including

> (1) the general desirability that a final judgment not be lightly disturbed, (2) where relief is sought from a judgment of dismissal or default, the relative interest of deciding cases on the merits and the interest in orderly procedure, (3) the opportunity the movant had to present his claim or defense, and (4) any intervening equities.[5]

Rule 60(b) is not intended to address a trial court's errors of law, and it is not to be used as a substitute for appeal,[6] even under the broad language of Rule 60(b)(6).[7] In general, the trial court's grant or denial of a Rule 60(b) motion is a matter of discretion, and the trial court's ruling will not be disturbed unless that discretion has been abused.[8]

---

4. *See, e.g.*, Brady v. Town of Chapel Hill, 277 N.C. 720, 724, 178 S.E.2d 446, 448 (1971) (noting that motions under Rule 60(b) are "analogous to former practice"); Tex. W. Fin. Corp. v. Mann, 36 N.C. App. 346, 349, 243 S.E.2d 904, 906 (1978) (same); Doxol Gas of Angier, Inc. v. Barefoot, 10 N.C. App. 703, 705, 179 S.E.2d 890, 891 (1971) (noting influence of pre-rules case law).

5. McGinnis v. Robinson, 43 N.C. App. 1, 10, 258 S.E.2d 84, 90 (1979) (quoting Standard Equip. Co. v. Albertson, 35 N.C. App. 144, 147, 240 S.E.2d 499, 501–02 (1978)).

6. McIntosh v. McIntosh, 184 N.C. App. 697, 704, 646 S.E.2d 820, 825 (2007); Baxley v. Jackson, 179 N.C. App. 635, 638–39, 634 S.E.2d 905, 907 (2006); Garrison *ex rel.* Chavis v. Barnes, 117 N.C. App. 206, 210, 450 S.E.2d 554, 557 (1994); Jenkins v. Richmond Cty., 118 N.C. App. 166, 169, 454 S.E.2d 290, 292–93 (1995); Hagwood v. Odom, 88 N.C. App. 513, 519, 364 S.E.2d 190, 193 (1988); Taylor v. Triangle Porsche-Audi, Inc., 27 N.C. App. 711, 717, 220 S.E.2d 806, 811 (1975) (distinguishing erroneous and irregular judgments). As discussed in Part I, Chapter 2, errors of law are properly addressed through Rule 59(a)(8) or timely appeal.

7. *See infra* section titled "Not a Substitute for Appellate Review of Legal Errors."

8. Davis v. Davis, 360 N.C. 518, 523, 631 S.E.2d 114, 118 (2006); Sink v. Easter, 288 N.C. 183, 198, 217 S.E.2d 532, 541 (1975); Goodwin v. Cashwell, 102 N.C. App. 275, 277, 401 S.E.2d 840, 842 (2001); Gallbronner v. Mason, 101 N.C. App. 362, 364, 399 S.E.2d 139, 140 (1991); Vuncannon v. Vuncannon, 82 N.C. App. 255, 258, 346 S.E.2d 274, 276 (1986). Some matters at issue on a Rule 60(b) motion may be questions of law to be reviewed

The following sections cover the jurisdictional principles governing the rule, discuss the law surrounding each of the six categories of relief, and explain the procedure.

"Final Judgment, Order, or Proceeding"

"By its express terms" Rule 60(b) applies only to *final* judgments, orders, or proceedings and does not, therefore, provide relief from interlocutory orders.[9] To that end, our courts have held that Rule 60(b) could not be used

- for relief from an order dismissing fewer than all the claims,[10]
- to challenge the denial of a motion to dismiss under Rule 12(b)(6),[11]
- to set aside an entry of default,[12]
- to seek relief from denial of a motion to disqualify counsel,[13]
- for relief from denial of a motion to dismiss a medical malpractice claim for failure to comply with Rule of Civil Procedure 9(j),[14]

---

de novo, such as the presence of "excusable neglect." Additional examples are discussed further in the relevant sections below.

9. *Sink,* 288 N.C. at 196, 217 S.E.2d at 540; O'Neill v. S. Nat'l Bank of N.C., 40 N.C. App. 227, 230, 252 S.E.2d 231, 234 (1979).

10. Pratt v. Staton, 147 N.C. App. 771, 775, 556 S.E.2d 621, 624 (2001); Hooper v. Pizzagalli Constr. Co., 112 N.C. App. 400, 408, 436 S.E.2d 145, 150–51 (1993).

11. *O'Neill,* 40 N.C. App. at 231, 252 S.E.2d at 234 (holding that trial court should not, as a matter of law, have considered the motion).

12. Bailey v. Gooding, 60 N.C. App. 459, 460, 299 S.E.2d 267, 269 (1983) (noting that Rule 60(b) is appropriate to set aside default *judgment* but that *entry* of default should be challenged only under Rule 55(d)'s good cause standard).

13. Adams Creek Assocs. v. Davis, 186 N.C. App. 512, 525, 652 S.E.2d 677, 685 (2007).

14. Rupe v. Hucks-Follis, 170 N.C. App. 188, 191, 611 S.E.2d 867, 869 (2005).

- for reconsideration of a trial court's exclusion of affidavits in a summary judgment hearing,[15] or
- for relief from an arbitration award where the trial court had not yet entered judgment under the arbitration rules.[16]

Despite being subject to modification under the court's continuing jurisdiction, however, final adjudications in child support and child custody actions are considered final orders for purposes of Rule 60(b).[17]

A judge's announcement or "rendering" of a decision in open court is not a final order or judgment from which relief may be sought by a Rule 60(b) motion.[18] In a recent case, the Court of Appeals rejected an attempt to use Rule 60(b) to introduce new evidence after a hearing and before entry of a ruling. Although apparently the judge had orally announced his ruling before the Rule 60(b) motion was filed, he had not yet entered an order, and his decision was not, therefore, final.[19]

Rule 60(b) is an appropriate mechanism for seeking relief from a voluntary dismissal *with* prejudice.[20] If a party has dismissed its

---

15. Rockingham Square Shopping Ctr. v. Integon Life Ins. Corp., 52 N.C. App. 633, 641, 279 S.E.2d 918, 924 (1981).

16. Brock & Scott Holdings, Inc. v. West, 198 N.C. App. 357, 363, 679 S.E.2d 507, 512 (2009) ("Until the trial court entered judgment on the arbitration award, there was no final judgment of the court from which plaintiff could seek relief."). For more information about interlocutory orders see Appellate Rules Committee of the N.C. Bar Association, "Guide to Appealability of Interlocutory Orders" (2014), www.aoc.state.nc.us/www/public/html/ARResources.asp.

17. Coleman v. Coleman, 74 N.C. App. 494, 496–97, 328 S.E.2d 871, 872 (1985) (support); Dishman v. Dishman, 37 N.C. App. 543, 546, 246 S.E.2d 819, 822 (1978) (custody).

18. *See* G.S. 1A-1, Rule 58 (judgment must be "reduced to writing, signed, and filed with the clerk of court"); *see also In re Hayes*, 106 N.C. App. 652, 657, 418 S.E.2d 304, 307 (1992) (making a similar analysis under prior version of Rule 58).

19. Kingston v. Lyon Const., Inc., 207 N.C. App. 703, 709, 701 S.E.2d 348, 353 (2010).

20. Estate of Barber v. Guilford Cty. Sheriff's Dep't, 161 N.C. App. 658, 663–64, 589 S.E.2d 433, 437 (2003); Carter v. Clowers, 102 N.C. App. 247, 252, 401 S.E.2d 662, 665 (1991).

case *without* prejudice under Rule 41(a), however, that party may not seek relief from that dismissal under Rule 60(b) because a dismissal without prejudice is not a final order, at least during the one-year refiling period.[21] When the party seeking to have the plaintiff's dismissal without prejudice set aside is the opposing party, however, our appellate courts have approved the use of Rule 60(b).[22]

The North Carolina Industrial Commission has inherent authority analogous to Rule 60(b) to set aside its final judgments and orders,[23] and numerous appellate cases have analyzed commission decisions granting or denying such relief under Rule 60(b)'s standards.[24] Rule 60(b) is also an appropriate means of challenging final orders made in condemnation actions under Chapter 40A of the North Carolina General Statutes (hereinafter G.S.).[25] A trial court may not, however, entertain a Rule 60(b) motion to set aside a final decision of a local government

---

21. Troy v. Tucker, 126 N.C. App. 213, 215, 484 S.E.2d 98, 99 (1997); Robinson v. Gen. Mills Rests., Inc., 110 N.C. App. 633, 637, 430 S.E.2d 696, 698 (1993). *But see In re* E.H., 227 N.C. App. 525, 526, 742 S.E.2d 844, 847–48 (2013) (allowing a Rule 60(b) motion to relieve a dismissal without prejudice in a juvenile case because "[n]o judgment or order is ever truly 'final' in the juvenile context[.]").

22. Bradley v. Bradley, 206 N.C. App. 249, 254, 697 S.E.2d 422, 425 (2010) (citing *Carter* as authority without discussing fact that *Carter* dealt with dismissal *with* prejudice).

23. Hogan v. Cone Mills Corp., 315 N.C. 127, 137, 337 S.E.2d 477, 483 (1985).

24. *See, e.g.*, Ammons v. Goodyear Tire & Rubber Co., 209 N.C. App. 741, 744–45, 708 S.E.2d 127, 129 (2011) (discussing commission authority to entertain Rule 60(b) relief on own motion); Higgins v. Michael Powell Builders, 132 N.C. App. 720, 725, 515 S.E.2d 17, 21 (1999) (discussing excusable neglect), Moore v. City of Raleigh, 135 N.C. App. 332, 336–37, 520 S.E.2d 133, 137–38 (1999) (same); Grupen v. Thomasville Furniture Indus., 28 N.C. App. 119, 121, 220 S.E.2d 201, 202 (1975) (analyzing timing requirements).

25. City of Durham v. Woo, 129 N.C. App. 183, 187, 497 S.E.2d 457, 460 (1998).

board when the court is acting in an appellate role in review of the board's decision.[26]

The Court of Appeals has held that a court may not relieve a party from a final judgment under Rule 60(b) once the judgment has been affirmed on appeal.[27] In another opinion a few years later, however, the court in fact *required* Rule 60(b) relief from a judgment that had been affirmed on appeal directing reconveyance of property. The court held that because the property had since been foreclosed upon and sold to third persons, compliance with the earlier judgment was impossible and relief under Rule 60(b)(6) was necessary.[28] The trial court had denied relief on grounds that it lacked authority to grant a Rule 60(b) motion after a judgment had been upheld on appeal. Rejecting this notion, the Court of Appeals stated, "We have found nothing to indicate that a judgment upheld on appeal would not be subject to the provisions of Rule 60 under appropriate circumstances."[29]

The North Carolina Supreme Court has also recently addressed the extent to which Rule 60(b) may be used by a judgment debtor to defend against enforcement of a final foreign (out-of-state) judgment in North Carolina pursuant to the Uniform Enforcement of Foreign Judgments Act (UEFJA).[30] Given the limits the Full Faith and Credit Clause of the United States Constitution places on challenges to foreign judgments,

---

26. Bailey & Assocs., Inc. v. Wilmington Bd. of Adjustment, 202 N.C. App. 177, 193, 689 S.E.2d 576, 588 (2010) (court properly denied Rule 60(b) motion during review of a board of adjustment decision on a writ of certiorari).

27. Severance v. Ford Motor Co., 105 N.C. App. 98, 100–01, 411 S.E.2d 618, 620 (1992). The court noted that once the judgment was affirmed, the trial court could take no action that would "alter, modify, or remove the imposed penalty." *Id.* at 101, 411 S.E.2d at 620.

28. Lumsden v. Lawing, 117 N.C. App. 514, 518–20, 451 S.E.2d 659, 662–63 (1995).

29. *Id.* at 517, 451 S.E.2d at 661.

30. G.S. 1C-1703(c) states that a foreign judgment "has the same effect and is subject to the same defenses as a judgment of this State and shall be enforced or satisfied in like manner."

the court held that the defenses available under the UEFJA are only those

> directed at the enforcement of a foreign judgment, such as, that the judgment creditor committed extrinsic fraud, that the rendering state lacked personal or subject matter jurisdiction, that the judgment has been paid, that the parties have entered into an accord and satisfaction, that the judgment debtor's property is exempt from execution, that the judgment is subject to continued modification, or that the judgment debtor's due process rights have been violated.[31]

The debtor may not assert a defense related to the merits.[32] Those grounds in Rule 60(b) directed at challenges to the merits of the case, therefore, cannot be used to avoid enforcement of the foreign judgment.

Grounds for Relief

Mistake, Inadvertence, Surprise, Excusable Neglect—Rule 60(b)(1)

Mistake and Inadvertence

"Mistake" (or inadvertence) in the Rule 60(b) context does not include (1) mistakes of law or (2) unilateral mistakes[33] of fact not caused by misconduct of the other party. In general, the rule addresses mutual mistakes of fact.

The North Carolina Supreme Court long ago held, under the precursor to Rule 60(b), that "the statute does not afford relief from a judgment on the ground of mistake of law."[34] And in *Braun v. Grundman*,

---

31. DocRx, Inc. v. EMI Servs. of N.C., LLC, 367 N.C. 371, 382, 758 S.E.2d 390, 397, *cert. denied*, 135 S. Ct. 678, 190 L. Ed. 2d 390 (U.S. 2014).

32. *Id.*

33. A "unilateral mistake" is "a mistake or misunderstanding as to the term or effect of a contract, made or entertained by one of the parties to it but not by the other." *Unilateral Mistake*, Black's Law Dictionary (10th ed. 2014).

34. Crissman v. Palmer, 225 N.C. 472, 474, 35 S.E.2d 422, 423 (1945) (interpreting former G.S. 1-220).

the Court of Appeals reiterated more recently that relief on the basis of "mistake" is not available simply because the movant had "an erroneous view of the law."[35] A party's—or its attorney's—mistake of law has been addressed under the excusable neglect provision of Rule 60(b)(1) (discussed below), and relief tends to be elusive in that context as well.[36] A court's mistakes of law are addressed through appeal and, where appropriate, by motions for new trial on the basis of "error in law" under Rule 59(a)(8).[37] Rule 60(b)(6) may provide a remedy for a mistake of law that occurs because of a change in the law occurring so recently that neither the parties nor the court could reasonably have been notified of it.[38]

As to mistakes of fact, no relief is available unless the moving party proves either (1) mutual mistake or (2) unilateral mistake caused by misconduct, such as "fraud, imposition, undue influence, or like oppressive circumstances."[39] A mistake is "mutual" in this context "where the mistake is common to both parties and because of it each has done what neither intended."[40] The most common source of mistake-of-fact arguments are consent judgments and other agreements forming the basis for a court's final order. The court rejected an argument for relief from a consent judgment where defendants claimed that

---

35. 63 N.C. App. 387, 388, 304 S.E.2d 636, 637 (1983).

36. *See infra* section titled "What Is Excusable Neglect?"

37. *See* Part I, Chapter 2.

38. See Barnes v. Taylor, 148 N.C. App. 397, 559 S.E.2d 246 (2002), discussed *infra* in section titled "To Account for Certain Changes in the Law."

39. Goodwin v. Cashwell, 102 N.C. App. 275, 277, 401 S.E.2d 840, 842 (2001) (quoting Marriott Fin. Servs. v. Capitol Funds, 288 N.C. 122, 136, 217 S.E.2d 551, 560 (1975)); *see also* Thacker v. Thacker, 107 N.C. App. 479, 481, 420 S.E.2d 479, 480 (1992) (stating requirements); Blankenship v. Price, 27 N.C. App. 20, 22, 217 S.E.2d 709, 710 (1975) (same); *see generally* Hartsell v. Pickett Cotton Mills, Inc., 4 N.C. App. 67, 165 S.E.2d 792 (1969) (analyzing mutual mistake of fact under statutory precursor to Rule 60(b)).

40. Stevenson v. Stevenson, 100 N.C. App. 750, 752, 398 S.E.2d 334, 336 (1990) (quoting *Marriott Financial Services*, 288 N.C. at 135, 217 S.E.2d at 560); *see also* Harris v. Harris, 162 N.C. App. 511, 516, 591 S.E.2d 560, 563 (2004) (affirming modification of judgment under Rule 60(b)(6) to eliminate unintended language inserted through "inadvertence").

the parties mutually misunderstood the cost of an annuity that would be a key part of settlement. Finding that the settlement agreement made no reference to the value of the annuity, and finding no other evidence that the misunderstanding was mutual, the court properly refused to grant defendants relief from the judgment.[41] The court also denied relief in a will caveat case where the movant alleged that the existence of a will discovered after judgment was a mutual mistake of fact. The Court of Appeals noted that the will's existence "might have been an unknown fact, common to all parties," but it was not material to the consent judgment, did not motivate the parties to enter into the agreement, and, even had it been discovered, would have been of no consequence to the caveators.[42] In a divorce action, the trial court improperly granted relief from a consent judgment that had been altered several times after the parties' oral agreement because there was no evidence that any of those alterations has been done through mutual inadvertence or mistake.[43] And in another divorce settlement, the parties' differing interpretations of a term in a memorandum of agreement was not a mutual mistake of fact where the meaning of the term was not ambiguous.[44] Furthermore, the moving party was not entitled to relief because she ratified the terms of the memorandum eleven days later by signing the consent judgment.[45]

Further, a mistake by a party or its attorney in presenting the facts of its case or in formulating its case strategy is not the mistake contemplated by this rule.[46] The Court of Appeals rejected an argument that failure to present key evidence prior to judgment was a "mistake," noting that the movants "should have been aware of this deficiency in their case before judgment was entered and therefore relief under

---

41. *Goodwin*, 102 N.C. App. at 277–78, 401 S.E.2d at 842.

42. *In re* Will of Baity, 65 N.C. App. 364, 367–68, 309 S.E.2d 515, 517–18 (1983).

43. *Stevenson*, 100 N.C. App. at 752, 398 S.E.2d at 336.

44. Griffith v. Curtis, 205 N.C. App. 462, 464–65, 696 S.E.2d 701, 703 (2010) (mistake of fact argument analyzed under Rule 60(b)(6)).

45. *Id.* at 465, 696 S.E.2d at 703–04.

46. Hagwood v. Odom, 88 N.C. App. 513, 519, 364 S.E.2d 190, 193 (1988).

Rule 60(b)(1) is not justified."[47] In addition, the purported "mistake" of a party in seeking default judgment as to only part of that to which it was entitled was not grounds for relief from that judgment, and certainly not for modification of that judgment to include the additional relief.[48]

Finally, a few cases have addressed arguments regarding irregular court processes as "mistakes" under this rule. These arguments are more typically analyzed as "irregularities" under Rule 60(b)(6) or Rule 59(a)(1). In *Tepper v. Hoch*,[49] a trial court did not err in setting aside an order on its own initiative after finding that defendant's failure to request a timely hearing was "inadvertent." Because there was evidence that notice to defendant "contained somewhat conflicting instructions and could lead a reasonable person to believe he did not have the obligation to request a hearing," relief under Rule 60(b)(1) was appropriate.[50] In another case in which defendant sought relief from a default judgment, the court analyzed the alleged mistake of a clerk's office in reporting the status of service of process. Finding insufficient evidence of misreporting, the court properly concluded that "no mistake occurred" and that relief was not warranted.[51]

Surprise

Relief is not available on the basis of a party's "surprise" at the court's action,[52] the party's own misapprehension of applicable law,[53] or the unauthorized actions of the party's attorney.[54] The leading description for proper use of this rule is stated in *Endsley v. Wolfe Camera Supply*

---

47. *Id.*

48. Kimzay Winston-Salem, Inc. v. Jester, 103 N.C. App. 77, 80, 404 S.E.2d 176, 178 (1991).

49. 140 N.C. App. 354, 536 S.E.2d 654 (2000).

50. *Id.* at 358–59, 536 S.E.2d at 658.

51. Partridge v. Associated Cleaning Consultants & Servs., Inc., 108 N.C. App. 625, 632, 424 S.E.2d 664, 668 (1993).

52. Crissman v. Palmer, 225 N.C. 472, 474, 35 S.E.2d 422, 423 (1945).

53. *Id.*; Braun v. Grundman, 63 N.C. App. 387, 388, 304 S.E.2d 636, 637 (1983).

54. Endsley v. Wolfe Camera Supply Corp., 44 N.C. App. 308, 310–11, 261 S.E.2d 36, 38 (1979) (citing Hairston v. Garwood, 123 N.C. 345, 31 S.E. 653

Corp., in which the court explained that "the surprise contemplated by this statute is some condition or situation in which a party to a cause is unexpectedly placed to his injury, without any fault or negligence of his own, which ordinary prudence could not have guarded against."[55] In that case, on the second morning of trial in superior court, which was set to begin at 10:30 A.M., plaintiff's counsel was called unexpectedly to appear in district court in an adjacent county at 9:00 A.M. to enter a plea for another client. The district court judge was late, causing counsel to arrive back in superior court at 11:00 A.M. By that time, his client's case had been dismissed with prejudice for failure to appear. The trial court later set the judgment aside on grounds that counsel had been "surprised" by the course of events.[56] While noting that the proper basis for setting aside the judgment might have been excusable neglect or mistake, the Court of Appeals affirmed the relief, stating that "the main point is that the trial court found sufficient facts to show that there was a good excuse for the tardiness of plaintiff's counsel."[57]

One traditional basis for relief under this rule is the surprise of a party when its counsel withdraws unexpectedly, leaving the party unprepared to proceed or otherwise creating an adverse outcome for the party.[58] Similar scenarios have been addressed more recently in

---

(1898)). Unauthorized actions of counsel are addressed under the excusable neglect provision of Rule 60(b)(1), as discussed below.

55. *Endsley*, 44 N.C. App. at 310, 261 S.E.2d at 38. The court quoted the North Carolina Supreme Court's pre-rules decision in *Townsend v. Carolina Coach Co.*, in which the court affirmed an order setting aside default judgment against a defendant who, through no fault of its own, had failed to receive service of process. 231 N.C. 81, 85–86, 56 S.E.2d 39, 42–43 (1949).

56. *Endsley*, 44 N.C. App. at 309, 261 S.E.2d at 37.

57. *Id.* at 312, 261 S.E.2d at 39.

58. *See, e.g.*, Perkins v. Sykes, 233 N.C. 147, 153, 63 S.E.2d 133, 138 (1951) (relief appropriate where attorney withdrew without due notice to movant); Gosnell v. Hilliard, 205 N.C. 297, 301–02, 171 S.E. 52, 53–54 (1933) (relief appropriate where judgment granted against movant after attorney withdrew without her knowledge).

the context of motions for new trial under Rule 59(a); those cases are instructive in the Rule 60(b) context as well.[59]

If a court finds that a party was "surprised" under the meaning of this rule, the court must also find that the party has a meritorious claim or defense.[60] "Meritorious defense" is discussed in the next section in connection with excusable neglect.

Excusable Neglect

Perhaps the most commonly cited basis for relief from judgment—often default judgment[61]—is excusable neglect. As discussed below, if a party succeeds in the difficult task of showing excusable neglect, it must also show that it has a meritorious defense to the action. Whether excusable neglect has been shown is a question of law, not fact, and the trial court's determination is fully reviewable on appeal.[62] However, the facts found by the trial court necessary to make this legal determination are conclusive on appeal if supported by competent evidence.[63] A

---

59. *See* section in Part I, Chapter 2 titled "Accident or Surprise—Rule 59(a)(3)."

60. *Perkins*, 233 N.C. at 151, 63 S.E.2d at 136; Roediger v. Sapos, 217 N.C. 95, 100, 6 S.E.2d 801, 804 (1940).

61. The Court of Appeals has held that a party must move for relief from default judgment in trial court before the party can have the matter heard on appeal. As the court stated in *Golmon v. Latham*, "Defendants should have first filed a motion pursuant to N.C. R. Civ. P. 55(d) or 60(b). They would then have been able to appeal to this Court from any denial of that motion. Because Defendants failed to follow this procedure, we are precluded from reviewing the issues they raise." 183 N.C. App. 150, 152, 643 S.E.2d 625, 626 (2007).

62. Sellers v. FMC Corp., 216 N.C. App. 134, 141, 716 S.E.2d 661, 666 (2011); Monaghan v. Schilling, 197 N.C. App. 578, 584, 677 S.E.2d 562, 566 (2009); Engines & Equip., Inc. v. Lipscomb, 15 N.C. App. 120, 122, 189 S.E.2d 498, 499 (1972).

63. Norton v. Sawyer, 30 N.C. App. 420, 422, 227 S.E.2d 148, 151 (1976); McKinley Bldg. Corp. v. Alvis, 183 N.C. App. 500, 504, 645 S.E.2d 219, 222 (2007); Anderson Trucking Serv., Inc. v. Key Way Transp., Inc., 94 N.C. App. 36, 41, 379 S.E.2d 665, 668 (1989); Estate of Teel v. Darby, 129 N.C. App. 604, 607, 500 S.E.2d 759, 762 (1998); *see also* McIntosh v. McIntosh, 184 N.C. App. 697, 704–05, 646 S.E.2d 820, 825–26 (2007) (lengthy and detailed

motion made on the basis of excusable neglect must be made within a reasonable time and not more than one year after the judgment was entered.[64]

What is excusable neglect?

Although "there is no clear dividing line as to what falls within the confines of excusable neglect as grounds for the setting aside of a judgment,"[65] our courts have established some essential parameters. As a baseline, excusable neglect depends on what "may be reasonably expected of a party in paying proper attention to his case" under all the surrounding circumstances.[66] In an unusual case, the court did not err in finding excusable neglect on the basis that a defendant was "deficient in his usual mental processes" because he presented competent evidence of being partially disabled due to depression and prescription drugs that prevented him from having the "sound mind" to properly handle his affairs.[67] And in a contract action, the trial court erred in denying relief to a plaintiff whose counsel moved to withdraw from the case only a few days prior to the trial without securing a continuance, leaving plaintiff no reasonable opportunity to retain new counsel and put on an effective case.[68] In general, however, the prudent attention

---

findings supported conclusion that party's failure to retain counsel and prepare for hearing was not excusable); Boyd v. Marsh, 47 N.C. App. 491, 492, 267 S.E.2d 394, 395 (1980) (court's findings of fact not supported by the evidence).

64. Rule 60(b). *See infra* section titled "Time Limits."

65. Thomas M. McInnis & Assocs., Inc. v. Hall, 318 N.C. 421, 425, 349 S.E.2d 552, 555–56 (1986); *McIntosh*, 184 N.C. App. at 705, 646 S.E.2d at 825 (quotation omitted).

66. *Sellers*, 216 N.C. App. at 141, 716 S.E.2d at 666; *McIntosh*, 184 N.C. App. at 704, 646 S.E.2d at 825 (quotation omitted); Overnite Transport Co. v. Styer, 57 N.C. App. 146, 149, 291 S.E.2d 179, 181 (1982).

67. U.S.I.F. Wynnewood Corp. v. Soderquist, 27 N.C. App. 611, 615, 219 S.E.2d 787, 790 (1975).

68. Barclays Am. Corp. v. Howell, 81 N.C. App. 654, 657, 345 S.E.2d 228, 230 (1986); *see also* Callaway v. Freeman, 71 N.C. App. 451, 452, 322 S.E.2d 432, 433–34 (1984) (judgment properly set aside where defendant never received trial calendar and matter had been calendared in a manner contrary to court rules).

rule has rendered most cases of neglect *in*excusable, as in the following examples:

- A trial correctly denied relief where defendants failed to respond to a complaint two months after obtaining an extension of time to do so and failed to respond to plaintiff's subsequent motion for entry of default. Their counsel acknowledged that "errors and mistakes were made," but the "explanations were not sufficient to excuse the mistakes."[69]
- Defendants' failure to attend to their own defense during the period when they were not represented by counsel was not excusable.[70]
- It was error to relieve a plaintiff from a dismissal for failure to prosecute where she had consented to the withdrawal of her prior counsel, was aware of the scheduled trial, and showed no diligent efforts to secure other legal services.[71]
- A defendant's neglect was not excusable where he failed to respond to a complaint in hopes that the attorney who formerly represented him would do so after the attorney made it clear there was no longer an attorney–client relationship. The court held that defendant "did not give the [matter] the attention which an ordinary and prudent person would give to important business."[72]
- A party who failed to learn of a hearing date was not entitled to relief where the record showed he had ample time to do so and knew that his counsel was in the process of withdrawing.[73]

---

69. Monaghan v. Schilling, 197 N.C. App. 578, 585, 677 S.E.2d 562, 566–67 (2009).

70. McKinley Bldg. Corp. v. Alvis, 183 N.C. App. 500, 506–07, 645 S.E.2d 219, 223–24 (2007).

71. Campbell v. First-Citizens Bank & Trust Co., 23 N.C. App. 631, 634–35, 209 S.E.2d 556, 558–59 (1974).

72. Gallbronner v. Mason, 101 N.C. App. 362, 364–65, 399 S.E.2d 139, 140–41 (1991).

73. Trivette v. Trivette, 162 N.C. App. 55, 62–63, 590 S.E.2d 298, 304 (2004).

- Defendants who failed to timely respond to an answer because their insurer wanted first to evaluate the case for settlement possibilities could not, as a matter of law, be relieved from default judgment on the basis of excusable neglect.[74]
- It was not excusable neglect to fail to respond to a summons and complaint that had been accepted at defendant's residence by another defendant, where the other defendant's qualifications to receive service were unchallenged and defendant was aware of the service.[75]
- It was not error to find a lack of excusable neglect where defendant's 24-year-old manager, on the job less than a month, believed the insurance company would handle the complaint because the parties' insurers had been negotiating to resolve the conflict for more than a year.[76]
- Parties were not entitled to relief where confusion caused by receiving two different trial calendars could have been resolved by a simple call to the clerk of court.[77]
- In a personal injury action, defendants could not be excused from failure to file an answer where their insurer informed them of its refusal to defend the action two weeks before the answer was due; plaintiff thereafter waited an additional three months to seek entry of default; plaintiff then gave defendants

74. Gibson v. Mena, 144 N.C. App. 125, 129–130, 548 S.E.2d 745, 747–48 (2001); *see also* Tex. W. Fin. Corp. v. Mann, 36 N.C. App. 346, 349–50, 243 S.E.2d 904, 907 (1978) (error to find excusable neglect where only justification for not responding was that plaintiff's counsel said he would give defendant time to review defendant's files).

75. Grier *ex rel.* Brown v. Guy, 741 S.E.2d 338, 341 (N.C. Ct. App. 2012).

76. Commercial Union Assurance Cos. v. Atwater Motor Co., Inc., 35 N.C. App. 397, 399, 241 S.E.2d 334, 335 (1978); *see also* Estate of Teel v. Darby, 129 N.C. App. 604, 611, 500 S.E.2d 759, 764 (1998) ("A defendant must give its litigation matters that level of attention one gives important business matters; the primary duty of attending to litigation remains with the defendant.").

77. Harrington v. Harrington, 38 N.C. App. 610, 612, 248 S.E.2d 460, 461 (1978).

advance notice of intent to seek default; and defendants still "did nothing."[78]

A recurring theme in excusable neglect cases is a defendant's failure to maintain a registered agent or to keep the court apprised of a current service address. Such neglect generally is deemed inexcusable.[79] In a personal injury action, for example, defendant did not receive actual notice of substitute service from the secretary of state because defendant's address on file with the secretary's office was not current. The trial court did not err in finding that defendant's failure to appoint a registered agent and notify the secretary of state of its address change was inexcusable neglect.[80] In a similar scenario, default judgment was entered in an amount exceeding $300,000 against a Maryland corporation that conducted business in North Carolina but failed to maintain a registered agent for service in North Carolina. The Maryland service agent received and forwarded the summons and complaint, but the documents were lost in the mail and never received. The trial court properly denied the motion for relief, having found that the defendant neglected for years to properly designate a North Carolina registered agent.[81] In another such case, failure of a party's registered agent to be available to accept service after multiple

---

78. Hayes v. Evergo Tel. Co., Ltd., 100 N.C. App. 474, 481–82, 397 S.E.2d 325, 330 (1990).

79. *See* Standard Equip. Co. v. Albertson, 35 N.C. App. 144, 146–47, 240 S.E.2d 499, 501 (1978) (failure to keep court informed of new address after discharging counsel not excusable).

80. Partridge v. Associated Cleaning Consultants & Servs., Inc., 108 N.C. App. 625, 631, 424 S.E.2d 664, 667–68 (1993).

81. Anderson Trucking Serv., Inc. v. Key Way Transp., Inc., 94 N.C. App. 36, 41–42, 379 S.E.2d 665, 668–69 (1989); *see also* Smith *ex rel.* Strickland v. Jones, 183 N.C. App. 643, 646–47, 645 S.E.2d 198, 201 (2007) (inexcusable neglect to fail to keep a functional registered agent address); *cf.* Howard v. Williams, 40 N.C. App. 575, 580, 253 S.E.2d 571, 573–74 (1979) ("[S]tatutory provisions designed to protect plaintiffs from defendants who do not give reasonable attention to important business affairs such as lawsuits cannot be ignored.").

attempts also was deemed inexcusable.[82] Extenuating circumstances were found, however, where defendant neglected to inform the court of her new address—resulting in her failure to receive and answer requests for admission—due to "fear of continuing harassment and abuse" from plaintiff, her former husband, who had a documented history of domestic abuse against her.[83]

In addition, a party will not be excused from paying prudent attention to its case due to ignorance of the law, ignorance of court processes, or failure to obtain counsel.[84] Relief has, for example, been denied where

- defendants received two identical summonses sixteen days apart but assumed the thirty-day response deadline applied only to the second summons;[85]
- a self-represented litigant in a paternity proceeding had a ninth-grade education, could read and write, and had

82. Advanced Wall Sys., Inc. v. Highlande Builders, LLC, 167 N.C. App. 630, 633–34, 605 S.E.2d 728, 731 (2004).

83. Elliott v. Elliott, 200 N.C. App. 259, 262–63, 683 S.E.2d 405, 408–09 (2009) (distinguishing the facts of this case from *Strickland* and other cases). Furthermore, the documents, in violation of Rule of Civil Procedure 5, had not been served on any other party or counsel. *Id.* at 263, 683 S.E.2d at 409.

84. Grier *ex rel.* Brown v. Guy, 741 S.E.2d 338, 341 (N.C. Ct. App. 2012) ("Generally, this Court will not find excusable neglect where the party establishes merely that he was ignorant of the judicial process or misunderstood the nature of the action against him, even when the party has little education."); Creasman v. Creasman, 152 N.C. App. 119, 124, 566 S.E.2d 725, 729 (2002) ("This Court has . . . held that the failure of a party to obtain an attorney is not excusable neglect."); Moore v. City of Raleigh, 135 N.C. App. 332, 336–37, 520 S.E.2d 133, 137 (1999) (claimant's ignorance of judicial process and lack of counsel not grounds for setting aside Industrial Commission decision); Hall v. Hall, 89 N.C. App. 685, 688, 366 S.E.2d 882, 885 (1988) ("[A] party may not show excusable neglect by merely establishing that she failed to obtain an attorney and was ignorant of the judicial process."); Gregg v. Steele, 24 N.C. App. 310, 311, 210 S.E.2d 434, 435 (1974) (neglect not excused by lack of counsel or ignorance of legal process).

85. Grant v. Cox, 106 N.C. App. 122, 125–26, 415 S.E.2d 378, 381 (1992).

previously hired counsel in other matters but did not attend to his case because "he did not believe plaintiffs could prevail";[86]

- defendant failed to respond to a complaint and summons because he thought the documents were a "prelude" to litigation and did not comprehend that an actual court case had been filed;[87]
- a party failed to retain new counsel because she believed that "nothing was happening" in the case and that the opposing party would inform her of important developments;[88] and
- defendant received a summons and complaint but did not obtain counsel or respond because he assumed plaintiff's counsel would contact him with a hearing date.[89]

In an exceptional case, the Supreme Court affirmed relief for a defendant who relied on her husband's assurances that judgment had been paid and that she did not need to respond to the summons and complaint.[90] As the Court of Appeals recently explained, however, this family reliance exception has been construed narrowly and has not been expanded beyond husband and wife.[91]

---

86. Boyd v. Marsh, 47 N.C. App. 491, 492, 267 S.E.2d 394, 395 (1980).

87. Scoggins v. Jacobs, 169 N.C. App. 411, 415, 610 S.E.2d 428, 432 (2005).

88. Milton M. Croom Charitable Remainder Unitrust v. Hedrick, 188 N.C. App. 262, 267–68, 654 S.E.2d 716, 720–21 (2008).

89. JMM Plumbing & Utils., Inc. v. Basnight Constr. Co., Inc., 169 N.C. App. 199, 203, 609 S.E.2d 487, 490–91 (2005).

90. Thomas M. McInnis & Assocs., Inc. v. Hall, 318 N.C. 421, 425–26, 349 S.E.2d 552, 555 (1986); *see also* Hickory White Trucks, Inc. v. Greene, 34 N.C. App. 279, 281–82, 237 S.E.2d 862, 864 (1977) (wife—the "feme defendant"—who relied on her husband's assurances granted relief as to part of claims). Actual reliance on the assurances, however, is required. Gregg v. Steele, 24 N.C. App. 310, 311, 210 S.E.2d 434, 435 (1974).

91. Grier *ex rel.* Brown v. Guy, 741 S.E.2d 338, 341 (N.C. Ct. App. 2012) (citing Mitchell Cty. Dep't of Soc. Servs. v. Carpenter, 127 N.C. App. 353, 356–57, 489 S.E.2d 437, 439 (1997)). It is questionable whether even a husband–wife reliance exception remains valid in modern times.

In addition, a party will not be relieved from judgment on grounds that its attorney was the cause of the neglect.[92] In *Briley v. Farabow*, the North Carolina Supreme Court held that "[c]learly, an attorney's negligence in handling a case constitutes inexcusable neglect and should not be grounds for relief under the 'excusable neglect' provision of Rule 60(b)(1)."[93] The court explained,

> In enacting Rule 60(b)(1), the General Assembly did not intend to sanction an attorney's negligence by making it beneficial for the client and to thus provide an avenue for potential abuse. . . . Looking only to the attorney to assume responsibility for the client's case, however, leads to undesirable results. . . . If the lawyer's neglect protected the client from ill consequences, neglect would become all too common. It would be a free good—the neglect would protect the client, and because the client could not suffer the lawyer would not suffer either. Thus, we hold that an attorney's negligent conduct is not "excusable neglect" under Rule 60(b)(1) and that in determining such, the court must look at the behavior of the attorney.[94]

Under this imputation rule, the Court of Appeals has repeatedly declined to grant relief on the basis of excusable neglect, such as when counsel

- failed to ensure a notice of appeal had been filed;[95]

92. *See, e.g.*, Vaglio v. Town & Campus Int'l, Inc., 71 N.C. App. 250, 254, 322 S.E.2d 3, 6 (1984) (attorney's failure to submit summary judgment briefs not excusable where there was ample time to do so).

93. 348 N.C. 537, 546, 501 S.E.2d 649, 655 (1998).

94. *Id.* at 546–47, 501 S.E.2d at 655 (internal quotation and citations omitted). The court went on to deny relief because the cause of the dismissal was the attorney's inexcusable negligence in failing to comply with deadlines to designate expert witnesses. *Id.* at 547–48, 501 S.E.2d at 655–56.

95. Sellers v. FMC Corp., 216 N.C. App. 134, 141–42, 716 S.E.2d 661, 666–67 (2011) ("The test for excusable neglect generally does not allow for

- failed to note the date of entry of dismissal, resulting in a missed deadline for refiling the action;[96]
- entered into a settlement agreement on defendants' behalf without defendants' knowledge or consent;[97]
- failed to meet court-ordered deadlines for service of discovery responses;[98]
- failed to inform trustee of a deposition date;[99]
- did not forward requests for admission to plaintiffs in order to obtain their timely responses or request an extension of time to respond;[100]
- mistakenly failed to take note of the order for sanctions that formed the basis of the judgment and thought that the motion for sanctions that appeared on the court docket pertained to another defendant;[101]

---

attorney negligence.").

96. Nieto-Espinoza v. Lowder Constr., Inc., 748 S.E.2d 8, 12 (N.C. Ct. App. 2013) (holding that such "carelessness if not negligence" was not excusable).

97. Purcell Int'l Textile Grp., Inc. v. Algemene AFW N.V., 185 N.C. App. 135, 139–40, 647 S.E.2d 667, 671–72 (2007) (noting that *Briley* is the "controlling authority on the issue of excusable neglect" rather than older cases where relief was allowed despite attorney neglect).

98. Parris v. Light, 146 N.C. App. 515, 521–22, 553 S.E.2d 96, 99–100 (2001); *cf.* Rose v. Forester, 201 N.C. App. 159, 688 S.E.2d 118, 2009 WL 3818848, *3–4 (2009) (unpublished) (where defendant Maryland corporation's North Carolina process agent failed to forward a complaint to defendant, the agent's inexcusable neglect was imputed to defendant).

99. Henderson v. Wachovia Bank of N.C., N.A., 145 N.C. App. 621, 627–28, 551 S.E.2d 464, 469 (2001) (citing *Briley*).

100. Brown v. Foremost Affiliated Ins. Servs., Inc., 158 N.C. App. 727, 729, 582 S.E.2d 335, 337 (2003). Plaintiffs were not entitled to a finding of excusable neglect because their argument was "predicated on the errors of [their] former counsel." *Id.* at 732, 582 S.E.2d at 339 (citing *Briley*).

101. Clark v. Penland, 146 N.C. App. 288, 292, 552 S.E.2d 243, 245 (2001) ("Ignorance, inexcusable negligence, or carelessness on the part of an attorney will not provide grounds for relief under Rule 60(b)(1)."); *see also* Estate of Carlsen v. Carlsen, 165 N.C. App. 674, 679, 599 S.E.2d 581, 585 (2004) ("[A]lthough attorney error may qualify as a reason for granting relief . . .

- did not comprehend the legal ramifications of voluntarily dismissing a defendant from the lawsuit.[102]

Meritorious defense.

In addition to demonstrating excusable neglect, the moving party must also show the court that it has a "meritorious defense" to the underlying cause of action.[103] As the Court of Appeals has explained, "The defendant must have a real or substantial defense on the merits, otherwise the court would engage in the vain work of setting a judgment aside when it would be its duty to enter again the same judgment on motion of the adverse party."[104] In addition, "it would be a waste of judicial economy to vacate a judgment or order when the movant could not prevail on the merits of the civil action."[105] To that end, there is authority for a trial court to grant relief as to only that portion of the action for which the defendant has demonstrated a meritorious

---

under certain conditions, neither ignorance nor carelessness on the part of an attorney will provide grounds for such relief.").

102. Couch v. Private Diagnostic Clinic, 133 N.C. App. 93, 103–04, 515 S.E.2d 30, 38 (1999) (holding it was error to reinstate the party and noting that "mistakes of legal advice or mistakes of law are not within the contemplation of Rule 60(b)(1)."). In a similar recent case in the context of Rule 6(b), lack of familiarity with rules governing time limits on refiling claims did not provide a basis for arguing excusable neglect to gain relief from dismissal of plaintiff's action with prejudice. Glynne v. Wilson Med. Ctr., 762 S.E.2d 645, 652 (N.C. Ct. App. 2014) ("[C]arelessness or negligence or ignorance of the rules of procedure . . . does not constitute 'excusable neglect.'").

103. Norton v. Sawyer, 30 N.C. App. 420, 423, 227 S.E.2d 148, 152 (1976); Doxol Gas of Angier, Inc. v. Barefoot, 10 N.C. App. 703, 704, 179 S.E.2d 890, 891 (1971). The court need not, of course, reach the question of meritorious defense if there is not first a showing of excusable neglect. Scoggins v. Jacobs, 169 N.C. App. 411, 413, 610 S.E.2d 428, 431 (2005); Estate of Teel v. Darby, 129 N.C. App. 604, 611, 500 S.E.2d 759, 764 (1998); Howard v. Williams, 40 N.C. App. 575, 580, 253 S.E.2d 571, 574 (1979)).

104. *Norton*, 30 N.C. App. at 423, 227 S.E.2d at 152 (quotation omitted).

105. Oxford Plastics v. Goodson, 74 N.C. App. 256, 259, 328 S.E.2d 7, 9 (1985).

defense.[106] While the term meritorious *defense* is the commonly used phrase to describe this requirement, a meritorious claim (or counterclaim) is appropriate if the party moving for relief was a claimant rather than a defendant.[107]

In determining the existence of a meritorious defense, the court's task is to examine whether the movant has in good faith presented a valid *prima facie* defense.[108] The court does not actually weigh the evidence and thereby deprive the movant of his right to a jury trial.

> Where a party, in good faith, shows facts which raise an issue sufficient to defeat his adversary, if it be found in his favor, it is for the jury to try the issue and not for the judge, who merely finds whether on their face the facts show a good defense in law; otherwise, the defendant, though he establish ever so clear a case of excusable neglect entitling him to have the judgment set aside, would be deprived of the right of trial by the jury of the issue thus raised.[109]

A proper prima facie meritorious defense was alleged in a debt case where defendant did more than merely deny the indebtedness but

---

106. *See, e.g.*, Emdur Metal Prods, Inc. v. Super Dollar Stores, Inc., 55 N.C. App. 668, 670, 286 S.E.2d 642, 643 (1982) (portion of default judgment set aside); Hickory White Trucks, Inc. v. Greene, 34 N.C. App. 279, 282, 237 S.E.2d 862, 864 (1977) (relief granted as to the cause of action for which there was a meritorious defense and denied as to the other).

107. Baker v. Baker, 115 N.C. App. 337, 340, 444 S.E.2d 478, 480–81 (1994) (citing Brady v. Town of Chapel Hill, 277 N.C. 720, 178 S.E.2d 446 (1971); *see, e.g.*, Barclays Am. Corp. v. Howell, 81 N.C. App. 654, 657–58, 345 S.E.2d 228, 230 (1986) (discussing existence of plaintiff's meritorious case).

108. *Oxford Plastics*, 74 N.C. App. at 260, 328 S.E.2d at 10.

109. *Id.* at 260, 328 S.E.2d at 10 (citations omitted); *see also* Chaparral Supply v. Bell, 76 N.C. App. 119, 120, 331 S.E.2d 735, 736 (1985) ("[T]he trial court does not hear the facts but determines only whether the movant has pleaded a meritorious defense."); Thelen v. Thelen, 53 N.C. App. 684, 692, 281 S.E.2d 737, 742 (1981) ("At a hearing for a Rule 60(b) motion it is not required that a meritorious defense be proved, only that a prima facie defense exists.") (citing U.S.I.F. Wynnewood Corp. v. Soderquist, 27 N.C. App. 611, 219 S.E.2d 787 (1975)).

instead also contended that the debt had been repaid as part of a separate transaction. The court explained that "[p]laintiffs' contention that the transaction defendant relies on makes little business sense is not dispositive. The trial court should not attempt to resolve the factual dispute but should determine only if the movant has sufficiently forecast a meritorious defense."[110] Defendants showed a prima facie defense in a contract case by making sufficient allegations that a partner's actions were not authorized by the partnership.[111] A trial court also properly granted relief from a judgment of absolute divorce where defendant showed she could put forth a counterclaim for equitable distribution.[112] And in a support action, a meritorious defense was shown by allegations of need for increased support for the minor children and that the former husband had incorrectly represented the plaintiff's financial circumstances in his submissions to the court.[113]

Newly Discovered Evidence—Rule 60(b)(2)

Rule 60 also provides relief for "[n]ewly discovered evidence which by due diligence could not have been discovered in time to move for a new trial under Rule 59(b)."[114] If a party could have based a timely new trial motion under Rule 59 on the evidence at issue, relief under

---

110. Dollar v. Tapp, 103 N.C. App. 162, 165, 404 S.E.2d 482, 484 (1991); *see also* PYA Monarch, Inc. v. Ray Lackey Enters., Inc., 96 N.C. App. 225, 229, 385 S.E.2d 170, 172 (1989) (mere denial of indebtedness was not sufficient assertion of meritorious defense in action to collect money owed on account); Holcombe v. Bowman, 8 N.C. App. 673, 675–76, 175 S.E.2d 362, 364 (1970) (mere denial of plaintiff's allegations, with no supporting facts, insufficient to constitute meritorious defense).

111. *Oxford Plastics*, 74 N.C. App. at 261–62, 328 S.E.2d at 10–11; *see also Barclays*, 81 N.C. App. at 657–58, 345 S.E.2d at 230 (meritorious claim for breach of contract shown where plaintiff presented contract in question, pertinent account statements, and affidavits with relevant allegations).

112. *Baker*, 115 N.C. App. at 341–42, 444 S.E.2d at 481–82.

113. *Thelen*, 53 N.C. App. at 692, 281 S.E.2d at 742.

114. Rule 60(b)(2).

Rule 60(b) is inappropriate.[115] A motion under Rule 60(b)(2) must be brought within a reasonable time[116] and not later than one year after entry of the judgment or order.[117] The trial court's decision to grant or deny relief from judgment for newly discovered evidence is reviewed for abuse of discretion.[118]

Evidence is newly discovered if it existed prior to the entry of the order or judgment but could not have been discovered by the moving party through reasonable diligence.[119] In a nuisance action, evidence that plaintiffs purchased additional land adjacent to the alleged nuisance could not qualify as a basis for relief because the purchase occurred after judgment.[120] In a worker's compensation action, evidence of plaintiff's physical activity after the Industrial Commission's final award was not in existence at the time of the order and, therefore, did not qualify as newly discovered evidence.[121] In another case before the

---

115. Jacobsen v. McMillan, 124 N.C. App. 128, 136, 476 S.E.2d 368, 372 (1996); Conrad Indus., Inc. v. Sonderegger, 69 N.C. App. 159, 162, 316 S.E.2d 327, 328 (1984). For a discussion of motions for new trial under Rule 59(a)(4) based on newly discovered evidence, see section in Part I, Chapter 2 titled "Newly Discovered Evidence—Rule 59(a)(4)." Because the two rules are subject to very similar analyses, the cases cited in that section are instructive in the Rule 60(b) context as well.

116. Rule 60(b); *see, e.g.*, *Sonderegger*, 69 N.C. App. at 160–63, 316 S.E.2d at 328–30 (motion filed months after the verdict but shortly after discovery of new evidence was reasonable).

117. Rule 60(b); *see, e.g.*, Grupen v. Thomasville Furniture Indus., 28 N.C. App. 119, 121, 220 S.E.2d 201, 202 (1975) (motion not filed within one year of North Carolina Industrial Commission's order). As with all of Rule 60, this section provides post-judgment relief, so it is not an appropriate means for reopening the evidence before a final decision has been reached. Kingston v. Lyon Const., Inc., 207 N.C. App. 703, 709, 701 S.E.2d 348, 353 (2010).

118. *In re* L.H., 210 N.C. App. 355, 367, 708 S.E.2d 191, 199 (2011); *Kingston*, 207 N.C. App. at 709, 701 S.E.2d at 353 (citing Davis v. Davis, 360 N.C. 518, 523, 631 S.E.2d 114, 118 (2006)).

119. *L.H.*, 210 N.C. App. at 367, 708 S.E.2d at 199 (citing Broadbent v. Allison, 176 N.C. App. 359, 364, 626 S.E.2d 758, 762–63 (2006)).

120. *Broadbent*, 176 N.C. App. at 364, 626 S.E.2d at 762–63.

121. Hill v. Hanes Corp., 79 N.C. App. 67, 71, 339 S.E.2d 1, 4 (1986).

Industrial Commission, the results of a medical exam on plaintiff could not be considered under Rule 60(b) because the exam was conducted after the commission's order.[122] And in a paternity action, evidence that defendant fathered another child over a year after the judgment was not newly discovered evidence to prove that defendant's sterilization procedure had reversed itself.[123] The court explained that, if evidence arising *after* judgment could be considered newly discovered, "litigation would never come to an end."[124]

Rule 60 provides no relief if the evidence could have been discovered with reasonable diligence. For example, in *Robinson v. Trantham*,[125] a car accident case, the driver's estate sought relief on grounds that new evidence would compel a jury instruction as to plaintiff's contributory negligence. After judgment, defendant's estate learned that the driver's blood—held in the custody of the office of the chief medical examiner—could be analyzed. After receiving results showing alcohol, cocaine, and methamphetamines, the estate sought to use the analysis to show that plaintiff should have known the driver was intoxicated. The trial court denied relief under Rule 60(b), finding that the driver's blood analysis could have been obtained prior to judgment in the exercise of due diligence, and the Court of Appeals affirmed.[126] In *Waldrop v. Young*,[127] a lease dispute, defendant sought relief from judgment upon locating a witness to testify about the leaky condition of the building's roof. Although defendant had searched for the witness at her address, he had neither subpoenaed her nor attempted to contact her by mail despite evidence showing that he had her last known address.

---

122. Harris v. Frank L. Blum Constr. Co., 10 N.C. App. 413, 421, 179 S.E.2d 148, 153 (1971); *see also Grupen*, 28 N.C. App. at 121, 220 S.E.2d at 202 (new affidavit by physician testifying that injury was permanent not newly discovered because it was not evidence of facts existing at time of trial).

123. Cole v. Cole, 90 N.C. App. 724, 728–29, 370 S.E.2d 272, 274 (1988).

124. *Id.* at 728, 370 S.E.2d at 274.

125. 195 N.C. App. 687, 673 S.E.2d 771 (2009).

126. *Id.* at 695, 673 S.E.2d at 777.

127. 104 N.C. App. 294, 408 S.E.2d 883 (1991).

Under these facts, defendant's lack of diligence foreclosed relief under Rule 60(b).[128] By contrast, in *Conrad Industries, Inc. v. Sonderegger*,[129] a trade secrets case, the trial court did not abuse its discretion in setting aside a judgment in defendant's favor after a key defense witness came forward to plaintiff some months after the verdict and admitted to lying about material issues in the case. The trial court found facts establishing that there was no reasonable action the plaintiff could have taken to discover before or during trial that the evidence was perjured.[130]

---

128. *Id.* at 297, 408 S.E.2d at 884–85; *see also* Hodgin v. United Cmty. Bank, Franklin, 734 S.E.2d 630, 633 (N.C. Ct. App. 2012) (court erred in granting relief from judgment confirming arbitration award because evidence existed and was known to plaintiffs up to four years before hearing); Baker v. Charlotte Motor Speedway, Inc., 180 N.C. App. 296, 302, 636 S.E.2d 829, 833–34 (2006) (evidence from plaintiff's work and medical history could not form basis for relief where he had failed to supply the information to his own counsel); Deer Corp. v. Carter, 177 N.C. App. 314, 329, 629 S.E.2d 159, 170 (2006) (relief denied where movants had opportunity to obtain evidence prior to the hearing but failed to do so); Parks v. Green, 153 N.C. App. 405, 412–13, 571 S.E.2d 14, 19 (2002) (defendant did not show why he could not have procured his own affidavit in context of earlier hearing); Higgins v. Michael Powell Builders, 132 N.C. App. 720, 725, 515 S.E.2d 17, 21 (1999) (evidence regarding employment status was no basis for relief because it was reasonably ascertainable prior to commission's award); Staples by Staples v. Woman's Clinic of Albemarle, P.A., 73 N.C. App. 617, 618–19, 327 S.E.2d 58, 59 (1985) (no abuse of discretion to deny relief based on later discovery of standard of care expert); Harris v. Family Med. Ctr., 38 N.C. App. 716, 719, 248 S.E.2d 768, 770 (1978) (evidence to establish accrual date, thus preventing dismissal based on statute of limitations, could have been located before judgment with due diligence); Grupen v. Thomasville Furniture Indus., 28 N.C. App. 119, 121, 220 S.E.2d 201, 203 (1975) (relief denied where plaintiff was not diligent in developing his presentation of medical evidence); Lattimore v. Powell, 15 N.C. App. 522, 523–24, 190 S.E.2d 288, 289–90 (1972) (no relief based on existence of prior action tolling the statute of limitations because information was readily available to plaintiff prior to judgment).

129. 69 N.C. App. 159, 316 S.E.2d 327 (1984).

130. *Id.* at 160–63, 316 S.E.2d at 328–30.

Relief also will not be granted based on newly discovered evidence if the evidence does not materially impact the judgment. In general, evidence that is largely cumulative, corroborative, or intended simply to impeach a witness's credibility will not suffice.[131] In *Waldrop* (discussed above), the testimony of the newly located witness merely corroborated earlier evidence about the leaky roof and, thus, was not enough to justify setting aside the judgment.[132] And in a case alleging multiple business torts, the trial court did not err in denying relief upon determining that the new evidence corroborated its prior findings and would not have materially affected the outcome.[133] But in *Davis v. Sellers*,[134] the trial court erred in concluding that newly discovered evidence regarding defendant's status as a real estate broker did not affect the judgment. The Court of Appeals concluded that the new evidence brought the matter under the unfair trade practices act as a matter of law and relief from judgment was therefore required.[135]

Fraud, Misrepresentation, or Other Misconduct of an Adverse Party—Rule 60(b)(3)

As the language of Rule 60(b)(3) makes clear, relief based on fraud, misrepresentation, or other misconduct is available only for behavior of an adverse party (or, by extension, its counsel).[136] The rule has not

---

131. Cole v. Cole, 90 N.C. App. 724, 727, 370 S.E.2d 272, 273–74 (1988) (discussing pre-rules guidance from Brown v. Sheets, 197 N.C. 268, 273–74, 148 S.E.233, 236 (1929)).

132. 104 N.C. App. at 296–97, 408 S.E.2d at 884.

133. *Deer Corp.*, 177 N.C. App. at 329, 629 S.E.2d at 170; *see also* Broadbent v. Allison, 176 N.C. App. 359, 365, 626 S.E.2d 758, 763 (2006) (evidence not a basis for relief where it did not clearly contradict plaintiff's earlier testimony); *cf.* Chandak v. Elec. Interconnect Corp., 144 N.C. App. 258, 265, 550 S.E.2d 25, 30 (2001) (new deposition testimony revealed information already available to the parties).

134. 115 N.C. App. 1, 443 S.E.2d 879 (1994).

135. *Id.* at 7–9, 443 S.E.2d at 883–84.

136. Autry v. Autry, 207 N.C. App. 514, 518, 700 S.E.2d 141, 143–44 (2010) (relief based on misrepresentations by opposing counsel); Harbin Yinhai Tech. Dev. Co., Ltd. v. Greentree Fin. Grp., Inc., 196 N.C. App. 615, 625–26, 677 S.E.2d 854, 861 (2009) (trial court erred in concluding it had no

been broadened to address, for example, misconduct by the moving party's own counsel[137] or a third-party witness.[138]

As to fraud specifically, the rule also states that either intrinsic or extrinsic fraud may be raised in a motion brought under Rule 60(b)(3).[139] Intrinsic fraud is fraud pertaining to the trial itself and affecting the court's or the jury's determination of the issues on the merits.[140] Perjury, for example, is intrinsic fraud,[141] as is manufacture of false evidence[142] and concealment or misrepresentation of evidence.[143]

---

jurisdiction to address conduct of adverse party's attorney); *see also* Carter v. Carr, 68 N.C. App. 23, 26–27, 314 S.E.2d 281, 283–84 (1984) (analyzing alleged opposing counsel misconduct but finding no material misconduct).

137. Henderson v. Wachovia Bank of N.C., N.A., 145 N.C. App. 621, 628, 551 S.E.2d 464, 469 (2001); Chandak v. Elec. Interconnect Corp., 144 N.C. App. 258, 265, 550 S.E.2d 25, 30 (2001).

138. McGinnis v. Robinson, 43 N.C. App. 1, 7, 258 S.E.2d 84, 88 (1979). Typically, misconduct by others should be addressed as a potential irregularity under the more general scope of Rule 60(b)(6). *See infra* section titled "Misconduct of Others."

139. Rule 60(b)(3) ("whether heretofore denominated intrinsic or extrinsic"); Textile Fabricators, Inc. v. C.R.C. Indus., Inc., 43 N.C. App. 530, 532, 259 S.E.2d 570, 571–72 (1979).

140. Caswell Realty Assocs. I, L.P. v. Andrews Co., Inc., 121 N.C. App. 483, 486, 466 S.E.2d 310, 312 (1996); *In re* Will of Evans, 46 N.C. App. 72, 75–76, 264 S.E.2d 387, 389 (1980).

141. McCoy v. Justice, 199 N.C. 602, 605, 155 S.E.2d 452, 454 (1930); Johnson v. Herbie's Place, 157 N.C. App. 168, 175, 579 S.E.2d 110, 116 (2003); *Textile Fabricators,* 43 N.C. App. at 532, 259 S.E.2d at 571 (citing Horne v. Edwards, 215 N.C. 622, 3 S.E.2d 1 (1939)). Although perjury is recognized as a potential basis for relief, our courts traditionally have been very hesitant to consider it, and in a relatively recent case the Court of Appeals reasserted older case language stating that "judgment cannot be vacated because of perjured testimony unless the party charged with perjury has been indicted or convicted or . . . has passed beyond the jurisdiction of courts and is not amendable to criminal process." *Herbie's Place,* 157 N.C. App. at 176, 579 S.E.2d at 116 (citing Gilliken v. Springle, 254 N.C. 240, 244, 118 S.E.2d 611, 614 (1961)). *But see* Conrad Indus., Inc. v. Sonderegger, 69 N.C. App. 159, 160–63, 316 S.E.2d 327, 328–30 (1984) (allowing relief based on discovery that key testimony was perjured).

142. *Herbie's Place,* 157 N.C. App. at 175, 579 S.E.2d at 116.

143. *Intrinsic Fraud,* Black's Law Dictionary (10th ed. 2014).

Extrinsic fraud—or collateral fraud—is fraud that "deprives the unsuccessful party of an opportunity to present his case to the court" and prevents full participation in the proceeding.[144] Although both types of fraud may be addressed by motion under Rule 60(b)(3), only *extrinsic* fraud may be the subject of a separate action to challenge the judgment.[145] Arguments based on intrinsic fraud, therefore, are limited to the Rule 60 context and must be brought within the applicable one-year time limit.[146]

To seek relief based on an adversary's misconduct, the moving party must show a material effect on the course of the proceedings—typically that the misconduct prevented that party from properly presenting its case or defense. The Court of Appeals has noted that "[t]o obtain relief under Rule 60(b)(3), the moving party must 1) have a meritorious defense, 2) that he was prevented from presenting prior to judgment,

---

144. *Caswell,* 121 N.C. App. at 486, 466 S.E.2d at 312 (quoting Stokley v. Stokley, 30 N.C. App. 351, 354–55, 227 S.E.2d 131, 134 (1976)); *Will of Evans,* 46 N.C. App. at 75–76, 264 S.E.2d at 389.

145. Smith v. Smith, 334 N.C. 81, 86, 431 S.E.2d 196, 199 (1993); Hooks v. Eckman, 159 N.C. App. 681, 685, 587 S.E.2d 352, 354 (2003); *Caswell,* 121 N.C. App. at 486, 466 S.E.2d at 312; *Textile Fabricators,* 43 N.C. App. at 532, 259 S.E.2d at 572; *Stokley,* 30 N.C. App. at 354–55, 227 S.E.2d at 134.

146. *Textile Fabricators,* 43 N.C. App. at 532, 259 S.E.2d at 572; *Stokley,* 30 N.C. App. at 354–55, 227 S.E.2d at 134. It should be noted, however, that *foreign* judgments may not be challenged on the basis of intrinsic fraud under Rule 60 or otherwise. Lang v. Lang, 108 N.C. App. 440, 450–51, 424 S.E.2d 190, 195 (1993) ("[T]o make a successful attack upon a foreign judgment on the basis of fraud, it is necessary that *extrinsic* fraud be alleged."); Hewett v. Zegarzewski, 90 N.C. App. 443, 446–47, 368 S.E.2d 877, 878–89 (1988) (intrinsic misrepresentations about assets in procuring settlement were not a basis for setting aside a foreign judgment). Recently, in *DocRx, Inc. v. EMI Services of North Carolina, LLC,* the North Carolina Supreme Court held that "the defenses preserved under North Carolina's [Uniform Enforcement of Foreign Judgments Act] are limited by the Full Faith and Credit Clause to those defenses which are directed to the validity and enforcement of a foreign judgment"—such as extrinsic fraud, jurisdictional matters, and accord and satisfaction—and not to defenses on the merits or other matters that could have been litigated in the rendering court. 367 N.C. 371, 382, 758 S.E.2d 390, 397, *cert. denied,* 135 S. Ct. 678, 190 L. Ed. 2d 390 (U.S. 2014).

3) because of fraud, misrepresentation or misconduct by the adverse party."[147] In *Autry v. Autry*, the court affirmed the trial court's decision to grant relief based on the misrepresentations of defendant's counsel in a court proceeding because those misrepresentations induced plaintiff to enter into a settlement agreement resolving a post-settlement support action.[148] In a similar case, a former wife was entitled to have a prior order for alimony and equitable distribution set aside after discovering that her former husband had deliberately failed to inform the court about certain material debts that would have affected the

---

147. Milton M. Croom Charitable Remainder Unitrust v. Hedrick, 188 N.C. App. 262, 268, 654 S.E.2d 716, 721 (2008) (concluding that opposing counsel's failure to inform an unrepresented party of a hearing date was not misconduct where counsel had no duty to do so). This causation language in *Croom* is identical to that of the Fourth Circuit Court of Appeals interpreting the parallel provision in Federal Rule of Civil Procedure 60(b)(3). *See, e.g.*, Green v. Foley, 856 F.2d 660, 665 (4th Cir. 1998) (citing Square Constr. Co. v. Washington Metro. Area Transit Auth., 657 F.2d 68, 71 (4th Cir. 1981)). In *Green*, the court found that a material misrepresentation by plaintiff throughout the litigation—which was not corrected until it was too late for defendant to present his meritorious defense based on that information—compelled relief under Federal Rule of Civil Procedure 60(b)(3). Plaintiff's failure to disclose the information "struck at the very heart of the fact finding process that is entrusted to the [trial] court." *Green*, 856 F.2d at 666–67 (quotations omitted); *see also* Static Control Components, Inc. v. Darkprint Imaging, Inc., 240 F. Supp. 2d 465, 476 (M.D.N.C. 2002) (relief appropriate under Rule 60(b)(3) when a party fails to disclose "'obviously pertinent requested discovery material'"). A similar requirement for challenging a judgment for misconduct exists in the arbitration context, where there must be a "nexus between the alleged fraud and the basis for the panel's decision." Trafalgar House Constr., Inc. v. MSL Enters., Inc., 128 N.C. App. 252, 258, 494 S.E.2d 613, 617 (1998) (finding no such nexus where the arbitrators did not consider the alleged misrepresentations in making their decision).

148. 207 N.C. App. 514, 517–18, 700 S.E.2d 141, 143–44 (2010). By contrast, in the unpublished case of *Washburn v. Washburn*, relief was denied because defendant failed to show how the false testimony prevented him from fully and fairly litigating his claim for equitable distribution. 749 S.E.2d 112, 2013 WL 4004123, *3 (N.C. Ct. App. 2013).

distribution.[149] And a consent judgment was properly set aside where the evidence supported a conclusion that the movant was under duress from the adverse party due to threats of harm to and loss of visitation with her children.[150] By contrast, a trial judge did not abuse his discretion in declining to set aside a custody order after finding that the false testimony of a witness—allegedly suborned by the adverse party—did not materially affect the judge's custody decision.[151]

Void Judgments—Rule 60(b)(4)

Rule 60(b)(4) allows a party to seek relief if "the judgment is void." The time limits set in Rule 60(b) do not apply to motions based on void judgments.[152] A judgment is void if the court lacks subject matter jurisdiction over the matter, personal jurisdiction over a party subject to the order, or authority to enter the order.[153] A judgment generally is not void merely because it is based on an error or misapplication of law, fact, or procedure or is otherwise irregular: For an order to be void, the court must lack legal authority to hear or determine the matter or lack jurisdictional control over one or more parties to the controversy.[154]

---

149. Sloan v. Sloan, 151 N.C. App. 399, 405, 566 S.E.2d 97, 101–02 (2002). This case analyzed adverse party misconduct but was decided under Rule 60(b)(6) because the fraud was discovered after the one-year time limit for bringing actions under Rule 60(b)(3).

150. Coppley v. Coppley, 128 N.C. App. 658, 667, 496 S.E.2d 611, 618 (1998); *see also* Yurek v. Shaffer, 198 N.C. App. 67, 79–81, 678 S.E.2d 738, 746–47 (2009) (noting that relief under Rule 60(b) may be granted based on duress or undue influence but finding insufficient evidence based on the facts).

151. Vuncannon v. Vuncannon, 82 N.C. App. 255, 259–60, 346 S.E.2d 274, 276–77 (1986).

152. *See infra* section titled "Time Limits."

153. Ottway Burton, P.A. v. Blanton, 107 N.C. App. 615, 616, 421 S.E.2d 381, 382 (1992); Vaughn v. Vaughn, 99 N.C. App. 574, 576, 393 S.E.2d 567, 568 (1990); Allred v. Tucci, 85 N.C. App. 138, 142, 354 S.E.2d 291, 294 (1987).

154. Hillard v. Hillard, 223 N.C. App. 20, 22, 733 S.E.2d 176, 179 (2012); *Blanton*, 107 N.C. App. at 617, 421 S.E.2d at 383; *Vaughn*, 99 N.C. App. at 576, 393 S.E.2d at 568–69; Windham Distrib. Co., Inc. v. Davis, 72 N.C. App. 179, 181, 323 S.E.2d 506, 508 (1984); Howell v. Tunstall, 64 N.C. App.

Lack of Subject Matter Jurisdiction or Authority

Judgments have been properly challenged as void under this rule where the trial judge who entered the order was disqualified from presiding,[155] there was no jurisdiction without a prior valid consent judgment as to a separate legal issue,[156] the trial court was not authorized by statute to enter the order absent specific findings of fact required by statute,[157] a contempt order was not authorized with respect to a non-domestic consent order,[158] a petition in a juvenile proceeding was not verified in the manner specifically required by statute,[159] and a debtor did not first receive proper notice and service of exemption rights prior to issuance of execution order.[160] Also, a trial court was unauthorized to enter an order enforcing a memorandum of judgment because the memorandum was so vague in its terms that it failed to apprise the parties of their rights and obligations under it.[161]

703, 705, 308 S.E.2d 454, 456 (1983); *see also* Autry v. Autry, 207 N.C. App. 514, 519, 700 S.E.2d 141, 144 (2010) ("[A] void judgment [is] 'one which has a mere semblance but is lacking in some of the essential elements which would *authorize the court to proceed to judgment.*'"); Chandak v. Elec. Interconnect Corp., 144 N.C. App. 258, 263–64, 550 S.E.2d 25, 29–30 (2001) (analyzing authority of district court to issue sanctions related to small claims action).

155. Alpine Motors Corp. v. Hagwood, 233 N.C. 57, 59–60, 62 S.E.2d 518, 519–20 (1950) (under then-existing law); *see also* Smith v. Gupton, 110 N.C. App. 482, 485–86, 429 S.E.2d 737, 739 (1993) (under then-existing law, judgment void where entered out of session and district without consent); *cf.* Vance Constr. Co., Inc. v. Duane White Land Corp., 127 N.C. App. 493, 495–96, 490 S.E.2d 588, 589–90 (1997) (court's order void where judge not authorized to hold session of court at time order was entered).

156. Collar v. Collar, 86 N.C. App. 105, 108, 356 S.E.2d 407, 408–09 (1987).

157. *Allred*, 85 N.C. App. at 143–44, 354 S.E.2d at 295.

158. Hemric v. Groce, 154 N.C. App. 393, 399, 572 S.E.2d 254, 258 (2002).

159. *In re* T.R.P., 360 N.C. 588, 593, 636 S.E.2d 787, 792 (2006).

160. First Union Nat'l Bank v. Rolfe, 83 N.C. App. 625, 629, 351 S.E.2d 117, 119–20 (1986).

161. Morrow v. Morrow, 94 N.C. App. 187, 190, 379 S.E.2d 705, 707 (1989).

In several cases, default judgments have been declared void because the statutory prerequisites to the court's authority to enter such a judgment were not met. In a recent case, for example, there was no authority for a clerk of court to enter a default judgment under Rule 55(b)(1) if the evidence showed that the defendant had made a prior appearance.[162] In a similar scenario, a clerk had no jurisdiction to enter a default judgment because the complaint did not establish a demand for damages in a "sum certain" as required by Rule 55(b)(1).[163] A court's entry of default judgment also was void because it was based on an unverified complaint and an affidavit that made no representations regarding personal jurisdiction as required by G.S. 1-75.11.[164] Default judgments also have been declared void where entered prior to an entry of default[165] and where the answer had been served prior to entry of default.[166]

Lack of Personal Jurisdiction

An order also is void if the court lacked personal jurisdiction over a party at the time of entry.[167] Courts typically obtain personal jurisdiction over a party through proper service of process, so when service is invalid, orders entered thereafter may be challenged as void under

---

162. Coastal Fed. Credit Union v. Falls, 217 N.C. App. 100, 106, 718 S.E.2d 192, 196 (2011). The Court of Appeals remanded the matter to the trial court for findings of fact as to whether defendant had appeared. *Id.* at 108, 718 S.E.2d at 197.

163. Basnight Const. Co., Inc. v. Peters & White Constr. Co., 169 N.C. App. 619, 623–24, 610 S.E.2d 469, 472 (2005).

164. McIlwaine v. Williams, 155 N.C. App. 426, 430, 573 S.E.2d 262, 264–65 (2002); *see also* Lemon v. Combs, 164 N.C. App. 615, 625, 596 S.E.2d 344, 350 (2004) (default judgment void where court had no proof of personal jurisdiction over defendant pursuant to statutory requirement).

165. *McIlwaine*, 155 N.C. App. at 430, 573 S.E.2d at 264–65; *see also* Hyder v. Dergance, 76 N.C. App. 317, 320, 332 S.E.2d 713, 715 (1985) (judgment entered prior to expiration of time to plead is void).

166. Quaker Furniture House, Inc. v. Ball, 31 N.C. App. 140, 141, 228 S.E.2d 475, 475–76 (1976).

167. Woods v. Billy's Auto., 174 N.C. App. 808, 812, 622 S.E.2d 193, 196 (2005) ("For a court to render a valid judgment against a defendant, it is

Rule 60(b)(4).[168] Examples have included failure to serve a summons,[169] service of a summons outside the time permitted for service under Rule 4,[170] improper service because documents were delivered to the wrong address,[171] service upon a corporation by a method not authorized under Rule 4,[172] and use of service by publication where the serving party did not meet the statutory prerequisites.[173] If, however, the service method in question established a presumption of proper service, the party moving for relief under Rule 60(b)(4) must rebut that presumption in order to show that the order is void.[174] If the record provides support for the trial court's findings as to whether the mov-

---

essential that jurisdiction of the party has been obtained . . . in some way allowed by law.").

168. Gibby v. Lindsey, 149 N.C. App. 470, 473, 560 S.E.2d 589, 591 (2002) ("A defect in service of process is jurisdictional rendering any judgment or order obtained thereby void."); Estate of Teel v. Darby, 129 N.C. App. 604, 608, 500 S.E.2d 759, 762 (1998). If the lack of proper service or notice is to a third party, however, and thus has no bearing on the authority of the court to enter judgment as to the movant, the judgment is not void. Barton v. Sutton, 152 N.C. App. 706, 708–09, 568 S.E.2d 264, 266 (2002).

169. Van Engen v. Que Sci., Inc., 151 N.C. App. 683, 688–89, 567 S.E.2d 179, 183 (2002).

170. Cole v. Cole, 37 N.C. App. 737, 738, 247 S.E.2d 16, 16–17 (1978).

171. Town of Cary v. Stallings, 97 N.C. App. 484, 488, 389 S.E.2d 143, 145 (1990).

172. Huggins v. Hallmark Enters., Inc., 84 N.C. App. 15, 21, 351 S.E.2d 779, 783 (1987).

173. Connette v. Jones, 196 N.C. App. 351, 353–54, 674 S.E.2d 751, 752–53 (2009); Cotton v. Jones, 160 N.C. App. 701, 703–04, 586 S.E.2d 806, 808 (2003); Cty. of Wayne v. Whitley, 72 N.C. App. 155, 160–61, 323 S.E.2d 458, 463 (1984); Thomas v. Thomas, 43 N.C. App. 638, 646–47, 260 S.E.2d 163, 169 (1979). In the recent case of *Chen v. Zou*, 780 S.E.2d 571, 575 (N.C. Ct. App. 2015), the Court of Appeals also held that it was proper to attack a divorce judgment as void under Rule 60(b)(4) where the plaintiff misrepresented to the court that his wife was properly served by publication.

174. Freeman v. Freeman, 155 N.C. App. 603, 607–08, 573 S.E.2d 708, 711–12 (2002) (movant successfully rebutted presumption of valid service established by acceptance of service); Gibby v. Lindsey, 149 N.C. App. 470, 473, 560 S.E.2d 589, 592 (2002) (movant failed to rebut the presumption).

ant rebutted the presumption, those findings will not be overturned on appeal.[175]

Even in the absence of valid service, however, a court may obtain jurisdiction over a party by general appearance or consent.[176] A corporation, for example, made a general appearance by attending a hearing and thereby waived its argument that the judgment was void for plaintiff's failure to properly serve the summons.[177] If the evidence as to service or appearance is conflicting, the trial court's findings, if supported by the competence evidence in the record, are conclusive on appeal.[178] Due process also requires that a non-party who will be subject to a court order be given notice and an opportunity to be heard. Thus a trial court's injunction order was void where it was entered without notice or hearing against a non-party who had communicated threats to a party outside the courtroom.[179]

---

175. *Freeman*, 155 N.C. App. at 607–08, 573 S.E.2d at 711–12 (trial court's findings of fact sufficient); Latimer v. Latimer, 136 N.C. App. 227, 229–30, 522 S.E.2d 801, 802–03 (1999) (trial court made findings based on sufficient evidence that acceptance of service had been backdated, rendering divorce judgment void).

176. Van Engen v. Que Sci., Inc., 151 N.C. App. 683, 690, 567 S.E.2d 179, 183 (2002) ("Jurisdiction of the court over the person of a defendant is obtained by service of process, voluntary appearance, or consent."); Wilson v. Wilson, 98 N.C. App. 230, 231, 390 S.E.2d 354, 355 (1990) (defendant submitted to court's jurisdiction by making a general appearance through a consent judgment). As G.S. 1-75.7 states,

> A court of this State having jurisdiction of the subject matter may, without serving a summons upon him, exercise jurisdiction in an action over a person . . . [w]ho makes a general appearance in an action; provided, that obtaining an extension of time within which to answer or otherwise plead shall not be considered a general appearance.

177. Woods v. Billy's Auto., 174 N.C. App. 808, 813–14, 622 S.E.2d 193, 197 (2005).

178. Macher v. Macher, 188 N.C. App. 537, 540–41, 656 S.E.2d 282, 284 (2008) (conflicting evidence regarding defendant's signing of answer); *Woods*, 174 N.C. App. at 811, 622 S.E.2d at 196.

179. Helbein v. S. Metals Co., Inc., 119 N.C. App. 431, 433, 458 S.E.2d 518, 519 (1995); *cf.* Nicks v. Nicks, 774 S.E.2d 365, 374–75 (N.C. Ct. App. 2015) (trial court had no authority to order equitable distribution of trust

Lack of Authority to Enter Consent Judgment

A court's authority to sign and enter a consent judgment depends on the unqualified consent of the parties to the agreement, and the judgment is void if consent does not exist at the time the court approves the agreement and enters it as judgment.[180] If a party's consent is withdrawn before entry, the consent judgment is void.[181] In many cases, parties have challenged consent judgments as void on grounds that their lawyers were unauthorized to enter into the agreements. Attorneys have no *inherent* authority to enter into settlement agreements or consent judgments that are binding on their clients.[182] When attorneys do act on behalf of their clients, however, they are presumed by the court to have their clients' authority to do so.[183] If this presumption of authority is rebutted, the consent judgment will be deemed void.[184] The party challenging the attorney's authority has the burden to rebut the

---

property where trust was not added as party); Campbell v. Campbell, 773 S.E.2d 93, 96 (N.C. Ct. App. 2015) (trial court had no authority to enter judgment requiring transfer of assets of entity that had not been added as a party).

180. Tevepaugh v. Tevepaugh, 135 N.C. App. 489, 492, 521 S.E.2d 117, 120 (1999); Hill v. Hill, 97 N.C. App. 499, 501, 389 S.E.2d 141, 142 (1990); *cf.* Alexander v. Iredell Cty. Bd. of Educ., 6 N.C. App. 92, 99–100, 169 S.E.2d 549, 554 (1969) (noting that a petition filed without knowledge and consent of person in whose name it was filed would be void).

181. Daniel v. Moore, 164 N.C. App. 534, 538, 596 S.E.2d 465, 468 (2004); *Tevepaugh*, 135 N.C. App. at 493, 521 S.E.2d at 120–21; Milner v. Littlejohn, 126 N.C. App. 184, 187, 484 S.E.2d 453, 456 (1997); *In re* Estate of Peebles, 118 N.C. App. 296, 298, 454 S.E.2d 854, 856 (1995).

182. Royal v. Hartle, 145 N.C. App. 181, 183, 551 S.E.2d 168, 170 (2001); Butler v. Weisler, 23 N.C. App. 233, 240, 208 S.E.2d 905, 910 (1974) (citing Howard v. Boyce, 254 N.C. 255, 118 S.E.2d 897 (1961)).

183. Guilford Cty. v. Eller, 146 N.C. App. 579, 581, 553 S.E.2d 235, 237 (2001); *Royal*, 145 N.C. App. at 183, 551 S.E.2d at 170; Nye, Mitchell, Jarvis & Bugg v. Oates, 109 N.C. App. 289, 292, 426 S.E.2d 291, 294 (1993).

184. *Tevepaugh*, 135 N.C. App. at 493, 521 S.E.2d at 120–21 (trial court did not first review the agreement with the parties as required by its terms); *Hill*, 97 N.C. App. at 501, 389 S.E.2d at 143 (record replete with evidence that party's consent not obtained).

presumption.[185] The mere lack of a party's signature on the agreement or consent judgment, or lack of the party's presence at time of entry, is not enough to show absence of consent to the judgment.[186] On disputed facts, a trial court's determination regarding the absence of consent will not be reversed on appeal if it is supported by competent evidence in the record.[187] Where the evidence is in dispute, and the trial court has made no findings as to the consent question, the Court of Appeals has remanded the matter to the trial court for those findings.[188]

Judgment Satisfied; Prior Judgment Reversed; No Longer Equitable—Rule 60(b)(5)

This category is an accumulation of traditional, practical grounds for equitable relief from a judgment. While still valid, they seldom appear in modern cases, at least by comparison to their counterparts.

Judgment Satisfied, Released, or Discharged

Once a judgment is paid, the creditor is not entitled to additional satisfaction,[189] and the debtor is entitled to have the judgment docket reflect that the judgment has been satisfied. The General Statutes

185. *Daniel*, 164 N.C. App. at 538–39, 596 S.E.2d at 468–69 (burden of showing consent withdrawn was met); *Eller*, 146 N.C. App. at 582, 553 S.E.2d at 237; *Royal*, 145 N.C. App. at 183, 551 S.E.2d at 171; *Peebles*, 118 N.C. App. at 299, 454 S.E.2d at 856–57 (presumption not rebutted); *Nye*, 109 N.C. App. at 292, 426 S.E.2d at 294; Nickels v. Nickels, 51 N.C. App. 690, 277 S.E.2d 577 (1981) (burden not met).

186. *Eller*, 146 N.C. App. at 581, 553 S.E.2d at 237 (lack of signature and presence); *Nye*, 109 N.C. App. at 293, 426 S.E.2d at 294 (lack of signature).

187. *Royal*, 145 N.C. App. at 184, 551 S.E.2d at 171; Greenhill v. Crabtree, 45 N.C. App. 49, 52–53, 262 S.E.2d 315, 317 (1980).

188. *Nye*, 109 N.C. App. at 293, 426 S.E.2d at 294; Caudle v. Ray, 69 N.C. App. 543, 546, 316 S.E.2d 909, 910 (1984). *But see Eller*, 146 N.C. App. at 582, 553 S.E.2d at 237 (where no findings by trial court, appellate court proceeded to review record and declined to hold that presumption had been rebutted).

189. Kavanau Real Estate Trust v. Debnam, 299 N.C. 510, 514, 263 S.E.2d 595, 598 (1980) (citing Bowen v. Iowa Nat'l Mut. Ins. Co., 270 N.C. 486, 155 S.E.2d 238 (1967)); Brown v. Vance, 55 N.C. App. 387, 389, 285 S.E.2d 333, 335 (1982).

provide a ready mechanism for the clerk of court to note payments made toward docketed judgments[190] as well as discharges of those judgments in bankruptcy.[191] In addition, there is a specific statutory procedure for filing a motion to have the clerk credit payments made or to note reversal or modification of a judgment on appeal.[192] These procedures likely capture most scenarios in which a party seeks to have the judgment docket reflect a judgment's satisfaction. Where it does not, however, Rule 60(b)(5) provides an equitable remedy in the trial court. For example, in *Witten Supply Co. v. Redmond*,[193] a motion under Rule 60(b)(5) was an appropriate means of challenging execution of a judgment through a foreclosure sale prior to confirmation of that sale. The trial court in that case properly granted a permanent injunction of the sale on grounds that the defendants had satisfied the debt through payments made under an earlier installment payment agreement.[194]

Prior Judgment Reversed or Vacated

This section of Rule 60 allows relief when a prior *judgment* upon which it is based has been reversed or otherwise vacated. Note that this language does not encompass arguments about changes in the *legal authority* upon which the court based its determination in the underlying action. Changes in applicable law have been addressed under the requirements of Rule 60(b)(6)[195] and under the general language of Rule 60(b)(5).

---

190. *See* G.S. 1-239.

191. *See* G.S. 1-245.

192. *See* G.S. 1-242.

193. 11 N.C. App. 173, 180 S.E.2d 487 (1971).

194. *Id.* at 175–76, 180 S.E.2d at 489.

195. *See* Hamby v. Profile Prods., LLC, 197 N.C. App. 99, 110, 676 S.E.2d 594, 601 (2009) ("Rule 60(b)(6) is properly employed to revisit a judgment affected by a subsequent change in the law."); and cases discussed *infra* in section titled "To Account for Certain Changes in the Law."

Prospective Application No Longer Equitable

Judgments generally have "prospective application" when they involve a permanent injunction or require long-term or ongoing payments. To that end, the Court of Appeals held that equitable relief from a permanent injunction contained in a prior summary judgment order was required under Rule 60(b)(5) because the injunction, which barred plaintiffs from further legal action, was the result of a pattern of gross negligence of their attorney.[196] In so holding, the Court of Appeals noted that, "[u]nquestionably, North Carolina courts have the equitable powers to dissolve or modify, on the grounds of change in circumstance, the type of injunction contained in [this] order[.]"[197] Likewise, a trial court properly exercised its discretion on equitable grounds to modify the terms of an earlier order of specific performance of a support agreement under Rule 60(b)(5). As the court stated, "An order directing specific performance may be modified if it is for specific performance in the future at various times, such as an order to perform pursuant to the terms of a contract with a long period to run."[198] It also was appropriate for a trial court to review on equitable grounds an earlier order that properly required destruction of a building foundation pursuant to a restrictive covenant. The appellate court remanded the matter to the trial court for consideration of the Rule 60(b) motion after the trial judge declined to do so under the mistaken impression that he lacked legal authority.[199] Also, a party was properly relieved from prospective application of a consent judgment resolving a dispute

---

196. Poston v. Morgan, 83 N.C. App. 295, 300–01, 350 S.E.2d 108, 111 (1986).

197. *Id.* at 299–300, 350 S.E.2d at 111 (citing McGuinn v. High Point, 219 N.C. 56, 13 S.E.2d 48 (1941)).

198. Harris v. Harris, 307 N.C. 684, 687–88, 300 S.E.2d 369, 372 (1983). The court also noted that a court may relieve a party from prospective application of the order and at the same time hold that party in contempt for past violations. *Id.* For a discussion of the propriety of modifying (rather than relieving a party from) a judgment under Rule 60(b), *see* discussion *infra* in section titled "Type of Relief Allowed."

199. Buie v. Johnston, 313 N.C. 586, 590–91, 330 S.E.2d 197, 199–200 (1985).

over enforcement of an order requiring defendant to pay plaintiff a portion of his retirement pay. Shortly after the consent judgment was entered, the United States Supreme Court issued a decision invalidating the legal argument for including the retirement pay in the consent judgment. With the legal basis for entering into the consent judgment no longer present, defendant was entitled to relief on equitable grounds.[200]

"Any Other Reason Justifying Relief"—Rule 60(b)(6)

Beyond the five specific categories just discussed is the broadly worded, general sixth category, which allows a court to relieve a party for "[a]ny other reason justifying relief from the operation of the judgment."[201] Rule 60(b)(6) has long been called "a grand reservoir of equitable power to do justice in a particular case."[202] To one seeking escape from a final order, this is promising language by any measure. In practice, though, this general category of Rule 60 is not a "catch-all."[203] As discussed below, Rule 60(b)(6)'s application is limited, providing relief only in "extraordinary circumstances" where the ends of justice require it and where the moving party forecasts a meritorious defense.

Not a Substitute for Appellate Review of Legal Errors

Although the language of Rule 60(b)(6) is broad, it is clear that—like all of Rule 60—it is not to be used to correct errors of law.[204] It is not, therefore, a substitute for bringing a timely appeal or making a motion for relief from an erroneous judgment under Rule 59: "The appropriate remedy for errors of law committed by the court is either appeal or a

---

200. Gardner v. Gardner, 63 N.C. App. 678, 681–82, 306 S.E.2d 496, 498 (1983).

201. Rule 60(b)(6).

202. Norton v. Sawyer, 30 N.C. App. 420, 426, 227 S.E.2d 148, 153 (1976) (quotation omitted).

203. *Id.*

204. Brown v. Cavit Scis., Inc., 749 S.E.2d 904, 908 (N.C. Ct. App. 2013) (citing Baxley v. Jackson, 179 N.C. App. 635, 638, 634 S.E.2d 905, 907 (2006)).

timely motion for relief under . . . Rule 59(a)(8)."[205] This restriction has been applied to legal errors related to the substance of an underlying claim, to application of procedural rules, and to methods of calculating damages and fees. In *Wallis v. Cambron*,[206] after a number of their claims were dismissed, plaintiffs filed a Rule 60(b)(6) motion asserting that the trial court misapplied the law related to shareholder demands and erred in determining there was no cause of action for civil conspiracy.[207] The Court of Appeals affirmed the trial court's denial of this motion, stating that "judgments involving misapplication of the law may be corrected only by appeal and Rule 60(b) motions cannot be used as a substitute for appeal."[208] In a medical malpractice action involving bariatric surgery, the trial court ordered plaintiff to produce complete medical records from all known medical providers, including mental health providers.[209] The Court of Appeals ordered plaintiff to produce the medical records, noting that the trial court's application of the discovery rules should have been challenged by a timely appeal

---

205. Hagwood v. Odom, 88 N.C. App. 513, 519, 364 S.E.2d 190, 193 (1988). By contrast, in *Petty v. Housing Authority of the City of Charlotte*, relief from a pre-judgment interest award under Rule 60(b)(6) was appropriate because the issue could not have been appealed prior to co-defendant's settlement with the plaintiff. 90 N.C. App. 559, 563, 369 S.E.2d 612, 615 (1988).

206. 194 N.C. App. 190, 194, 670 S.E.2d 239, 241 (2008).

207. *Id.* at 194, 670 S.E.2d 241.

208. *Id.* at 194–95, 670 S.E.2d at 242 (quotation omitted); *see also Baxley*, 179 N.C. App. at 638–39, 634 S.E.2d at 907 (denying a "second bite at the apple" under Rule 60 where defendants failed to perfect their appeal of a contempt order); Draughon v. Draughon, 94 N.C. App. 597, 599, 380 S.E.2d 547, 548 (1989) (where plaintiff had failed to make a timely appeal, Rule 60(b)(6) could not be used to set aside an order simply because the plaintiff was dissatisfied with it); Garrison *ex rel.* Chavis v. Barnes, 117 N.C. App. 206, 208–10, 450 S.E.2d 554, 556–58 (1994) (denying relief to a defendant who argued he had right to obtain blood paternity test prior to adjudication of paternity).

209. Spangler v. Olchowski, 187 N.C. App. 684, 687–88, 654 S.E.2d 507, 510–11 (2007).

rather than through Rule 60.[210] And in *Lang v. Lang*,[211] the court properly rejected a motion for relief from enforcement of a foreign divorce decree where defendant argued that the wrong exchange rate had been used in calculating the judgment amount.[212]

The restriction against use of the rule to correct errors of law had a harsh result where the court took an inflexible view of the rule designation. The trial court in *Catawba Valley Bank v. Porter*[213] entered judgment and a separate order denying attorney fees to the prevailing plaintiff. The same day, the defendant filed a motion to reconsider under Rule 60.[214] The trial court amended its order awarding attorney fees, finding that it had "applied the wrong legal standard upon Defendants' initial Motion for Attorney Fees and Costs and erroneously held that a failed attempt to settle the action after its institution was a necessary finding in awarding a prevailing party attorney's fees and costs . . . pursuant to N.C. Gen. Stat. § 75-16.1."[215] The plaintiff appealed the amended judgment on grounds it corrected an error of law. The Court of Appeals agreed with the plaintiff and held that

> the trial court's amended order was entered, not pursuant to its inherent authority nor under N.C. Gen. Stat. § 1A-1, Rule 59 (2005), but in an order granting Defendants' motion under Rule 60. As discussed above, Rule 60 is an improper mechanism for obtaining review of alleged legal error. For the reasons discussed above, the trial court's order awarding attorney's fees to Plaintiff's counsel is Vacated.[216]

---

210. *Id.* at 689, 654 S.E.2d at 512.

211. 108 N.C. App. 440, 424 S.E.2d 190 (1993).

212. *Id.* at 452–53, 424 S.E.2d at 196–97; *see also* McKyer v. McKyer, 182 N.C. App. 456, 459–62, 642 S.E.2d 527, 530–31 (2007) (rejecting Rule 60(b)(6) motion for relief from attorney fee award and order dismissing notices of appeal).

213. 188 N.C. App. 326, 655 S.E.2d 473 (2008).

214. *Id.* at 327–28, 655 S.E.2d at 474.

215. *Id.* at 329, 655 S.E.2d at 474.

216. *Id.* at 329–30, 655 S.E.2d 475 (citations omitted).

The Rule 60 motion was made well within the ten days allowed for a motion to alter or amend the judgment under Rule 59(a). If the movant had invoked this rule by name instead of Rule 60, the outcome of this case would surely have been different. As it stands, *Catawba* reminds parties to observe all relevant time limits and to carefully designate motions for relief according to the proper rule.[217]

Not a Second Chance to Raise a Missed Trial Argument

Rule 60(b)(6) is also not to be used to raise arguments that could have been raised at trial but were not. It is not broad enough to provide a second chance to make a legal assertion or defense that was available to the party at the time of trial.[218] In *Concrete Supply Co. v. Ramseur Baptist Church*,[219] a supplier sued to enforce a lien against a church for money owed by a contractor in constructing the church's driveway. After a bench trial, the court found the church liable to the supplier. The church did not appeal, but some months later it filed a Rule 60(b)(6) motion arguing that it had paid the contractor in full and thus the supplier was not subrogated to the rights of the contractor and could not hold the church liable for the contractor's debts.[220] The Court of Appeals agreed with the church's legal point, but because the

---

217. By contrast, in the odd case of *Jorgensen v. Seeman*, the Court of Appeals reversed a trial court's denial of a Rule 60(b) motion brought on grounds that the court had erred in unilaterally reducing the jury's verdict. While the argument for relief seems clearly to have been based on an error of law that could have been appealed, the Court of Appeals deemed it an extraordinary circumstance warranting relief under Rule 60(b). 95 N.C. App. 767, 768–70, 383 S.E.2d 702, 703–04 (1989). It appears, however, that the Rule 60(b) motion was filed very soon after the erroneous judgment, so it seems practical that it was effectively treated as a proper motion for amendment of judgment.

218. Concrete Supply Co. v. Ramseur Baptist Church, 95 N.C. App. 658, 659–60, 383 S.E.2d 222, 223 (1989).

219. 95 N.C. App. 658, 383 S.E.2d 222 (1989).

220. *Id.* at 658–59, 383 S.E.2d at 223.

church "failed to assert this defense at trial and then failed to bring an appeal," Rule 60(b)(6) could not be used to seek relief on this basis.[221]

Not a Substitute for Other Rule 60 Grounds Not Timely Raised

All motions under Rule 60(b)(6) must be made within a "reasonable time." Motions under Rules 60(b)(1), (2), and (3), however, must also be made "not more than one year after the judgment, order, or proceeding was entered or taken."[222] When a party fails to meet this one-year limit, Rule 60(b)(6) cannot be used as a substitute when the basis for the motion is encompassed by one of the first three categories.[223] The defendant in a paternity action filed a motion to void the paternity order and support agreement on grounds that a later paternity test revealed he was not the father.[224] The motion was filed more than one year after the order was entered. Noting that the motion made allegations of fraud and mistake, the court stated that "the facts supporting the motion are facts which . . . more appropriately would support consideration pursuant to (b)(1) or (b)(3)."[225] Because the motion was filed outside the one-year limit, defendant's motion was untimely and Rule 60(b)(6) could not be used to extend the time limit. The court noted that the one-year limitation "is an explicit requirement which

---

221. *Id.* at 660, 383 at S.E.2d 223; *see also* Piedmont Rebar, Inc. v. Sun Constr., Inc., 150 N.C. App. 573, 576–77, 564 S.E.2d 281, 284 (2002) (Rule 60(b)(6) not available to property owner to assert that subcontractor had no right to enforce a lien where property owner did not make the argument/defense at trial.).

222. Rule 60(b); see discussion of timing *infra* in section titled "Time Limits."

223. Norton v. Sawyer, 30 N.C. App. 420, 426, 227 S.E.2d 148, 153 (1976). In *Norton,* defendant's counsel neglected to file an answer, resulting in default judgment. Defendant filed a Rule 60 motion more than one year later. Noting that defendant had missed the one-year deadline to bring an excusable neglect motion under Rule 60(b)(1), the Court of Appeals declined to interpret "grand reservoir of equitable power" to allow relief for the same basis under Rule 60(b)(6). *Id.* (citation omitted).

224. State *ex rel.* Richmond Cty. Child Support Agency v. Adams, 153 N.C. App. 512, 513, 571 S.E.2d 238, 239 (2002).

225. *Id.* at 515, 571 S.E.2d at 241.

our Court cannot ignore."[226] In *Bruton v. Sea Captain Properties, Inc.*,[227] a foreclosure action, out-of-state defendants moved for relief over sixteen months after judgment was entered against them. Defendants had retained Pennsylvania counsel, who then hired North Carolina counsel, but then the North Carolina attorneys resigned and no further North Carolina counsel were retained. Ultimately judgment by default was entered against defendants.[228] The court explained,

> [N]o one was "minding the shop" in North Carolina, including the appellants, and a judgment of nearly $500,000.00 was entered against them in this action. Defendants argue that because their Pennsylvania attorney had competently procured North Carolina counsel in the past, and had made representations to them in this case that "everything was taken care of" and "not to worry", they should be excused for failing to take further measures to keep informed about the status of their case.[229]

The court declined to grant relief, explaining that "[a]t its very best," their argument was based on excusable neglect under Rule 60(b)(1), and because they waited over one year after entry of judgment, their motion was not timely: "Rule 60(b)(6) cannot be the basis for a motion to set aside judgment if the facts supporting it are facts which more appropriately would support one of the five preceding clauses."[230]

---

226. *Id.* at 515, 571 S.E.2d at 240–41.

227. 96 N.C. App. 485, 386 S.E.2d 58 (1989).

228. *Id.* at 487–89, 386 S.E.2d at 58–60.

229. *Id.* at 488, 386 S.E.2d at 59.

230. *Id.* at 488, 386 S.E.2d at 59–60; *see also* DeLote Builders, LLC v. Conley, 223 N.C. App. 361, 734 S.E.2d 140, 2012 WL 5395276, *3 (2012) (unpublished) (providing a thorough discussion of whether a party's neglect of his case was "sufficient to draw water from the grand reservoir of Rule 60(b)(6)").

Not to Relax the Standards for Bases 1 through 5

Rule 60(b)(6) is not a mechanism to effectively widen the scope of the first five bases. For example, where 60(b)(1) allows relief for "excusable neglect," 60(b)(6) cannot be invoked where the neglect in question is something short of excusable. Along the same lines, in *Akzona, Inc. v. American Credit Indemnity Co. of New York,*[231] defendants sought relief from summary judgment based on new evidence. Rule 60(b)(2) requires that the purported new evidence "could not have been discovered by the exercise of due diligence in time to present it in the original proceeding." The defendants in *Akzona* could not make this showing, so they turned to (b)(6).[232] Affirming the trial court's denial of relief, the Court of Appeals explained,

> Defendants attempted to circumvent the definitional requirements for new evidence under Rule 60(b)(2) by designating their motion as one made under Rule 60(b)(6), which grants relief from a judgment or order for "any other reason justifying relief from the operation of the judgment." . . . Defendants' motion . . . was expressly based on newly discovered evidence, which brings it within the scope of Rule 60(b)(2), and not within the scope of Rule 60(b)(6), which speaks of any *other* reason, *i.e.,* any reason other than those contained in Rule 60(b)(1)–(5). Thus, this motion was not properly brought under Rule 60(b)(6), and defendants' discussion of Rule 60(b)(6) is inapposite.[233]

---

231. 71 N.C. App. 498, 505, 322 S.E.2d 623, 629 (1984).

232. *Id.* at 505, 322 S.E.2d at 629.

233. *Id.*; *see also* Hill v. Hanes Corp., 79 N.C. App. 67, 72, 339 S.E.2d 1, 4 (1986) ("[W]e decline to circumvent the "due diligence" requirement of Rule 60(b)(2) by indiscriminately entertaining any and all 'newly discovered evidence' under Rule 60(b)(6).").

Requirements: Extraordinary Circumstances and Meritorious Defense

Rule 60(b)(6) allows relief "for [a]ny other reason justifying relief from the operation of the judgment." Our courts have established that such justifications exist only if the movant shows that (1) extraordinary circumstances exist, (2) justice demands it, and (3) the movant has a meritorious defense to the underlying claims.[234] Our courts routinely discuss the first two requirements as a unified concept, so this section will refer to them together as "extraordinary circumstances."

Potential "extraordinary circumstances."

Our appellate courts have not specifically defined this term in the context of Rule 60. In the following circumstances, however, the courts have found that extraordinary circumstances exist.

IRREGULAR JUDGMENTS RELATED TO COURT PRACTICE

Unlike "erroneous" judgments—where the court's decision is based on an error of law—*irregular* judgments can form a basis for relief under Rule 60(b)(6). An irregular judgment in this context is one "rendered contrary to the cause and practice of the court."[235] Featuring prominently in this category are notice and calendaring errors that are not the fault of the movant. For example, a small claims appeal was dismissed when defendant did not appear.[236] The Court of Appeals held that defendant's Rule 60(b)(6) motion should have been granted because the only evidence was that there had been no notice: "It is clear that the court may give relief from a judgment pursuant to Rule 60(b)(6) if the party making the motion has not had notice that the case was duly calendared."[237] The policy behind such relief was

---

234. Oxford Plastics v. Goodson, 74 N.C. App. 256, 258–60, 328 S.E.2d 7, 9–10 (1985).

235. Taylor v. Triangle Porsche-Audi, Inc., 27 N.C. App. 711, 717, 220 S.E.2d 806, 811 (1975).

236. Windley v. Dockery, 95 N.C. App. 771, 771–72, 383 S.E.2d 682, 682 (1989).

237. *Id.* at 773, 383 S.E.2d at 683; *see also* Lowe's Charlotte Hardware, Inc. v. Howard, 18 N.C. App. 80, 82–83, 196 S.E.2d 53, 54–55 (1973)

well articulated in *LaRoque v. LaRoque*,[238] in which the defendant, who lived in Maryland, had received no notice of an early calendaring of a divorce case for trial, and judgment was entered in her absence.[239] The Court of Appeals held that this "irregular" judgment should have been vacated, stating,

> There is no . . . neglect of her lawsuit by the defendant in the present case. Furthermore, were we to apply the rule of constructive notice, that when a case is listed on the court calendar, a party has notice of the time and date of hearing, such a rule bends to embrace common sense and fundamental fairness. We think common sense and fundamental fairness required that before the divorce could be granted, notice be given defendant of the trial when the trial was had one day after an answer was filed by the out-of-state defendant who had no reason to know that the case had been listed on the calendar.[240]

In *Brady v. Town of Chapel Hill*,[241] a case was transferred from superior to district court. A clerk overlooked the order of transfer and placed the case on the superior court calendar. When called for trial, plaintiff did not appear, and the case was dismissed.[242] Without ruling on the question, the Court of Appeals noted that the proper remedy for this "mischance, which need not, and should not, have occurred," would be a motion under Rule 60, which the trial court could grant if plaintiff

---

(affirming relief under 60(b)(6) where trial court found that plaintiff and plaintiff's counsel had no notice that a case would be called for trial).

238. 46 N.C. App. 578, 265 S.E.2d 444 (1980).

239. *Id.* at 579, 265 S.E.2d at 445.

240. *Id.* at 582, 265 S.E.2d at 446–47 (citation omitted); *see also* Brown v. Ellis, 206 N.C. App. 93, 696 S.E.2d 813 (2010).

241. 277 N.C. 720, 178 S.E.2d 446 (1971).

242. *Id.* at 721, 178 S.E.2d at 447; *see also* Dollar v. Tapp, 103 N.C. App. 162, 164–65, 404 S.E.2d 482, 483–84 (1991) (relief appropriate for defendant who received only four days' notice of trial rather than four weeks).

could show he exercised proper diligence and had a meritorious defense.[243]

Perhaps the most striking fact scenario, however, comes from *Butler Service Co. v. Butler Service Group, Inc.*[244] Late on a Monday afternoon, plaintiff's case was called for trial at 9:30 the next morning in superior court. Plaintiff's counsel was set to try a non-jury case in district court starting at 9:00 the same morning. Plaintiff's attorney advised both courtroom clerks of the conflict and attempted to find the superior court judge and clerk of court to inform them as well. After learning of the conflict, the district court judge nevertheless ordered counsel to proceed with his client's case at 9:00 A.M. While counsel was proceeding in district court, he was informed that his case in superior court would be dismissed if he did not appear in five minutes. He was excused to go speak to the superior court judge, who then dismissed the case for failure to prosecute. In a scathing opinion, the Court of Appeals held that relief under Rule 60(b)(6) was required, noting,

> The harshness of a Rule 41 dismissal with prejudice is seldom more apparent than on the facts of this case. Plaintiff . . . was standing outside of superior courtroom #304, ready and willing to prosecute its case at the time the case was dismissed. . . . This case does not involve an attorney who has repeatedly taken action to delay the trial of its case. . . . In this case, plaintiff's counsel's failure to proceed did not arise out of a deliberate attempt to delay the progress of the action to its conclusion, but rather, arose out of a very typical and practically expected situation that was handled in an atypical manner.[245]

Note that many of the opinions discussing irregular judgments, including *Butler*, date from before electronic court records and communications, so the exact scenarios certainly are less likely to happen

---

243. *Id.* at 722–24, 178 S.E.2d at 447–48.
244. 66 N.C. App. 132, 310 S.E.2d 406 (1984).
245. *Id.* at 135–36, 310 S.E.2d at 408.

today. The general concept of an "irregular" judgment, however, is no less valid,[246] so it remains useful if, when comparing older cases to current ones, we adjust for modern court practices.

IRREGULAR JUDGMENTS DUE TO IMPROPER RELIEF

In *Sharyn's Jewelers, LLC v. Ipayment, Inc.*, relief from default judgment was required under Rule 60(b)(6) where the trial court awarded punitive damages, damages for unfair and deceptive trade practices, and corresponding attorney fees against a defendant from whom the complaint had not sought such relief.[247]

GROSS NEGLIGENCE BY MOVANT'S COUNSEL OR REPRESENTATIVE

In general, an attorney's inexcusable negligence is imputed to the client and is, therefore, not an "extraordinary circumstance" under Rule 60(b)(6).[248] In rare circumstances, however, an attorney's or representative's negligence may be considered so serious it constitutes an extraordinary circumstance.[249] In *Poston v. Morgan*,[250] the movants' attorney severely neglected and manipulated his clients' cases, including failing to perfect appeals in four different matters, failing to file appeal records, failing to appear at hearings, and systematically misleading the movants about the status of their cases.[251] The Court of Appeals held that the attorney's misdeeds resulted in movants' inability to explore all avenues of appeal, entitling them to Rule 60(b) relief.[252]

---

246. *See, e.g.*, Brown v. Ellis, 206 N.C. App. 93, 696 S.E.2d 813 (2010).

247. 196 N.C. App. 281, 287–88, 674 S.E.2d 732, 737 (2009). Certainly this case seems to involve relief from legal error. Given the bulk of the case law making clear that Rule 60(b) is not designed to be a remedy for legal errors, this case may best be viewed as unusual.

248. Henderson v. Wachovia Bank of N.C., N.A., 145 N.C. App. 621, 626, 551 S.E.2d 464, 468 (2001). See discussion of the imputation rule in the context of excusable neglect in the section *supra* titled "What Is Excusable Neglect?"

249. Royal v. Hartle, 145 N.C. App. 181, 185, 551 S.E.2d 168, 171–72 (2001).

250. 83 N.C. App. 295, 350 S.E.2d 108 (1986).

251. *Id.* at 297–300, 350 S.E.2d at 109–11.

252. *Id.* at 300, 350 S.E.2d at 111.

LOSS OF REMEDY THROUGH NO FAULT OF MOVANT

In *Fox v. Health Force, Inc.*,[253] a legally incapacitated plaintiff with multiple sclerosis sued a medical care center for alleged negligence that left her in a vegetative state. Originally her mother sued on her behalf, purportedly as her guardian ad litem, but the mother was never properly appointed guardian ad litem under Rule of Civil Procedure 17 and had not been appointed guardian under Chapter 35A. The attorney hired by plaintiff's mother neglected the case, causing plaintiff's claims to be dismissed as outside the statutes of limitation and an attorney fee award to be assessed against her. Later, new counsel was hired, plaintiff was properly adjudicated legally incompetent with a general guardian, and a guardian ad litem was appointed who soon filed a Rule 60 motion. The trial court found that Rule 60(b)(6) relief was proper.[254] The Court of Appeals affirmed, making clear that this was not a mere case of attorney neglect imputable to the client.

> The person representing [her] as her "guardian *ad litem*" was not in actuality her guardian or guardian *ad litem*. At that time, none of the parties was entitled to act on [her] behalf, as incompetent plaintiffs *must* be represented by a general or testamentary guardian or guardian *ad litem*. N.C. Gen. Stat. § 1A-1, Rule 17(b)(1) (1999). Moreover, . . . [counsel's] inexcusable negligence could not be charged against [her] because she is an incompetent "entitled to the greatest possible protection by this court."[255]

IMPOSSIBILITY OF ENFORCEMENT

In *Curran v. Barefoot*,[256] the trial court ordered specific performance of a contract, including conveyance of certain watercraft. The defendant moved for relief on grounds that he was not the record owner of some of the boats, and he presented new (apparently uncontroverted)

---

253. 143 N.C. App. 501, 547 S.E.2d 83 (2001).
254. *Id.* at 504–05, 547 S.E.2d at 85–86.
255. *Id.* at 506, 547 S.E.2d at 87.
256. 183 N.C. App. 331, 333, 645 S.E.2d 187, 189–90 (2007).

evidence in support of the motion. The trial court denied the relief.[257] The Court of Appeals reversed, holding that

> "extraordinary circumstances exist" and "justice demands" the judgment be modified. The trial court ordered defendant to convey personal property it did not own. "Specific performance may not be granted where the performance of the contract is impossible" and "specific performance will not be decreed against a defendant who is unable to comply with the contract even though the inability to perform is caused by the defendant's own act."[258]

Also, in a real property case the Court of Appeals required relief from a judgment directing reconveyance of property. The court held that because the property had been foreclosed upon and sold to third persons since the original judgment was entered, compliance with the earlier judgment was impossible and relief under Rule 60(b)(6) was necessary.[259]

TO CLARIFY THE JUDGMENT

In limited circumstances, Rule 60(b)(6) may support modification of a judgment to clarify the court's or parties' intentions.[260] In *Alston v. Federal Express Corp.*,[261] the trial court entered an order setting a statutory lien on October 12, 2007; on May 28, 2008, the plaintiff filed a motion to clarify, and the trial court subsequently amended the order.[262] The Court of Appeals affirmed, stating,

> Although the trial court's intentions regarding the distribution of attorney's fees is not clear from the record, subse-

257. *Id.* at 333, 645 S.E.2d at 189–90.

258. *Id.* at 343, 645 S.E.2d at 195 (citations omitted).

259. Lumsden v. Lawing, 117 N.C. App. 514, 518–20, 451 S.E.2d 659, 662–63 (1995).

260. *See, e.g.*, Harris v. Harris, 162 N.C. App. 511, 515–16, 591 S.E.2d 560, 562–63 (2004) (affirming modification of judgment under Rule 60(b)(6) to eliminate unintended language).

261. 200 N.C. App. 420, 684 S.E.2d 705 (2009).

262. *Id.* at 422, 684 S.E.2d at 706.

> quent correspondence by the parties suggested that neither [party] could agree on how to interpret the trial court's order. Pursuant to Rule 60(b)(6)'s "grand reservoir of equitable power," the trial court had jurisdiction to revisit its order so that its intentions could be made clear.[263]

Note that this particular circumstance would require review by the same judge who heard the evidence because only that judge would be able to clarify his or her own "intentions." Under most circumstances, clarifications of trial judgments typically should be sought within ten days of the judgment pursuant to Rules 59(e) or 52(b), as discussed in Part I, Chapter 3.

TO ACCOUNT FOR CERTAIN CHANGES IN THE LAW

The Court of Appeals has stated generally that "Rule 60(b)(6) is properly employed to revisit a judgment affected by a subsequent change in the law."[264] The court cited as authority the cases of *Barnes v. Taylor* and *McNeil v. Hicks*, so this language should be viewed through the relatively limited lens of those cases. In *Barnes v. Taylor*,[265] the trial court entered a judgment on October 8, 1997, ordering defendants to remove a manufactured home from a subdivision on grounds it violated the neighborhood's restrictive covenants prohibiting trailers. One day earlier, the Court of Appeals had filed an opinion setting forth the factors to determine if a structure is a trailer or a modular home. A third-party defendant shortly thereafter brought the appellate opinion to the trial court's attention on a Rule 60 motion. The trial court then determined that "'it is clear that [defendants'] home does not violate

---

263. *Id.* at 423–24, 684 S.E.2d at 707; *see also* Ammons v. Goodyear Tire & Rubber Co., 209 N.C. App. 741, 744–45, 708 S.E.2d 127, 129 (2011) (appropriate to amend a judgment on own motion under Rule 60(b) to clarify the judgment and alleviate confusion); *cf. Harris*, 162 N.C. App. at 516, 591 S.E.2d at 563 (affirming modification of judgment to reflect parties' true intentions).

264. Hamby v. Profile Prods., LLC, 197 N.C. App. 99, 110, 676 S.E.2d 594, 601 (2009).

265. 148 N.C. App. 397, 559 S.E.2d 246 (2002).

the restrictive covenants . . . and, therefore, the October 8, 1997 ruling was erroneous.'"[266] On appeal, the plaintiff argued that the trial court had no authority to set aside the order on the motion of a third-party defendant rather than the defendants against whom the order had been issued. The Court of Appeals rejected this argument, noting in any event that the court would have been authorized to grant relief under Rule 60(b)(6) on its own initiative where extraordinary circumstances exist. The court held that "due to the extraordinary circumstances present here, we reject plaintiff's contention that the trial court lacked authority to act on its own initiative in order to accomplish justice."[267]

In *McNeil v. Hicks*,[268] the plaintiff sued her insurance company under the uninsured motorist coverage of her policy when an unknown driver caused another car to collide with hers. The trial court granted partial summary judgment for the plaintiff. Not long after, the North Carolina Supreme Court issued an opinion holding that there must be physical contact with the unidentified vehicle in order for uninsured motorist coverage to apply. Based on this holding, the trial court granted the insurance company relief from the partial summary judgment order under Rule 60(b)(6), and the Court of Appeals affirmed.[269]

MISCONDUCT OF OTHERS

The misconduct of an adverse party is addressed by Rule 60(b)(3).[270] For third-party misconduct, Rule 60(b)(6) may provide a remedy. The Court of Appeals has affirmed relief for plaintiff based on the admitted false testimony of a witness for the defense and has noted that the equivalent Federal Rule of Civil Procedure 60(b)(6) "has been held

---

266. *Id.* at 398–99, 559 S.E.2d at 247–48.

267. *Id.* at 400, 559 S.E.2d at 248–49.

268. 119 N.C. App. 579, 580–81, 459 S.E.2d 47, 48 (1995).

269. *Id.* at 580–81, 459 S.E.2d at 48.

270. See discussion *supra* in section titled "Fraud, Misrepresentation, or Other Misconduct of an Adverse Party—Rule 60(b)(3)." *But see* Sloan v. Sloan, 151 N.C. App. 399, 405, 566 S.E.2d 97, 101–02 (2002) (order set aside under Rule 60(b)(6) based on discovery outside one-year time frame for Rule 60(b)(3) motion of adverse party's deliberate failure to disclose certain facts).

to permit relief from . . . nonadverse third party intrinsic fraud of perjury."[271]

GENERAL FAIRNESS

In a condemnation action, the trial court did not err in setting aside default judgment under Rule 60(b)(6) in favor of a city against a property owner where the city pursued default despite the owner's letter to the court contesting damages and despite ongoing negotiations between the city and the owner after the condemnation action was filed.[272] The Court of Appeals concluded that relief was appropriate "on the basis of the fundamental unfairness of allowing the city to go forward with default judgment in light of the documents of record filed in the case."[273] The apparent breadth of this decision appears unusual in light of the stringency of our courts' analyses of excusable neglect arguments in default judgment cases.[274]

No extraordinary circumstances.

In the following categories, the courts have rejected arguments that extraordinary circumstances exist to warrant relief under Rule 60(b)(6).

LACK OF UNDERSTANDING OF LAW; FAILURE TO PROCURE COUNSEL

Litigants typically have been unsuccessful when arguing that they were unsophisticated about the law or did not have counsel to prevent an unfortunate result. In *Thacker v. Thacker*,[275] for example, defendant wife executed a consent judgment dividing marital assets.[276] She later moved for relief pursuant to Rule 60(b), arguing that the judgment was

---

271. McGinnis v. Robinson, 43 N.C. App. 1, 10, 258 S.E.2d 84, 89 (1979) (citing McKinney v. Boyle, 404 F.2d 632 (9th Cir. 1968)). The distinction between intrinsic and extrinsic fraud is discussed *supra* in section titled "Fraud, Misrepresentation, or Other Misconduct of an Adverse Party—Rule 60(b)(3)."

272. City of Durham v. Woo, 129 N.C. App. 183, 187–88, 497 S.E.2d 457, 460 (1998).

273. *Id.* at 187, 497 S.E.2d at 460.

274. *See* discussion *supra* in section titled "What Is Excusable Neglect?"

275. 107 N.C. App. 479, 420 S.E.2d 479 (1992).

276. *Id.* at 480, 420 S.E.2d at 479.

"patently unfair and inequitable" and that the plaintiff had fraudulently induced her to sign by telling her "we will work things out and we will get back together, but we still have to get these papers done to keep from going to court."[277] The Court of Appeals stated, "This Court has held on numerous occasions that a lack of counsel and/or an ignorance of the law does not amount to 'extraordinary circumstances' without some showing that the lack of counsel or ignorance was due to reasons beyond control of the party seeking relief."[278] In *Baylor v. Brown*,[279] the Court of Appeals reversed a grant of relief under Rule 60(b)(6) where defendants had repeatedly ignored plaintiff's counsel's warning that plaintiffs would seek default judgment if defendants did not obtain new counsel and file an answer.[280] Defendants essentially argued an inability to pay counsel's retainer and fee and failure to procure help from Legal Aid because Legal Aid already represented plaintiffs. The court said, "To us, defendants made a free choice to take the risk of not defending the action against them and to use [available funds] for another purpose other than defending the action in question."[281]

FAILURE TO PROSECUTE OR DEFEND

The courts have regularly rejected requests for relief when the litigant has not diligently attended to its case. During a custody modification court date that the defendant and his attorney did not attend (but had notice of), defendant's case was continued to the following month.[282] Defendant discovered the new schedule on the Friday before the new Monday court date, but he was booked on a flight out of state and could not attend. He called the court twice but proceeded to go on vacation without making a proper continuance motion.[283] To the Court of Appeals, "Defendant's telephone calls requesting a continu-

---

277. *Id.*

278. *Id.* at 482, 420 S.E.2d at 481 (citing Wilson v. Wilson, 98 N.C. App. 230, 390 S.E.2d 354 (1990)).

279. 46 N.C. App. 664, 266 S.E.2d 9 (1980).

280. *Id.* at 666–67, 266 S.E.2d at 10–12.

281. *Id.* at 671, 266 S.E.2d at 14.

282. Trivette v. Trivette, 162 N.C. App. 55, 57, 590 S.E.2d 298, 301 (2004).

283. *Id.* at 57–58, 590 S.E.2d at 301.

ance three days before the scheduled hearing were not sufficient to excuse his failure to attend the hearing or mandate a setting aside of the judgment pursuant to Rule 60(b)(6)."[284]

Self-represented litigants, perhaps particularly those with some business acumen, are not excused from the requirement to pay proper attention to court deadlines. In *Sides v. Reid*, the Court of Appeals reversed an order granting relief from default judgment.[285] Defendant had argued to the trial court that he received and understood the complaint and summons and that "he mailed a handwritten note to the court which he thought would be sufficient answer, but does not remember when or to what court he mailed it."[286] There was, however, no evidence in the record of the letter's existence. Noting the defendant's "failure to use proper diligence," the Court of Appeals stated that

> although defendant owned and managed three corporations and admitted reading and generally understanding the summons and complaint, he made no effort to consult an attorney until after the supplemental proceeding. In fact, defendant took no action other than the handwritten note for which he cannot account until this time, some thirteen months after he was personally served with process.[287]

In a similar scenario, the trial court dismissed a case for plaintiff's failure to prosecute the action during the discovery phase.[288] Another trial court judge later set aside the dismissal because "plaintiff was not represented by counsel during the period February 1, 1974 to

---

284. *Id.* at 63, 590 S.E.2d at 305; *see also* Parks v. Green, 153 N.C. App. 405, 413, 571 S.E.2d 14, 19 (2002) (no relief where defendant failed to attend arbitration or be properly represented at arbitration despite a rule requiring attendance).

285. 35 N.C. App. 235, 237–38, 241 S.E.2d 110, 111–12 (1978).

286. *Id.* at 236, 241 S.E.2d at 111.

287. *Id.* at 238, 241 S.E.2d at 112.

288. Campbell v. First-Citizens Bank & Trust Co., 23 N.C. App. 631, 632, 209 S.E.2d 556, 557 (1974).

and including February 17, 1974 but made this Motion with diligence upon retaining substitute counsel."[289] The Court of Appeals disagreed, holding,

> Plaintiff was aware of her scheduled trial and the need to obtain legal counsel in sufficient time to procure such representation. She had consented to the court order on 1 February 1974 which relieved her attorneys from their obligation to appear for her, and there is no finding that any diligent effort was made to secure other legal services. The absence of counsel for plaintiff was before the court and considered when the original judgment of dismissal was entered. Plaintiff did not appeal from that dismissal order or petition for certiorari, but chose to present to a second superior court judge upon motion to set aside the judgment the identical circumstances which resulted in the original dismissal for failure to prosecute her action.[290]

NOTICE ISSUES WHERE FAULT SHARED BY MOVANT OR MOVANT'S AGENT OR ATTORNEY

A lack of proper notice can amount to an irregularity warranting relief from judgment.[291] If the movant shares the blame for the lack of notice, however, the courts typically deny relief.[292] Many such cases relate to a party's failure to keep a current registered agent or to provide an up-to-date notice address. For example, where defendant, a self-represented litigant, provided a confusing array of addresses to

---

289. *Id.* at 633, 209 S.E.2d at 557–58.

290. *Id.* at 634–35, 209 S.E.2d at 558.

291. *See supra* section titled "Irregular Judgments Related to Court Practice."

292. *See, e.g.,* Milton M. Croom Charitable Remainder Unitrust v. Hedrick, 188 N.C. App. 262, 269–70, 654 S.E.2d 716, 721–22 (2008) (failure to receive calendar was not an "extraordinary circumstance" where her prior counsel's knowledge was imputed to her and she was not diligent in obtaining new counsel); Huggins v. Hallmark Enters., Inc., 84 N.C. App. 15, 25, 351 S.E.2d 779, 785 (1987) (failure to comply with requirements regarding service addresses contributed to lack of notice).

which service could be made upon him, and plaintiff was diligent in attempting service and did not violate Rules 4 and 5 of the Rules of Civil Procedure, defendant did not establish extraordinary circumstances entitling him to relief from default judgment in the amount of $13,000.[293]

More than once this type of scenario has left out-of-state defendants responsible for sizable default judgments. In *Partridge v. Associated Cleaning Consultants & Services, Inc.*,[294] a Pennsylvania corporation was sued for negligence in North Carolina; plaintiff made service on the North Carolina registered agent, but the registered agent was no longer in contact with defendant, and process was returned unserved.[295] Plaintiff then made service on the secretary of state's office, which forwarded process to the registered address, but defendant had since moved. Defendant later learned of the lawsuit from the city of Charlotte, a co-defendant, but defendant was informed by the clerk's office that plaintiff had not yet obtained service on defendant. Plaintiff had, however, received entry of default against defendant in a sum exceeding $100,000 and later moved for and received default judgment. Defendant never received the summons and complaint.[296] The court held that defendant's neglect in failing to keep an up-to-date registered agent and a current business address on file in North Carolina constituted inexcusable neglect and that the circumstances did not warrant a finding of extraordinary circumstances under Rule 60(b)(6).[297] In a similar case, default judgment was entered in an amount exceeding $300,000 against a Maryland corporation that conducted business in North Carolina but failed to maintain a registered agent for service in North Carolina.[298] The Maryland service agent received the summons

293. Venters v. Albritton, 184 N.C. App. 230, 237–38, 645 S.E.2d 839, 844–45 (2007).

294. 108 N.C. App. 625, 424 S.E.2d 664 (1993).

295. *Id.* at 627, 424 S.E.2d at 665–66.

296. *Id.* at 627–28, 424 S.E.2d at 665–66.

297. *Id.* at 630–33, 424 S.E.2d at 667–69.

298. Anderson Trucking Serv., Inc. v. Key Way Transp., Inc., 94 N.C. App. 36, 38–40, 379 S.E.2d 665, 666–67 (1989).

and complaint and then forwarded them to defendant, but they were lost in the mail and never received. The trial court denied the motion for relief, finding that defendant "failed for eight years to designate a new registered agent, and further failed, for at least five years, to honor [its agent's] request to be replaced by another registered agent."[299] The Court of Appeals affirmed, stating,

> Had this simply been a "lost mail" case, particularly in light of the large judgment awarded, we might be inclined to say that extraordinary circumstances existed and that justice demanded relief from the judgment. We will not do so when, as here, the evidence suggests that the corporation exhibited a longstanding pattern of irresponsibility and disregard of legal matters and failed to respond to *two* communications about a pending suit, only one of which allegedly was lost in the mail. Under circumstances such as this, we cannot say that the trial judge's discretionary ruling allowing the judgment to stand was "manifestly unsupported by reason."[300]

In addition, a party that has not received notice is certainly not guaranteed to get relief by asserting that its counsel is at fault. In *Henderson v. Wachovia Bank of North Carolina, N.A.*,[301] the trustee defendant failed to obey two orders to appear at depositions, and the trial court entered judgment against him. The trustee moved for relief from the judgment on grounds that his attorneys never informed him of the deposition notices or orders. The motion was denied.[302] After a discussion of whether an attorney's inexcusable neglect of a case is imputed to the client, the court rejected the defendant's Rule 60(b)(1) arguments

---

299. *Id.* at 41, 379 S.E.2d at 668.

300. *Id.* at 43, 379 S.E.2d at 669 (citation omitted); *see also* Rose v. Forester, 201 N.C. App. 159, 688 S.E.2d 118, 2009 WL 3818848,*4 (2009) (unpublished) (no relief where defendant's registered agent in North Carolina failed to forward complaint to defendant; agent's inexcusable neglect was imputed to defendant).

301. 145 N.C. App. 621, 551 S.E.2d 464 (2001).

302. *Id.* at 622–23, 551 S.E.2d at 466.

and then addressed whether the attorney's actions amounted to fraud, thereby entitling the defendant to relief under Rule 60(b)(6).[303] The court rejected the fraud argument.

> At most the affidavits show that defendant's attorneys did not fully apprise defendant of court orders to appear for depositions. Without so holding today, there may be situations so egregious that would entitle a party to be relieved of fraud on it by its own attorney, but this is not one of those situations.[304]

UNILATERAL MISTAKE (WITHOUT MISREPRESENTATION)

Rule 60(b)(6) also cannot be used to relieve a party who is vexed by or has failed to comprehend the impact of a judgment. In *Griffith v. Curtis,*[305] plaintiff moved to set aside a mediated settlement agreement incorporated into a duly executed consent judgment on grounds that the result of one of the provisions was "completely and utterly unfair."[306] Because she showed only a unilateral mistake, not a mutual mistake or a unilateral mistake procured by misconduct, there was no basis for finding extraordinary circumstances.[307]

---

303. *Id.* at 627–28, 551 S.E.2d at 469–70.

304. *Id.* at 628, 551 S.E.2d at 469.

305. 205 N.C. App. 462, 696 S.E.2d 701 (2010).

306. *Id.* at 463–64, 696 S.E.2d at 702.

307. *Id.* at 465, 696 S.E.2d at 703–04. A "unilateral mistake" is "a mistake or misunderstanding as to the term or effect of a contract, made or entertained by one of the parties to it but not by the other." *Unilateral Mistake,* BLACK'S LAW DICTIONARY (10th ed. 2014). The discovery of new evidence or circumstances, even by both parties, is not necessarily a "mutual mistake" that will allow relief. In a will contest case, the parties reached a settlement agreement and executed a consent judgment. *In re* Will of Baity, 65 N.C. App. 364, 365, 309 S.E.2d 515, 516 (1983). They later discovered a hand-written will and moved to be relieved from the consent judgment. The Court of Appeals held that the existence of the will was not a mutual mistake that would allow relief under Rule 60(b)(6) and did not motivate the parties' consent to the settlement agreement. *Id.* at 367–68, 309 S.E.2d at 517–18. The court noted that a "unilateral mistake, unaccompanied by fraud, imposition, undue influence, or like oppressive circumstances, is

PROCEDURAL BLUNDER NOT AMOUNTING TO GROSS NEGLIGENCE

Defendants could not show gross negligence establishing "extraordinary circumstances" where defendants' counsel allegedly entered into a consent agreement resolving an easement dispute without defendants' knowledge or permission.[308]

FORESEEABLE CHANGE IN CIRCUMSTANCES

In *Lee v. Lee,*[309] a divorce case, a qualified domestic relations order was entered, part of which provided the wife with the greater of a lump sum of approximately $400,000 or one half of the value of a retirement account. By the date of distribution, the value of the account had dropped to $498,000.00, effectively giving the wife—who had opted for the lump sum—a far greater than one-half share of the original value. The husband moved for relief under Rule 60(b)(6), citing the "extraordinary circumstance" of the stock market downturn.[310] The Court of Appeals rejected this argument, stating, "A change in the value of the stock market over the course of five years does not amount to an extraordinary or even unforeseeable circumstance. There was therefore no abuse of discretion by the trial court in its denial of defendant's Rule 60(b) motion[.]"[311]

MODIFICATION OF JUDGMENT MERELY TO RESOLVE DISSATISFACTION

In *Draughon v. Draughon,*[312] the trial court allowed a Rule 60(b)(6) motion to set aside an equitable distribution order where the parties

---

not sufficient to avoid a contract or conveyance." *Id.* at 368, 309 S.E.2d at 518 (citation omitted). *But see* City of Durham v. Woo, 129 N.C. App. 183, 187–88, 497 S.E.2d 457, 460 (1998) (discussed *supra* in section titled "General Fairness").

308. Royal v. Hartle, 145 N.C. App. 181, 185, 551 S.E.2d 168, 171–72 (2001); *see also* Purcell Int'l Textile Grp., Inc. v. Algemene AFW N.V., 185 N.C. App. 135, 139, 647 S.E.2d 667, 671 (2007) (no extraordinary circumstances where movant's attorney entered into a settlement agreement without the movant's knowledge or consent).

309. 167 N.C. App. 250, 257–58, 605 S.E.2d 222, 227 (2004).

310. *Id.* at 257–58, 605 S.E.2d at 227.

311. *Id.* at 258, 605 S.E.2d at 227.

312. 94 N.C. App. 597, 598, 380 S.E.2d 547, 547 (1989).

were both dissatisfied but could not agree on a resolution, and the plaintiff had let his appeal period run. The Court of Appeals rejected this use of Rule 60(b)(6), explaining,

> The parties' failure to agree as to the order's modification is not a justifiable reason for setting the order aside; for they resorted to the court in the first place because of their inability to agree and the stability of the judicial order arrived at after an adversarial hearing cannot be made to depend upon their agreement to it. And setting the order aside because plaintiff lost his right to appeal through his own oversight amounted to using Rule 60(b)(6) as a substitute for appeal, which our law does not permit. If the order remained set aside we have no reason to suppose that the next equitable distribution order would be acquiesced in by both parties; and under the circumstances recorded the integrity and stability of our judicial process requires that the duly entered and presumably correct order be reinstated and upheld.[313]

Meritorious defense.

In addition to demonstrating extraordinary circumstances, a Rule 60(b)(6) movant also must show the court that it has a "meritorious defense" to the underlying cause of action.[314] The standard for assessing a party's meritorious defense, which applies equally in the context of excusable neglect, is discussed previously in the section titled "Excusable Neglect."

313. *Id.* at 599, 380 S.E.2d at 548 (citation omitted).
314. Royal v. Hartle, 145 N.C. App. 181, 184, 551 S.E.2d 168, 171 (2001).

Procedure and Jurisdiction

The Motion

Who May Seek Relief

Any party to an action who is affected by the order in question may seek relief under Rule 60(b) if there are adequate grounds.[315] The party does not have to be the party who lost on the merits.[316] The right to bring a motion for relief, however, is expressly reserved for "a party or his legal representative."[317] The Court of Appeals has on many occasions applied this language to prohibit motions by non-parties—or "strangers"—to the underlying action.[318] The court recently noted that "we have strictly construed Rule 60(b)'s requirement that only a party to the original action may seek relief."[319] The court acknowledged,

---

315. Wood v. Wood, 297 N.C. 1, 7, 252 S.E.2d 799, 803 (1979).

316. Love v. Moore, 54 N.C. App. 406, 408, 283 S.E.2d 801, 803 (1981), ("Rule 60(b) has no language suggesting that the movant for relief . . . must be the losing party."), *vacated on other grounds*, 305 N.C. 575, 291 S.E.2d 141 (1982).

317. Rule 60(b). The right of a party to bring a Rule 60(b) motion extends to intervenors: "After intervention, an intervenor is as much a party to the action as the original parties are and has rights equally as broad[.]" Williams v. Walker, 185 N.C. App. 393, 397, 648 S.E.2d 536, 539 (2007) (holding that grandparents who intervened in custody action had standing to bring Rule 60(b) motion).

318. *See* Edmunds v. Edmunds, 194 N.C. App. 425, 431–32, 669 S.E.2d 874, 878 (2008), *aff'd*, 363 N.C. 740, 686 S.E.2d 150 (2009); Watson v. Ben Griffin Realty & Auction, Inc., 128 N.C. App. 61, 63–64, 493 S.E.2d 331, 333 (1997) (non-party to easement action had no standing to seek order setting aside judgment even though property rights affected by it); Sotelo v. Drew, 123 N.C. App. 464, 468, 473 S.E.2d 379, 381 (1996) (vacating order in which the non-party Attorney General of North Carolina moved to set aside judgment in child support action), *aff'd*, 345 N.C. 750, 483 S.E.2d 439 (1997); Lawyers Title Ins. Corp. v. Langdon, 91 N.C. App. 382, 385, 371 S.E.2d 727, 730 (1988) (non-party condominium owners precluded from bringing motion challenging lien); Browne v. Catawba Cty. Dep't of Soc. Servs., 22 N.C. App. 476, 478, 206 S.E.2d 792, 793 (1974) (non-party foster parents had no standing to raise challenges to parental rights action); *cf.* State v. Smith, 130 N.C. App. 600, 600, 503 S.E.2d 674, 675 (1998) (vacating expungement stay orders entered at request of non-party insurance company).

319. *Edmunds*, 194 N.C. App. at 432, 669 S.E.2d at 878.

however, that the rule was relaxed under the narrow facts of *Bowling v. Combs*, where strict construction would have been unnecessarily technical.[320] In *Bowling*,[321] the decedent's widow succeeded the original estate administrator and moved under Rule 60(b) to set aside a voluntary dismissal the administrator had earlier filed in a wrongful death action. At the same time the widow filed the Rule 60(b) motion, she also filed a motion to be substituted as party plaintiff. The trial court granted the Rule 60(b) motion and three months later granted the substitution motion.[322] Noting that the widow was "the only person entitled to function as plaintiff in the action," the Court of Appeals concluded that the "technicality" of the delay in substituting her as a party was not sufficient reason to invalidate the Rule 60(b) order.[323]

Although prevented from filing a Rule 60(b) motion, a non-party may file an independent action to seek relief from a judgment affecting its rights.[324] In dicta, the Court of Appeals has also suggested that, under the right circumstances, a non-party could file a post-judgment motion to intervene in order to have standing to challenge a judgment.[325] The court noted that post-judgment intervention motions are disfavored

---

320. *Id.*

321. 60 N.C. App. 234, 298 S.E.2d 754 (1983).

322. *Id.* at 235–36, 298 S.E.2d at 754–55.

323. *Id.* at 239, 298 S.E.2d at 758. Along similar lines, in *Helbein v. Southern Metals Co., Inc.*, a non-party was allowed to challenge—on the basis of lack of notice and hearing—an order enjoining him from further participation in an action after he threatened one of the parties in the hallway outside the courtroom. Although the Court of Appeals did not directly address the question of the movant's standing, his motion presumably was deemed valid because he was the only person subject to the order and thus the only one who would have reason to challenge it. 119 N.C. App. 431, 433, 458 S.E.2d 518, 519 (1995).

324. *Edmunds*, 194 N.C. App. at 431, 669 S.E.2d at 878; Watson v. Ben Griffin Realty & Auction, Inc., 128 N.C. App. 61, 63–64, 493 S.E.2d 331, 333 (1997); State v. Smith, 130 N.C. App. 600, 600, 503 S.E.2d 674, 675 (1998); Lawyers Title Ins. Corp. v. Langdon, 91 N.C. App. 382, 385, 371 S.E.2d 727, 730 (1988). See further discussion of independent actions *infra* in section titled "Independent Action."

325. *Smith*, 130 N.C. App. at 602, 503 S.E.2d at 676 (discussing the concurring opinion in *Watson*, 128 N.C. App. at 64–65, 493 S.E.2d at

but may be granted under extraordinary circumstances or "a strong showing of entitlement and justification."[326]

Time Limits

The outer time limit for making a Rule 60(b) motion depends on the grounds for the motion. The trial court has no authority under Rule of Civil Procedure 6(b) to extend the time for making a Rule 60(b) motion.[327] Nor may the parties agree to extend the deadline by stipulation or otherwise.[328]

Rules 60(b)(1), (2), and (3) motions brought on the basis of mistake, surprise, or excusable neglect, newly discovered evidence, or fraud must be made (a) within a reasonable time and (b) within one year after entry of the order or judgment.[329] Under Rule of Civil Procedure 58, "a judgment is entered when it is reduced to writing, signed by the judge, and filed with the clerk of court."[330] It should be carefully noted

---

333). Motions to intervene are governed by Rule of Civil Procedure 24. *See* G.S. 1A-1, Rule 24.

326. *Smith*, 130 N.C. App. at 602, 503 S.E.2d at 676; Proctor v. City of Raleigh Bd. of Adjustment, 133 N.C. App. 181, 183, 514 S.E.2d 745, 746 (1999) (allowing intervention after judgment where intervenors had been involved in proceedings from an early stage).

327. Rule 6(b). This rule gives the trial court broad discretion to extend deadlines established in the Rules of Civil Procedure, but it explicitly excludes most significant post-trial motions for relief: "[N]either the court nor the parties may extend the time for taking any action under Rules 50(b), 52, 59(b), (d), (e), 60(b), except to the extent and under the conditions stated in them." Rule 60(b) includes no extension provisions of its own.

328. Rule 6(b).

329. Rule 60(b); Kavanau Real Estate Trust v. Debnam, 299 N.C. 510, 514, 263 S.E.2d 595, 598 (1980) (motion brought outside one-year limit could not be considered); State *ex rel.* Richmond Cty. Child Support Agency v. Adams, 153 N.C. App. 512, 515, 571 S.E.2d 238, 241 (2002) ("The one-year limitation is . . . an explicit requirement which our court cannot ignore."); Huggins v. Hallmark Enters., Inc., 84 N.C. App. 15, 24, 351 S.E.2d 779, 784 (1987) (no exception could be made even where plaintiff deliberately waited one year to collect so the movants would not discover judgments in time).

330. G.S. 1A-1, Rule 58; *cf.* Guilford Cty. *ex rel.* Child Support Enf't Unit v. Holbrook, 190 N.C. App. 188, 192, 660 S.E.2d 175, 177 (2008) (in paternity

that the one-year time limit is an *outside* limit, not a guaranteed time provision. A "reasonable time" under one of these grounds depends on all the facts of a case and is a matter for the court's discretion; a reasonable time may, therefore, be less than one year.[331] The one-year time limit for a motion under Rules (60)(b)(1) through (3) may not be circumvented by restyling it as a motion for "any other reason" under Rule 60(b)(6).[332] In addition, the one-year limit is not tolled during the period of time during which the underlying judgment is on appeal.[333]

Rules 60(b)(5) and (6) motions brought on one of the grounds stated in (b)(5) or for "any other reason" as provided in (b)(6) are not subject to a one-year outside limit but nevertheless must be made within a reasonable time.[334] Whether a motion made on these grounds has been made in a reasonable time depends on all the facts of a case.[335] Motions have been properly rejected when brought as little as six months after

---

action, one-year period began to run at time of filing of affidavit of parentage, not when affidavit of parentage was executed).

331. *See, e.g.*, Brown v. Windhom, 104 N.C. App. 219, 221, 408 S.E.2d 536, 537 (1991) (motion not reasonable even though filed within two days of the one-year time limit where movant gave no explanation for delay other than confusion about legal rights); *see also* Clendening v. Sears, Roebuck & Co., 152 N.C. App. 477, 567 S.E.2d 840 (2002) (unpublished) (motion filed eleven months after judgment held unreasonable).

332. *Adams*, 153 N.C. App. at 515, 571 S.E.2d at 241; Bruton v. Sea Captain Props., Inc., 96 N.C. App. 485, 488–89, 386 S.E.2d 58, 60 (1989); Norton v. Sawyer, 30 N.C. App. 420, 426, 227 S.E.2d 148, 153 (1976). For further discussion, see *supra* section titled "Not a Substitute for Other Rule 60 Grounds Not Timely Raised."

333. Talbert v. Mauney, 80 N.C. App. 477, 479, 343 S.E.2d 5, 7 (1986); Wiggins v. Bunch, 280 N.C. 106, 111, 184 S.E.2d 879, 881–82 (1971). See discussion *infra* of trial court's authority to issue a conditional ruling after appeal of the underlying judgment in section titled "Effect of Appeal of Underlying Judgment; Conditional Ruling."

334. Rule 60(b).

335. J & M Aircraft Mobile T-Hangar, Inc. v. Johnston Cty. Airport Auth., 166 N.C. App. 534, 538, 603 S.E.2d 348, 351 (2004); Sloan v. Sloan, 151 N.C. App. 399, 405, 566 S.E.2d 97, 101 (2002); *Brown*, 104 N.C. App. at 221, 408 S.E.2d at 537; McGinnis v. Robinson, 43 N.C. App. 1, 8, 258 S.E.2d 84, 88 (1979).

judgment;[336] have been properly reviewed when filed as much as seventeen months after judgment;[337] and have been subject to various analyses in between.[338]

Although Rule 60(b), by its terms, imposes a "reasonable time" requirement on *all* motions, there is a well-established exception for motions made pursuant to Rule 60(b)(4). Rule 60(b)(4) applies to motions brought on the basis of void judgments. Because a void judgment is a legal nullity, it may be challenged at any time; the reasonable time requirement therefore does not apply to motions properly made under 60(b)(4).[339]

---

336. Sea Ranch II Owners Ass'n, Inc. v. Sea Ranch, Inc., 180 N.C. App. 226, 230, 636 S.E.3d 332, 335 (2006) (court did not err in finding that motion filed under Rule 60(b)(6) six months after the order was not reasonable).

337. Sharyn's Jewelers, LLC v. Ipayment, Inc., 196 N.C. App. 281, 285, 674 S.E.2d 732, 735 (2009) (timing not unreasonable under circumstances where movant's notice of judgment was constructive rather than actual).

338. *See, e.g.*, Adams Creek Assocs. v. Davis, 186 N.C. App. 512, 522, 652 S.E.2d 677, 684 (2007) (motion filed twenty months after order and fourteen months after dismissal of appeal unreasonable); *J & M Aircraft*, 166 N.C. App. at 538, 603 S.E.2d at 351 (motion brought fifteen months after notice of judgment not presumed unreasonable); Branch Banking & Trust Co. v. Tucker, 131 N.C. App. 132, 137, 505 S.E.2d 179, 183 (1998) (motion eleven months after judgment reasonable when plaintiff himself took one year to get judgment signed and entered after hearing and there was no indication defendants knew of its entry); Jenkins v. Richmond Cty., 118 N.C. App. 166, 169, 454 S.E.2d 290, 292 (1995) (court erred in granting relief under Rules (b)(5) and (b)(6) where the motion was brought one year after the order and then not pursued for yet another year); Poston v. Morgan, 83 N.C. App. 295, 301, 350 S.E.2d 108, 111 (1986) (motions not unreasonable where filed within one year of order and four months after denial of writs of certiorari); Nickels v. Nickels, 51 N.C. App. 690, 693, 277 S.E.2d 577, 579 (1981) (23-month delay in bringing motion to challenge consent judgment unreasonable).

339. Hillard v. Hillard, 223 N.C. App. 20, 22, 733 S.E.2d 176, 179 (2012); Freeman v. Freeman, 155 N.C. App. 603, 606, 573 S.E.2d 708, 711 (2002); Van Engen v. Que Sci., Inc., 151 N.C. App. 683, 689, 567 S.E.2d 179, 184 (2002); Nye, Mitchell, Jarvis & Bugg v. Oates, 109 N.C. App. 289, 291, 426 S.E.2d 291, 293 (1993); Allred v. Tucci, 85 N.C. App. 138, 141, 354 S.E.2d 291, 294 (1987). *But see* Prescott v. Prescott, 83 N.C. App. 254, 261–62,

Court's Own Motion

Rule 60(b) states that a court may grant relief "on motion." Our courts have held, however, that, under this rule, the court may act on its own initiative where necessary to accomplish justice.[340] If the court considers granting relief in the absence of a party's motion it may not so do without first providing notice to the parties and an opportunity for them to be heard.[341]

---

350 S.E.2d 116, 121 (1986) (32-month delay unreasonable where movant acquiesced to consent judgment during that time and trial court found evidence of lack of consent not credible); *Nickels*, 51 N.C. App. at 693–94, 277 S.E.2d at 579 (23-month delay in bringing motion was unreasonable due to partial compliance with order and lack of evidence that order was void).

340. Barnes v. Taylor, 148 N.C. App. 397, 400–401, 559 S.E.2d 246, 249 (2002) (court properly granted relief under Rule 60(b)(6) due to change in applicable law); Taylor v. Triangle Porsche-Audi, Inc., 27 N.C. App. 711, 717, 220 S.E.2d 806, 811 (1975) (court has "power to act in the interest of justice in an unusual case where its attention has been directed to the necessity for relief by means other than a motion"); *see also* Ammons v. Goodyear Tire & Rubber Co., 209 N.C. App. 741, 744–45, 708 S.E.2d 127, 129 (2011) (appropriate for commissioner to modify judgment on own motion to clarify ruling); Jenkins v. Piedmont Aviation Servs., 147 N.C. App. 419, 424, 557 S.E.2d 104, 108 (2001) (extending this authority to the Industrial Commission); Tepper v. Hoch, 140 N.C. App. 354, 359, 536 S.E.2d 654, 658 (2000) (noting that Rule 60(b) relief may be "upon the trial court's own initiative"); *In re* Estate of English, 83 N.C. App. 359, 363, 350 S.E.2d 379, 382 (1986) (clerk of court has corresponding authority in matters over which it has jurisdiction).

341. Utica Mut. Ins. Co. v. Johnson, 41 N.C. App. 299, 301, 254 S.E.2d 643, 644 (1979) (a court has "no power to amend or vacate an order or judgment so as to affect the rights of the parties" without notice and hearing); Vandooren v. Vandooren, 27 N.C. App. 279, 281, 218 S.E.2d 715, 717 (1975) (court corrected a substantive provision in alimony order without notice); *see also* Plomaritis v. Plomaritis, 222 N.C. App. 94, 108–09, 730 S.E.2d 784, 793 (2012) (court set aside stipulations without notice).

Form and Notice

Rule 60(b) does not provide its own procedural provisions by which a motion is "made" but, instead, states that "[t]he procedure for obtaining any relief from a judgment, order, or proceeding shall be by motion as prescribed in these rules or by an independent action."[342] Rule of Civil Procedure 7(b)(1) provides that

> an application to the court for an order shall be by motion which, unless made during a hearing or trial or at a session at which a cause is on the calendar for that session, shall be made in writing, shall state with particularity the grounds therefor, and shall set forth the relief or order sought. The requirement of writing is fulfilled if the motion is stated in a written notice of the hearing of the motion.

A Rule 60(b) motion may, therefore, be made orally when the underlying matter is properly before the court. Our courts have acknowledged this practice.[343] Much more commonly, however, Rule 60(b) motions are in writing, as required by Rule 7(b)(1), with a statement of the specific grounds and relief sought. The motion is filed in the action in which the relevant order or judgment was entered. The "technical requirements" of a Rule 60(b) motion are that it identify the error (or other basis) and identify the relief sought.[344] Ideally the motion will identify both Rule 60(b) and, as precisely as possible, the relevant subsection. But if it is clear that the motion seeks relief available under Rule 60(b), a failure to state a specific rule or identify the proper rule

---

342. Rule 60(b).

343. *See, e.g.*, Wood v. Wood, 297 N.C. 1, 5, 252 S.E.2d 799, 801–02 (1979) (noting that an oral motion made during the session in which the case was calendared was "clearly permitted by Rule 7."); Sloan v. Sloan, 151 N.C. App. 399, 404, 566 S.E.2d 97, 101 (2002) (court did not err in considering oral motion made in other party's presence during duly noticed hearing); Lee v. Jenkins, 57 N.C. App. 522, 524, 291 S.E.2d 797, 798 (1982) (treating an oral motion in open court to set aside as a Rule 60(b) motion "in substance.").

344. State *ex rel.* Richmond Cty. Child Support Agency v. Adams, 153 N.C. App. 512, 514, 571 S.E.2d 238, 240 (2002); Carter v. Clowers, 102 N.C. App. 247, 253, 401 S.E.2d 662, 665 (1991).

may be overlooked.[345] In *Carter v. Clowers*,[346] the trial court did not err in treating a motion to amend a notice of dismissal as a Rule 60(b) motion because the motion adequately identified the basis for relief. The court noted that " . . . moving papers that are mislabeled in other ways may be treated as motions under Rule 60(b) when relief would otherwise be proper under that Rule."[347] And the Court of Appeals has noted, "If a party is unsure under which of subsections (1), (2) and (3) or (6) of Rule 60(b) to proceed, he need not specify if his motion is timely and the reason justifies relief."[348] Where, however, a motion failed completely to make mention of Rule 60(b) and failed to specify in substance any of the grounds set forth in the rule, the court properly declined to entertain it, particularly because the record showed that the judge "did not understand on what theory the [movants] were proceeding[.]"[349]

Rule of Civil Procedure 5(a) requires service of a written Rule 60(b) motion.[350] The method of service also is governed by Rule 5.[351] Pursuant to Rule 6(d), if a party has also filed a notice of hearing of the Rule 60(b) motion, service must occur not later than five days before

---

345. *See, e.g.*, *Adams*, 153 N.C. App. at 514, 571 S.E.2d at 240 (motion reviewed under Rule 60(b) despite movant's failure to refer to any statute).

346. 102 N.C. App. 247, 401 S.E.2d 662 (1991).

347. *Id.* at 253, 401 S.E.2d at 665.

348. McGinnis v. Robinson, 43 N.C. App. 1, 7, 258 S.E.2d 84, 88 (1979) (quotations omitted) (citing Brady v. Town of Chapel Hill, 277 N.C. 720, 723, 178 S.E.2d 446, 448 (1971)); *see also* Sides v. Reid, 35 N.C. App. 235, 237, 241 S.E.2d 110, 111 (1978) (a party need not specify between basis (1) and (6) if not sure of proper basis). Rule 6 of the general practice rules also requires parties to state the rule number or numbers on which their motions are based. GEN. R. P. SUPER. & DIST. CTS. 6. In the Rule 60(b) context, however, this rule is applied flexibly where the court and parties are aware of the basis for the motion. Wood v. Wood, 297 N.C. 1, 6–7, 252 S.E.2d 799, 802 (1979).

349. Sherman v. Myers, 29 N.C. App. 29, 30–31, 222 S.E.2d 749, 750 (1976).

350. *See* Rule 5(a); Doxol Gas of Angier, Inc. v. Barefoot, 10 N.C. App. 703, 705, 179 S.E.2d 890, 892 (1971).

351. *See* Rules 5(a), (b), and (b1).

the hearing, unless the court has more exacting requirements.[352] Any affidavits filed in support of a Rule 60(b) motion must be served with the motion.[353] Opposing affidavits, if any, must be served at least two days before the hearing, unless the court otherwise permits.[354] The method of serving opposing affidavits is "personal delivery, facsimile transmission, or other means such that the party actually receives the affidavit within the required time."[355] Written motions under Rule 60(b) must also be filed with the court either before service or within five days after service.[356]

---

352. *See* Rule 6(d).

353. *Id.* Rule of Civil Procedure 6(b) may be used to obtain extensions of time to present such affidavits. Rule 60 does not *require* affidavits in support of Rule 60(b) motions, but they are often necessary to demonstrate a basis for relief depending on the grounds for the motion.

354. See Rule 6(d), which states,

> If the opposing affidavit is not served on the other parties at least two days before the hearing on the motion, the court may continue the matter for a reasonable period to allow the responding party to prepare a response, proceed with the matter without considering the untimely served affidavit, or take such other action as the ends of justice require.

Rule 6(e) also appears to provide for an additional three days of time to serve opposing affidavits if the movant's affidavits were served by mail. *See* Rule 6(e).

355. Rule 6(d).

356. Rule 5(d). In general, filing with the court means filing with the clerk of court unless the judge permits the motion to be filed with the judge. Rule 5(e)(1).

Effect on Appeal Deadline

A motion for relief under Rule 60(b) does not toll the time for filing a notice of appeal of the underlying judgment.[357] The appeal deadlines set forth in Rule of Appellate Procedure 3 are jurisdictional, and failure to follow them requires dismissal of the appeal.[358]

Court's Authority and Order

Who May Rule

Unlike decisions under Rules 50 and 59,[359] Rule 60(b) motions may be heard and determined by a judge other than the judge who issued the order.[360] The general rule that "one trial judge may not overrule another"[361] does not apply to Rule 60(b) motions.[362] As the Court of Appeals has explained, "A 60(b) order does not overrule a prior order but, consistent with statutory authority, relieves parties from the effect of an order."[363] On several occasions, the Court of Appeals has

---

357. Mitchell Cty. Dep't of Soc. Servs. v. Carpenter, 127 N.C. App. 353, 356, 489 S.E.2d 437, 439 (1997); Parrish v. Cole, 38 N.C. App. 691, 695, 248 S.E.2d 878, 880 (1978); *see* N.C. R. App. P. 3(c)(3); G.S. 1-279.1.

358. Wallis v. Cambron, 194 N.C. App. 190, 193, 670 S.E.2d 239, 241 (2008) (citing Abels v. Renfro Corp., 126 N.C. App. 800, 802, 486 S.E.2d 735, 737 (1997)).

359. *See* Part I, Chapters 1 and 2.

360. Van Engen v. Que Sci., Inc., 151 N.C. App. 683, 690, 567 S.E.2d 179, 184 (2002).

361. *See* First Fin. Ins. Co. v. Commercial Coverage Inc., 154 N.C. App. 504, 507, 572 S.E.2d 259, 262 (2002); *see also* Michael Crowell, *One Trial Judge Overruling Another*, Admin. of Just. Bull. 2015/06 (UNC School of Government, Dec. 2015).

362. Hoglen v. James, 38 N.C. App. 728, 731, 248 S.E.2d 901, 904 (1978) (in excusable neglect context); *see also* Charleston Capital Corp. v. Love Valley Enters., Inc., 10 N.C. App. 519, 523, 179 S.E.2d 190, 193 (1971) (stating the rule in a Rule 60(b) context with specific application to void judgments).

363. Charns v. Brown, 129 N.C. App. 635, 639, 502 S.E.2d 7, 10 (1988) (also noting that the second trial judge "certainly would have had grounds to grant [the] motion because [the] order was void as a matter of law."). In *Whitfield v. Wakefield*, however, the Court of Appeals determined that a second judge did not have authority to grant Rule 60(b) relief from a default

remanded cases for hearing where the trial judge apparently declined to rule on a Rule 60(b) motion, believing he or she had no authority to do so.[364] This rule is practical also because some Rule 60(b) motions may be filed long after judgment,[365] and the issuing judge may be presiding in a different district—making a hearing by that judge unwieldy—or may no longer be on the bench.

Hearing

If a court has authority to consider (to "hear") and to rule on a Rule 60(b) motion, the court abuses its discretion if it declines to do so.[366] In addition, Rule 60 motions may not be heard and disposed of *ex parte*.[367] Rule 60, however, contains no specific requirement that the court conduct a formal or evidentiary hearing before ruling on the motion. Such hearings may occur by operation of court practice if they are duly noticed by a party pursuant to Rule of Civil Procedure 6(d) or if they appear on a motions calendar pursuant to court calendaring rules or policy. But the Court of Appeals declined to find that the trial court abused its discretion by ruling on Rule 59 and 60 motions

---

judgment where, in doing so, the second judge necessarily substituted his own judgment for that of the first judge on the factual question of whether the defendant had "appeared" in the action. 51 N.C. App. 124, 127–28, 275 S.E.2d 263, 265–66 (1981). The Court of Appeals appeared to conclude that Rule 60(b) was being used as an appeal of the judgment rather than as a proper request for equitable relief.

364. *See* Novak v. Daigle, 226 N.C. App. 253, 256, 741 S.E.2d 890, 892–93 (2013); Boseman v. Jarrell, 199 N.C. App. 128, 133–34, 681 S.E.2d 374, 377–78 (2009), *rev'd in part on other grounds*, 364 N.C. 537, 704 S.E.2d 494 (2010); Trent v. River Place, LLC, 179 N.C. App. 72, 79, 632 S.E.2d 529, 534 (2006) (by declining to hear the Rule 60 motion, the second judge failed to "exercise the discretion conferred on him by law"); *Hoglen*, 38 N.C. App. at 731, 248 S.E.2d at 904 ("Because [the judge] erroneously believed he lacked the power to grant the relief requested, plaintiff has never had the proper hearing on his Rule 60(b) motion to which he is entitled.").

365. *See supra* section titled "Time Limits."

366. *See* cases cited *supra* at note 364.

367. Doxol Gas of Angier, Inc. v. Barefoot, 10 N.C. App. 703, 705, 179 S.E.2d 890, 892 (1971) ("Defendant's written motion to set aside the default judgment was not one which might be heard ex parte.").

without a hearing where the moving party argued that a hearing would have been her only opportunity to subpoena her supporting witness.[368] Before granting a written motion without a hearing, however, the court should give the opposing party a reasonable time to respond and should observe the time allowances in Rule of Civil Procedure 6(d) for service of opposing affidavits.

If the court conducts a hearing on a Rule 60 motion, there must, of course, be adequate notice to the parties and an opportunity to respond.[369] In a case decided in the similar context of a new trial motion, the trial court granted plaintiff's motion after conducting a hearing without defendants or their counsel present, and the record revealed no actual notice or attempted notice to defendants of the hearing date.[370] The Court of Appeals reversed and remanded for a new hearing, holding that the lack of notice deprived defendants of an opportunity to object, a violation of their right to due process.[371] When hearing a Rule 60(b) motion the court may—in addition to considering any affidavits or exhibits the parties may have presented—take live testimony or consider deposition testimony.[372]

---

368. Ollo v. Mills, 136 N.C. App. 618, 625, 525 S.E.2d 213, 217 (2000).

369. Rule of Civil Procedure 5(a) requires service of every written notice applicable to the action. *See* G.S. 1A-1, Rule 5(a). Rule 6(d) sets out the general timing requirements for notices of hearing. *See* G.S. 1A-1, Rule 6(d). Many local court rules include preferred procedures and forms for requesting a hearing on a motion. *See, e.g.*, Local Rules for Civil Superior Court, Tenth Judicial District, North Carolina, Local Form 1, www.nccourts.org/Courts/CRS/Policies/LocalRules.

370. Otto v. Certo, 210 N.C. App. 468, 472–73, 708 S.E.2d 183, 186 (2011).

371. *Id.* at 473, 708 S.E.2d at 186. Notice and an opportunity to be heard are particularly important when the trial court contemplates Rule 60(b) relief on its *own* motion. *See supra* section titled "Court's Own Motion."

372. *See* G.S. 1A-1, Rule 43(e), which states: "When a motion is based on facts not appearing of record the court may hear the matter on affidavits presented by the respective parties, but the court may direct that the matter be heard wholly or partly on oral testimony or depositions." The evidence upon which a Rule 60(b) decision is based must be competent evidence. Highfill v. Williamson, 19 N.C. App. 523, 533, 199 S.E.2d 469, 475 (1973).

Timing of Order; Stay of Execution; Restitution

There is no time frame specified in the Rules of Civil Procedure within which the court must enter an order on a Rule 60(b) motion.[373] As with all orders, the court should dispose of post-judgment motions as soon as reasonably possible in the interests of fairness, judicial efficiency, and the parties' need for finality—a need that may be particularly acute if the motion was filed long after judgment.[374] The court may enter an order on a Rule 60 motion after expiration of the session of court in which the motion was heard.[375]

Rule 60(b) states that "a motion under this section does not affect the finality of a judgment or suspend its operation." A Rule 60(b) motion does not automatically stay enforcement of the underlying judgment past the automatic (thirty-day) stay allowed in Rule 62(a).[376] The trial court, therefore, has discretion under Rule 62(b) to stay execution of proceedings to enforce the judgment while a Rule 60(b) motion

---

373. As always, local court rules may dictate certain time requirements where not provided by statute.

374. In an extreme situation, the failure to make a timely ruling could result in reversal and remand on appeal. *See, e.g.*, Plomaritis v. Plomaritis, 222 N.C. App. 94, 109, 730 S.E.2d 784, 794–95 (2012) (discussing the impact of an eighteen-month delay in the context of changed circumstances in an equitable distribution matter); Wall v. Wall, 140 N.C. App. 303, 313–14, 536 S.E.2d 647, 654 (2000) (nineteen months was "more than a *de minimus* delay" in the context of equitable distribution).

375. Rule of Civil Procedure 6(c) provides as follows:

> The period of time provided for the doing of any act or the taking of any proceeding is not affected or limited by the continued existence or expiration of a session of court. The continued existence or expiration of a session of court in no way affects the power of a court to do any act or take any proceeding, but no issue of fact shall be submitted to a jury out of session.

G.S. 1A-1, Rule 6(c). For a discussion of a court's ability to enter an order after a term or session of court has ended, see Michael Crowell, *Out-of-Term, Out-of-Session, Out-of-County*, ADMIN. OF JUST. BULL. 2008/05 (UNC School of Government, Nov. 2008).

376. *See* G.S. 1A-1, Rule 62(a).

is pending.[377] In the event that a judgment is set aside under Rule 60 *after* that judgment has been subject to collection or similar enforcement, G.S. 1-108 provides a remedy in the form of restitution. The statute gives certain protections to good faith purchasers and provides as follows:

> If a judgment is set aside pursuant to Rule 60(b) or (c) of the Rules of Civil Procedure and the judgment or any part thereof has been collected or otherwise enforced, such restitution may be compelled as the court directs. Title to property sold under such judgment to a purchaser in good faith is not thereby affected. No fiduciary officer or trustee who has made distribution of a fund under such judgment in good faith is personally liable if the judgment is changed by reason of such defense made after its rendition; nor in case the judgment was rendered for the partition of land, and any persons receiving any of the land in such partition sell it to a third person; the title of such third person is not affected if such defense is successful, but the redress of the person so defending after judgment shall be had by proper judgment against the parties to the original judgment and their heirs and personal representatives, and in no case affects persons who in good faith have dealt with such parties or their heirs

---

377. *See* Rule 62(b), which provides as follows:

> In its discretion and on such conditions for the security of the adverse party as are proper, the court may stay the execution of or any proceedings to enforce a judgment pending the disposition of a motion for . . . relief from a judgment or order made pursuant to Rule 60. If the time provided in the controlling statute or rule of appellate procedure for giving notice of appeal from the judgment had not expired before a stay under this subsection was entered, that time shall begin to run immediately upon the expiration of any stay under this section, and no execution shall issue nor shall proceedings be taken for enforcement of the judgment until the expiration of that time.

This rule applies also to motions under Rules 50, 59, and 52(b).

or personal representatives on the basis of such judgment being permanent.[378]

Written Findings of Fact and Conclusions of Law

Rule 52(a)(2) states, "Findings of fact and conclusions of law are necessary on decisions of any motion or order *ex mero motu* only when requested by a party[.]"[379] Consistent with this rule, our courts hold that trial judges are not required to include findings of fact and conclusions of law in their Rule 60(b) orders, *unless requested by a party* pursuant to Rule 52(a).[380] Inclusion of findings of fact may be the preferred practice,[381] but when they are absent, the appellate court will review the record to determine "whether, on the evidence before it, the court could have made findings of fact sufficient to support its legal conclusion."[382]

---

378. G.S. 1-108.

379. G.S. 1A-1, Rule 52(a)(2). Subsection (a)(3) further states that "[i]f an opinion or memorandum of decision is filed, it will be sufficient if the findings of fact and conclusions of law appear therein."

380. *See* Monaghan v. Schilling, 197 N.C. App. 578, 582–83, 677 S.E.2d 562, 564–65 (2009); Milton M. Croom Charitable Remainder Unitrust v. Hedrick, 188 N.C. App. 262, 266, 654 S.E.2d 716, 719 (2008); Brown v. Foremost Affiliated Ins. Servs., Inc., 158 N.C. App. 727, 732, 582 S.E.2d 335, 339 (2003); Creasman v. Creasman, 152 N.C. App. 119, 124, 566 S.E.2d 725, 729 (2002); Gibson v. Mena, 144 N.C. App. 125, 128, 548 S.E.2d 745, 747 (2001); Condellone v. Condellone, 137 N.C. App. 547, 550, 528 S.E.2d 639, 642 (2000); Haiduven v. Cooper, 23 N.C. App. 67, 69, 208 S.E.2d 223, 224–25 (1974).

381. McLean v. Mechanic, 116 N.C. App. 271, 276–77, 447 S.E.2d 459, 462 (1994) (noting that making findings of fact would be "a better practice" but is not required absent request); Nations v. Nations, 111 N.C. App. 211, 214, 431 S.E.2d 852, 855 (1993) (same); Grant v. Cox, 106 N.C. App. 122, 125, 415 S.E.2d 378, 380 (1992) (same).

382. Novak v. Daigle, 226 N.C. App. 253, 255, 741 S.E.2d 890, 892 (2013); *Croom*, 188 N.C. App. at 266, 654 S.E.2d at 719–20; *see also Brown*, 158 N.C. App. at 732, 582 S.E.2d at 339 ("[W]hen a trial court is not required to find facts, and does not do so, it is presumed that the court on proper evidence implicitly found facts to support its judgment."); *Nations*, 111 N.C. App. at 215, 431 S.E.2d at 855 (appeal court's task is to examine record to determine whether findings could have been made to support the decision).

Note, however, that in 2014 the General Assembly amended G.S. 7A-45.3 to require the presiding business court judge in a complex business case to "issue a written opinion in connection with any order granting or denying a motion under G.S. 1A-1, Rule . . . 59 or 60, or any order finally disposing of a complex business case, other than an order effecting a settlement agreement or jury verdict."[383]

While written findings of fact and conclusions of law are not, as just discussed, required in the absence of a party's request, it certainly seems important that the court at least specify its basis for granting Rule 60(b) relief.

Type of Relief Allowed

By its plain language, Rule 60(b) allows the court to "relieve" a party from the judgment or order in question. The rule provides for relief "upon such terms as are just," but typically such relief entails setting aside the judgment entirely or in relevant part.[384] In some circumstances, however, modification of the judgment has been permitted, such as when necessary to relieve a party from an impossible specific

---

Note that in the 1978 case of *Hoglen v. James* the court stated, "It is the duty of the judge presiding at a Rule 60(b) hearing to make findings of fact and to determine from such facts whether the movant is entitled to relief from a final judgment or order." 38 N.C. App. 728, 731, 248 S.E.2d 901, 903 (1978). This statement, however, did not specify a requirement that findings of fact be *included in a written order*, and it was drawn from an earlier case that itself cited language long predating enactment of the Rules of Civil Procedure. U.S.I.F. Wynnewood Corp. v. Soderquist, 27 N.C. App. 611, 614–15, 219 S.E.2d 787, 790 (1975) (citing Johnson v. Sidbury, 225 N.C. 208, 34 S.E.2d 67 (1945)). It was also made in the context of a proceeding in which the trial judge, under a mistaken belief that he had no authority to do so, had failed to consider the Rule 60(b) motion and, thus, had necessarily made no determination (or "findings"), written or otherwise. *Hoglen*, 38 N.C. App. at 731, 248 S.E.2d at 904. The language of *Hoglen*, while occasionally cited, has not been expressly interpreted to mandate written findings and conclusions absent a request by a party.

383. S.L. 2014-102 (S.B. 853), sec. 2.

384. For information regarding the posture of a case after relief is granted, see the section titled "Appealability of Rule 60(b) Order," *infra*, and cases cited at note 414.

performance requirement;[385] to relieve a party of part of a specific performance order due to a change in circumstances;[386] where the court had inserted unintended language "due to inadvertence";[387] and to remedy an inappropriate pre-judgment interest award that could not have been raised during appeal.[388] Modification of a judgment under Rule 60(b) is not permitted, however, when it merely corrects an error of law that could have been raised in a new trial motion or on appeal;[389] when it effectively grants the moving party additional affirmative relief;[390] or when it purports to nullify a legal effect of a judgment without vacating the judgment itself.[391]

---

385. Curran v. Barefoot, 183 N.C. App. 331, 343, 645 S.E.2d 187, 195 (2007).

386. Harris v. Harris, 307 N.C. 684, 687–88, 300 S.E.2d 369, 372 (1983).

387. Harris v. Harris, 162 N.C. App. 511, 516, 591 S.E.2d 560, 563 (2004).

388. Petty v. Hous. Auth. of City of Charlotte, 90 N.C. App. 559, 563, 369 S.E.2d 612, 615 (1988).

389. Town of Sylva v. Gibson, 51 N.C. App. 545, 548, 277 S.E.2d 115, 117 (1981) (reversing a modification reducing the amount of attorney fees allowed in earlier judgment based on perceived error in application of fee statute).

390. Cty. of Durham v. Daye, 195 N.C. App. 527, 533, 673 S.E.2d 683, 688–89 (2009) (error for court to award damages and fees through a Rule 60(b) motion to set aside default for non-payment of taxes); White v. White, 152 N.C. App. 588, 592, 568 S.E.2d 283, 285 (2002) (court properly declined to address motion under Rule 60(b) to modify a qualified domestic relations order to increase movant's share of retirement pay); Kimzay Winston-Salem, Inc. v. Jester, 103 N.C. App. 77, 79–80, 404 S.E.2d 176, 177 (1991) (error for court to allow additional damages for future rents, thus impermissibly keeping the judgment in effect while permitting its enlargement); Coleman v. Arnette, 48 N.C. App. 733, 735, 269 S.E.2d 755, 756 (1980) (amendment of divorce judgment to allow movant to claim children as dependents not permitted under Rule 60(b)(6)); *see also* Baker v. Tucker, 768 S.E.2d 874, 877 (N.C. Ct. App. 2015) (noting that Rule 60(b) was not the appropriate procedural mechanism for substantive amendments to judgment after bench trial).

391. Howell v. Howell, 321 N.C. 87, 91, 361 S.E.2d 585, 588 (1987) (reversing order relieving movant only from *effect* of divorce judgment on her equitable distribution claim); Carter v. Carter, 102 N.C. App. 440, 446, 402 S.E.2d 469, 472 (1991) (reversing order reaffirming divorce decree and reserving equitable distribution issue for future resolution).

Effect of Appeal of Underlying Judgment; Conditional Ruling

If the underlying judgment has been appealed, the trial court is divested of jurisdiction to enter a ruling on a Rule 60(b) motion made thereafter.[392] A trial court does, however, have "limited jurisdiction" to *hear and consider* a Rule 60(b) motion "to indicate what action it would be inclined to make were an appeal not pending."[393] One reason for this limited authority is practical: The trial judge's knowledge of the case and its facts puts it in a "far better position" to assess the motion than the appeals court.[394] A second reason is that an appeal of the underlying judgment does not toll the one-year time period for making motions under Rules 60(b)(1) through (b)(3);[395] if the court had no authority to make a conditional determination, some parties would lose the opportunity to seek Rule 60(b) relief during appeal.[396]

In the 1979 case of *Bell v. Martin*, the Court of Appeals set forth the procedure for a conditional ruling as follows:

- The Rule 60(b) motion is made in the trial court.
- The movant then notifies the appellate court.
- The appellate court delays consideration of the underlying appeal.
- The trial court considers the motion and indicates "by a proper entry in the record" how it would be inclined to rule.

---

392. Sink v. Easter, 288 N.C. 183, 197, 217 S.E.2d 532, 541 (1975); Talbert v. Mauney, 80 N.C. App. 477, 478, 343 S.E.2d 5, 7 (1986) (noting that the trial court is "functus officio" upon appeal of the judgment); York v. Taylor, 79 N.C. App. 653, 339 S.E.2d 830 (1986)); *see generally* G.S. 1-294. The trial court retains authority, however, to rule on the motion during the same term in which the judgment was entered. *Sink*, 288 N.C. at 197, 217 S.E.2d at 541 (noting the "in fieri" exception).

393. *Talbert*, 80 N.C. App. at 478–79, 343 S.E.2d at 7.

394. *Id.* at 479, 343 S.E.2d at 7 (citing Swygert v. Swygert, 46 N.C. App. 173, 181, 264 S.E.2d 902, 907–08 (1980)).

395. *Talbert*, 80 N.C. App. at 479, 343 S.E.2d at 7; Wiggins v. Bunch, 280 N.C. 106, 111, 184 S.E.2d 879, 881–82 (1971).

396. *Talbert*, 80 N.C. App. at 479, 343 S.E.2d at 7; *see also Sink*, 288 N.C. at 199, 217 S.E.2d at 542 (discussing this tension).

- The appellate court is notified [apparently by the moving party] of the trial court's conditional determination.
- If the trial court's determination
    - Favors granting the Rule 60(b) motion, the movant may seek remand to the trial court for entry of judgment on the motion. The proceedings would then continue in the trial court, as appropriate, until a final, appealable judgment is rendered.
    - Favors denying the Rule 60(b) motion, that determination would be "binding on that court" and the movant could then request the appellate court review the conditional Rule 60(b) determination at the same time it considers the issues in the underlying appeal.[397]

In the relatively recent case of *Hall v. Cohen*,[398] the Court of Appeals reiterated and summarized this procedure but also seemed to add a further step in the process that was not explicit in *Bell*: "Upon the appellate court's notification of a Rule 60(b) motion filed with the trial court, this Court *will remand the matter to the trial court* so the trial court may hold an evidentiary hearing and indicate 'how it [is] inclined to rule[.]'"[399] From this language, it appears that the appellate court must first be notified of the Rule 60(b) motion and then it also *must remand* the case to the trial court before the trial court's "limited jurisdiction" to consider the motion is invoked. In the recent unpublished opinion of *Knowles v. Bennett*, the Court of Appeals re-emphasized the remand language of *Hall*. In *Knowles*, a

397. Bell v. Martin, 43 N.C. App. 134, 142, 258 S.E.2d 403, 409 (1979), *rev'd on other grounds*, 299 N.C. 715, 264 S.E.2d 101 (1980). For an example of appellate review of a trial court's conditional denial of a post-appeal Rule 60(b)(2) motion, see Morgan v. Nash Cty., 735 S.E.2d 615, 625 (N.C. Ct. App. 2012). Some authority also exists for filing a Rule 60(b) motion directly with the appellate court, but this method is not favored. *See, e.g., Bell*, 43 N.C. App. at 142, 258 S.E.2d at 409 (noting that "this procedure should not be encouraged").

398. 177 N.C. App. 456, 628 S.E.2d 469 (2006).

399. *Id.* at 458, 628 S.E.2d at 471 (emphasis added).

self-represented appellant filed a Rule 60(b) motion after appeal but did not notify the Court of Appeals it had been filed. The trial court declined to rule on the motion on grounds of lack of jurisdiction. The Court of Appeals affirmed, stating, "In the present case, [appellant] failed to notify this Court that he had filed a Rule 60(b) motion with the trial court *and has not sought remand*. Accordingly, the trial court correctly determined that it lacked jurisdiction to consider father's Rule 60(b) motion after notice of appeal had been filed[.]"[400] A combined reading of *Hall* and *Knowles*—with due regard for the fact that *Knowles* is unpublished[401]—suggests that the trial court's limited jurisdiction to consider a Rule 60(b) motion is dependent on an actual remand by the appellate court.

For a Rule 60(b) motion filed *at the same time* as the notice of appeal of the underlying judgment, the Court of Appeals held, in *York v. Taylor*,[402] that the trial court is *not* divested of jurisdiction to enter a ruling on the motion.[403] And in a recent case, the court, citing *York*, stated that "the trial court is not divested of jurisdiction to entertain and may fully rule upon a Rule 60(b) motion that is filed *prior to* or contemporaneously with the notice of appeal.[404]

Judgments of Clerks and Magistrates

Clerks of Superior Court

Under Rule 60(c), a clerk of superior court may set aside a final order for the reasons set forth in Rule 60(b) if the clerk issued the order.[405] A judge in the appropriate division also may hear and decide a motion

---

400. Knowles v. Bennett, 762 S.E.2d 2, 2014 WL 2507787, *5 (N.C. Ct. App. 2014) (unpublished) (emphasis added).

401. *See* North Carolina Rule of Appellate Procedure 30(e)(3).

402. 79 N.C. App. 653, 339 S.E.2d 830 (1986).

403. *Id.* at 654–55, 339 S.E.2d at 831–32.

404. Town of Leland v. HWW, LLC, 725 S.E.2d 1, 4 (N.C. Ct. App. 2010) (emphasis added) (remanding to trial court for ruling on a motion filed prior to notice of appeal).

405. Rule 60(c) ("The clerk may, in respect of judgments rendered by himself, exercise the same powers authorized in sections (a) and (b)."); *see also In re* Ward, 337 N.C. 443, 448, 446 S.E.2d 40, 43 (1994) (clerk

under Rule 60(b) to be relieved from a clerk's order.[406] When a clerk makes a ruling on a Rule 60(b) motion pertaining to a clerk's order, appeals of that ruling "may be had to the judge in the manner provided by law."[407] Orders of the clerk of superior court are appealed to superior and district courts (according to the appropriate division), and the manner of appeal is set forth in Chapter 1, Article 27A of the General Statutes, which became effective in 2000.[408]

---

authorized to reopen incompetency proceeding under Rule 60(b) and (c)); *In re* Estate of Heffner, 61 N.C. App. 646, 301 S.E.2d 720 (1983) (clerk authorized under Rule 60(b) and (c) to set aside final accounting in estate matter); *In re* Estate of Snipes, 45 N.C. App. 79, 81–82, 262 S.E.2d 292, 294 (1980) (noting that the clerk is limited to the grounds set forth in Rule 60). A clerk has general authority under G.S. 7A-103(9) to "open, vacate, modify, set aside, or enter as of a former time, decrees or orders of [the clerk's] court."

Note also that there is confusion between the language of Rule 60(c) and Rule 55(d), the rule governing default judgments. Rule 55(d) states, "For good cause shown the court may set aside an entry of default, and, if a judgment by default has been entered, the judge may set it aside in accordance with Rule 60(b)." In conflict with Rule 60(c), this language suggests that only a judge may set aside a default judgment entered by a clerk. In practice, clerks seem to have reconciled the conflict in favor of exercising the authority to set aside their own default judgments under Rule 60(c). *See generally* Joan G. Brannon & Ann M. Anderson, 1 North Carolina Clerk of Superior Court Procedures Manual Chapter 31 (UNC School of Government 2d ed., Dec. 2012).

To further complicate the relationship between a clerk and Rule 60, G.S. 28A-2-6, enacted in 2011, excludes Rule 60 from the list of Rules of Civil Procedure that apply in an estate proceeding (as "estate proceeding" is defined in Chapter 28A). Instead, in any such proceeding, Rule 60 applies only if the clerk so specifies. G.S. 28A-2-6(e). For further discussion of estate proceedings, see Ann M. Anderson, *Estate Proceedings in North Carolina*, Admin. of Just. Bull. 2012/04 (UNC School of Government, Dec. 2012).

406. Rule 60(c) ("The judge has like powers in respect of such judgments.").

407. *Id.*

408. *See* Chapter 1, Article 27A, of the General Statutes, specifically secs. 1-301.1 (civil actions), 1-301.2 (special proceedings), and 1-301.3 (estate and trust matters); *see also* Auto. Equip. Distribs., Inc. v. Petroleum Equip. & Serv., Inc., 87 N.C. App. 606, 607, 361 S.E.2d 895, 896 (1987) (noting

Magistrate Judgments

If authorized by the chief district court judge, a magistrate may hear a motion to set aside an order or judgment entered in a small claims action but only if brought under Rule 60(b)(1)—for mistake, inadvertence, surprise, or excusable neglect. If the order is set aside, the magistrate then orders a new trial before a magistrate.[409] The statute does not limit a district court judge's authority to set aside a final small claims order or judgment on any Rule 60(b) grounds.[410] After final disposition of a matter by a magistrate, the exclusive avenue for appeal is to the district court for trial *de novo*.[411]

Appealability of Rule 60(b) Order

Orders denying relief under Rule 60(b) are final orders appealable to the appellate division.[412] Because the filing of a Rule 60(b) motion does not toll the period for appeal of the underlying judgment,[413] the appeal of a Rule 60(b) order relates only to the trial court's disposition of the motion itself. When Rule 60(b) relief is granted, the order generally is interlocutory because additional action is then required in the trial

---

authority of trial court to hear appeal of clerk's ruling on Rule 60 motion pursuant to former statute).

409. G.S. 7A-228(a).

410. *Id.*

411. *Id.*

412. Orders of the clerk of court and magistrate, however, are appealable to the trial division. Note that S.L. 2014-102 (S.B. 853) amended G.S. 7A-27 to make final judgments in mandatory and discretionary complex business cases appealable of right directly to the North Carolina Supreme Court.

413. *See supra* section titled "Effect on Appeal Deadline."

court to settle the remaining issues in the case.[414] Orders granting Rule 60(b) relief generally are not, therefore, immediately appealable.[415]

Independent Action

Rule 60(b) states,

> This rule does not limit the power of a court to entertain an independent action to relieve a party from a judgment, order, or proceeding, or to set aside a judgment for fraud

---

414. Campbell v. Campbell, 764 S.E.2d 630, 632 (N.C. Ct. App. 2014) (further action necessary to "settle and determine the entire controversy") (quoting Veazey v. City of Durham, 231 N.C. 357, 362, 57 S.E.2d 377, 381 (1950)); Robinson v. Gardner, 167 N.C. App. 763, 767, 606 S.E.2d 449, 452 (2005) (orders granting Rule 60(b) relief effectively "direct[ ] some further proceeding preliminary to final decree."); Banner v. Hatcher, 124 N.C. App. 439, 441, 477 S.E.2d 249, 250–51 (1996) (stating the principle in the child support context); *see also* Cty. of Durham v. Daye, 195 N.C. App. 527, 535, 673 S.E.2d 683, 688 (2009) (noting that relief from judgment "sets the stage for further proceedings in the case").

There may be situations in which the grant of relief under Rule 60(b) would not require further action in the trial court, such as when the court concludes that it is no longer equitable to require prospective application of a permanent injunction under Rule 60(b)(5). In such a case, the court's order may not be interlocutory.

415. *Robinson,* 167 N.C. App. at 767, 606 S.E.2d at 452; Braun v. Grundman, 63 N.C. App. 387, 388, 304 S.E.2d 636, 637 (1983); Bailey v. Gooding, 301 N.C. 205, 210, 270 S.E.2d 431, 434 (1980); Metcalf v. Palmer, 46 N.C. App. 622, 625, 265 S.E.2d 484, 485 (1980).

An interlocutory order is, however, immediately appealable in two circumstances: (1) if the trial court has properly certified the case for immediate appeal under Rule of Civil Procedure 54(b); and (2) when the order affects a substantial right that would be lost without immediate review. *Robinson,* 167 N.C. App. at 767, 606 S.E.2d at 452. As to the first exception, Rule 54(b) certification is appropriate when a court has entered final judgment on some but not all claims, a scenario not common in the context of an order granting Rule 60(b) relief. *See Campbell,* 764 S.E.2d at 632. As to the substantial rights exception, there may be some circumstances in which substantial rights would be implicated in the context of a Rule 60(b) order granting relief, but the right to avoid a trial on the merits generally is not a substantial right absent immunity or other special circumstances. *See id.* at 633–34; *Banner,* 124 N.C. App. at 442, 477 S.E.2d at 251.

> upon the court.[416] The procedure for obtaining any relief from a judgment, order, or proceeding shall be by motion as prescribed in these rules or by an independent action.[417]

This provision preserves an interested person's traditional right to challenge a judgment by independent action. It is not intended to expand that right beyond what is otherwise permitted by law.[418] So, while extrinsic fraud may be challenged by independent action, our courts hold that *intrinsic* fraud may not.[419] Intrinsic fraud, therefore, may be raised only by motion under Rule 60(b) and thus is subject to a one-year outside time limit.[420] A principal reason to challenge a judgment for extrinsic fraud—or another basis in 60(b)(1) through (3)—by

---

416. The Court of Appeals has noted that federal courts interpreting Federal Rule of Civil Procedure 60(b)(6) have described fraud on the court as "a deliberate, egregious scheme of directly subverting the judicial process which cannot be exposed by the normal adversarial process, such as bribery of a judge or juror or improper influence exerted by an attorney on the court." Henderson v. Wachovia Bank of N.C., N.A., 145 N.C. App. 621, 628, 551 S.E.2d 464, 469 (2001). For further cases discussing fraud on the court, see generally McLean v. McLean, 233 N.C. 139, 145, 63 S.E.2d 138, 143 (1951); Purcell Int'l Textile Grp., Inc. v. Algemene AFW N.V., 185 N.C. App. 135, 138, 647 S.E.2d 667, 670 (2007); Stokley v. Stokley, 30 N.C. App. 351, 354–55, 227 S.E.2d 131, 134 (1976); Alexander v. Iredell Cty. Bd. of Educ., 6 N.C. App. 92, 98, 169 S.E.2d 549, 553 (1969).

417. Rule 60(b).

418. *See, e.g.*, Hassell v. Wilson, 301 N.C. 307, 311–12, 272 S.E.2d 77, 80 (1980) (noting pre-rules law that service of process could be attacked by independent action only if defect appeared on face of the documents); Cty. of Durham v. Daye, 195 N.C. App. 527, 535–36, 673 S.E.2d 683, 689 (2009) (independent action to set aside foreclosure sale not permitted).

419. Smith v. Smith, 334 N.C. 81, 86, 431 S.E.2d 196, 199 (1993); Hooks v. Eckman, 159 N.C. App. 681, 685, 587 S.E.2d 352, 354 (2003); Caswell Realty Assocs. I, L.P. v. Andrews Co., Inc., 121 N.C. App. 483, 486, 466 S.E.2d 310, 312 (1996); Textile Fabricators, Inc. v. C.R.C. Industr., Inc., 43 N.C. App. 530, 532, 259 S.E.2d 570, 572 (1979); *Stokley*, 30 N.C. App. at 354–55, 227 S.E.2d at 134. For a discussion of the distinctions between intrinsic and extrinsic fraud, see *supra* section titled "Fraud, Misrepresentation, or Other Misconduct of an Adverse Party—Rule 60(b)(3)."

420. *Textile Fabricators*, 43 N.C. App. at 532, 259 S.E.2d at 572; *Stokley*, 30 N.C. App. at 354–55, 227 S.E.2d at 134. See *supra* section titled "Final

independent action is to avoid the explicit constraints of Rule 60(b)'s one-year time limit. However, other limitations, such as laches, still apply.

As discussed above,[421] Rule 60(b) is reserved for parties and their legal representatives. An independent action is the procedure by which a non-party to the underlying action may challenge a judgment that affects its rights,[422] and this provision makes clear that the right to do so is not foreclosed by Rule 60(b) itself.

Judgment, Order, or Proceeding" for a discussion of challenges to foreign judgments on the basis of fraud.

421. *See supra* section titled "Who May Seek Relief."

422. Edmunds v. Edmunds, 194 N.C. App. 425, 431, 669 S.E.2d 874, 878 (2008), *aff'd*, 363 N.C. 740, 686 S.E.2d 150 (2009); Watson v. Ben Griffin Realty & Auction, Inc., 128 N.C. App. 61, 63–64, 493 S.E.2d 331, 333 (1997); Lawyers Title Ins. Corp. v. Langdon, 91 N.C. App. 382, 385, 371 S.E.2d 727, 730 (1988).

Appendix A—Full Text of Relevant Rules of Civil Procedure

(Chapter 1A of the N.C. General Statutes)

North Carolina Rule of Civil Procedure 50 (G.S. 1A-1, Rule 50)

Rule 50. Motion for a directed verdict and for judgment notwithstanding the verdict.

(a) When made; effect.—A party who moves for a directed verdict at the close of the evidence offered by an opponent may offer evidence in the event that the motion is not granted, without having reserved the right so to do and to the same extent as if the motion had not been made. A motion for a directed verdict which is not granted is not a waiver of trial by jury even though all parties to the action have moved for directed verdicts. A motion for a directed verdict shall state the specific grounds therefor. The order granting a motion for a directed verdict shall be effective without any assent of the jury.

(b) Motion for judgment notwithstanding the verdict.—

(1) Whenever a motion for a directed verdict made at the close of all the evidence is denied or for any reason is not granted, the submission of the action to the jury shall be deemed to be subject to a later determination of the legal questions raised by the motion. Not later than 10 days after entry of judgment, a party who has moved for a directed verdict may move to have the verdict and any judgment entered thereon set aside and to have judgment entered in accordance with

his motion for a directed verdict; or if a verdict was not returned such party, within 10 days after the jury has been discharged, may move for judgment in accordance with his motion for a directed verdict. In either case the motion shall be granted if it appears that the motion for directed verdict could properly have been granted. A motion for a new trial may be joined with this motion, or a new trial may be prayed for in the alternative. If a verdict was returned the judge may allow the judgment to stand or may set aside the judgment and either order a new trial or direct the entry of judgment as if the requested verdict had been directed. If no verdict was returned the judge may direct the entry of judgment as if the requested verdict had been directed or may order a new trial. Not later than ten (10) days after entry of judgment or the discharge of the jury if a verdict was not returned, the judge on his own motion may, with or without further notice and hearing, grant, deny, or redeny a motion for directed verdict made at the close of all the evidence that was denied or for any reason was not granted.

(2) An appellate court, on finding that a trial judge should have granted a motion for directed verdict made at the close of all the evidence, may not direct entry of judgment in accordance with the motion unless the party who made the motion for a directed verdict also moved for judgment in accordance with Rule 50(b)(1) or the trial judge on his own motion granted, denied or redenied the motion for a directed verdict in accordance with Rule 50(b)(1).

(c) Motion for judgment notwithstanding the verdict—Conditional rulings on grant of motion.—

(1) If the motion for judgment notwithstanding the verdict, provided for in section (b) of this rule, is granted, the court shall also rule on the motion for new trial, if any, by determining whether it should be granted if the judgment is thereafter vacated or reversed, and shall specify the grounds for granting or denying the motion for the new trial. If the motion for new trial is thus conditionally granted, the order thereon does not affect the finality of the judgment. In case the motion for new trial has been conditionally granted and the judgment is reversed on appeal, the new trial shall proceed unless the appellate division has otherwise ordered.

In case the motion for new trial has been conditionally denied, the appellee on appeal may assert error in that denial; and if the judgment is reversed on appeal, subsequent proceedings shall be in accordance with the order of the appellate division.

(2) The party whose verdict has been set aside on motion for judgment notwithstanding the verdict may serve a motion for a new trial pursuant to Rule 59 not later than 10 days after entry of the judgment notwithstanding the verdict.

(d) Motion for judgment notwithstanding the verdict—Denial of motion.—If the motion for judgment notwithstanding the verdict is denied, the party who prevailed on that motion may, as appellee, assert grounds entitling him to a new trial in the event the appellate division concludes that the trial court erred in denying the motion for judgment notwithstanding the verdict. If the appellate division reverses the judgment, nothing in this rule precludes it from determining that the appellee is entitled to a new trial, or from directing the trial court to determine whether a new trial shall be granted. (1967, c. 954, s. 1; 1969, c. 895, s. 11.)

North Carolina Rule of Civil Procedure 52 (G.S. 1A-1, Rule 52)

Rule 52. Findings by the court

(a) Findings.—

(1) In all actions tried upon the facts without a jury or with an advisory jury, the court shall find the facts specially and state separately its conclusions of law thereon and direct the entry of the appropriate judgment.

(2) Findings of fact and conclusions of law are necessary on decisions of any motion or order ex mero motu only when requested by a party and as provided by Rule 41(b). Similarly, findings of fact and conclusions of law are necessary on the granting or denying of a preliminary injunction or any other provisional remedy only when required by statute expressly relating to such remedy or requested by a party.

(3) If an opinion or memorandum of decision is filed, it will be sufficient if the findings of fact and conclusions of law appear therein.

(b) Amendment.—Upon motion of a party made not later than 10 days after entry of judgment the court may amend its findings or make additional findings and may amend the judgment accordingly. The motion may be made with a motion for a new trial pursuant to Rule 59.

(c) Review on appeal.—When findings of fact are made in actions tried by the court without a jury, the question of the sufficiency of the evidence to support the findings may be raised on appeal whether or not the party raising the question has made in the trial court an objection to such findings or has made a motion to amend them or a motion for judgment, or a request for specific findings. (1967, c. 954, § 1. Amended by Laws 1969, c. 895, § 12.)

North Carolina Rule of Civil Procedure 59 (G.S. 1A-1, Rule 59)

Rule 59: New trials; amendment of judgments

(a) Grounds.—A new trial may be granted to all or any of the parties and on all or part of the issues for any of the following causes or grounds:

(1) Any irregularity by which any party was prevented from having a fair trial;
(2) Misconduct of the jury or prevailing party;
(3) Accident or surprise which ordinary prudence could not have guarded against;
(4) Newly discovered evidence material for the party making the motion which he could not, with reasonable diligence, have discovered and produced at the trial;
(5) Manifest disregard by the jury of the instructions of the court;
(6) Excessive or inadequate damages appearing to have been given under the influence of passion or prejudice;
(7) Insufficiency of the evidence to justify the verdict or that the verdict is contrary to law;
(8) Error in law occurring at the trial and objected to by the party making the motion, or
(9) Any other reason heretofore recognized as grounds for new trial.

On a motion for a new trial in an action tried without a jury, the court may open the judgment if one has been entered, take additional testimony, amend findings of fact and conclusions of law or make new findings and conclusions, and direct the entry of a new judgment.

(b) Time for motion.—A motion for a new trial shall be served not later than 10 days after entry of the judgment.

(c) Time for serving affidavits.—When a motion for new trial is based upon affidavits they shall be served with the motion. The opposing party has 10 days after such service within which to serve opposing affidavits, which period may be extended for an additional period not exceeding 30 days either by the court for good cause shown or by the parties by written stipulation. The court may permit reply affidavits.

(d) On initiative of court.—Not later than 10 days after entry of judgment the court of its own initiative, on notice to the parties and hearing, may order a new trial for any reason for which it might have granted a new trial on motion of a party, and in the order shall specify the grounds therefor.

(e) Motion to alter or amend a judgment.—A motion to alter or amend the judgment under section (a) of this rule shall be served not later than 10 days after entry of the judgment. (1967, c. 954, § 1. Amended by S.L. 2014-115, § 1, eff. Aug. 11, 2014.)

North Carolina Rule of Civil Procedure 60(b) (G.S. 1A-1, Rule 60(b))

Rule 60(b). Relief from judgment or order

(b) Mistakes; inadvertence; excusable neglect; newly discovered evidence; fraud, etc.—On motion and upon such terms as are just, the court may relieve a party or his legal representative from a final judgment, order, or proceeding for the following reasons:

(1) Mistake, inadvertence, surprise, or excusable neglect;

(2) Newly discovered evidence which by due diligence could not have been discovered in time to move for a new trial under Rule 59(b);

(3) Fraud (whether heretofore denominated intrinsic or extrinsic), misrepresentation, or other misconduct of an adverse party;

(4) The judgment is void;

(5) The judgment has been satisfied, released, or discharged, or a prior judgment upon which it is based has been reversed or otherwise vacated, or it is no longer equitable that the judgment should have prospective application; or

(6) Any other reason justifying relief from the operation of the judgment.

The motion shall be made within a reasonable time, and for reasons (1), (2) and (3) not more than one year after the judgment, order, or proceeding was entered or taken. A motion under this section does not affect the finality of a judgment or suspend its operation. This rule does not limit the power of a court to entertain an independent action to relieve a party from a judgment, order, or proceeding, or to set aside a judgment for fraud upon the court. The procedure for obtaining any relief from a judgment, order, or proceeding shall be by motion as prescribed in these rules or by an independent action.

(c) Judgments rendered by the clerk.—The clerk may, in respect of judgments rendered by himself, exercise the same powers authorized in sections (a) and (b). The judge has like powers in respect of such judgments. Where such powers are exercised by the clerk, appeals may be had to the judge in the manner provided by law. (1967, c. 954, § 1.)

Appendix B—Table of Authorities

U.S. Constitution

N.C. Constitution

North Carolina General Statutes (G.S.)

Chapter 1: Civil Procedure

Chapter 1A: Rules of Civil Procedure (G.S. 1A-1)

Article 2—Commencement of Action; Services of Process, Pleadings, Motions, and Orders

Article 3—Pleadings and Motions

Article 4—Parties

Article 5—Depositions and Discovery

Article 6—Trials

Article 7—Judgment

Chapter 1C: Enforcement of Judgments

Chapter 1D: Punitive Damages

Chapter 7A: Judicial Department

Chapter 8C: North Carolina Rules of Evidence (G.S. 8C-1)

Chapter 15A: Criminal Procedure Act

Chapter 28A: Administration of Decedents' Estates

Chapter 35A: Incompetency and Guardianship

Chapter 75: Monopolies, Trusts, and Consumer Protection

North Carolina Session Laws

Federal Rules of Civil Procedure (Fed. R. Civ. P.)

Cases

A

B

C

D

E

H

I

J

K

L

M

N

O

P

Q

R

S

T

U

V

W

Y

N.C. Rules of Appellate Procedure (N.C. R. App. P.)

General Rules of Practice for Superior & District Courts (Gen. R. P. Super & Dist. Cts.)

Local Rules for Civil Superior Court (Tenth Judicial District)

N.C. Code of Judicial Conduct

N.C. Pattern Instructions (N.C.P.I.)

Other Sources

www.ingramcontent.com/pod-product-compliance
Lightning Source LLC
LaVergne TN
LVHW052259200926
848481LV00002B/413
9781560118558